THE EVERYTHING
No Trans Fat Cookbook

Dear Reader,

When I think of all the trans fats I have consumed in my lifetime I can't help but shudder. Solid vegetable shortening was a staple in my kitchen for years, as in my mother's before me. Everyone used it. Everyone thought it was healthier than butter or lard. Everyone was wrong.

Many of the dietary recommendations that the government hands out are colored by politics and big business. One of the reasons that margarine was so highly touted as being "better than butter" is because of highly paid lobbyists. Now, I do have faith in the FDA and the USDA, but I don't take everything they say as gospel.

It's my philosophy that the more natural and less processed foods you can consume the better—whole grains, fresh (or frozen) fruits and vegetables, cereals, meats, and dairy products. That goes for fats, too. Butter, coconut oil, and extra-virgin cold-pressed olive oil are your best choices.

I developed the recipes in this book to use ingredients commonly found in supermarkets and grocery stores. I don't like cookbooks that call for unusual ingredients. The only thing you'll need to buy at a health food store to make the recipes in this book is coconut oil.

Other books about reducing trans fat usually include recipes made with sugar substitutes, egg substitutes, and no refined carbohydrates. While sugar, eggs, and carbs may be factors in our unhealthy lifestyle, this book is concerned with trans fat, and that is what I focused on. I hope you enjoy this book and the better health it will bring you!

Linda Larsen

The EVERYTHING® Series

Editorial

Publisher	Gary M. Krebs
Director of Product Development	Paula Munier
Managing Editor	Laura M. Daly
Associate Copy Chief	Sheila Zwiebel
Acquisitions Editor	Kerry Smith
Development Editor	Brett Palana-Shanahan
Associate Production Editor	Casey Ebert

Production

Director of Manufacturing	Susan Beale
Production Project Manager	Michelle Roy Kelly
Prepress	Erick DaCosta Matt LeBlanc
Interior Layout	Heather Barrett Brewster Brownville Colleen Cunningham Jennifer Oliveira
Cover Design	Erin Alexander Stephanie Chrusz Frank Rivera

Visit the entire Everything® Series at *www.everything.com*

THE

EVERYTHING®

No Trans Fat Cookbook

From store shelves to your kitchen table—
healthy meals your family will love

Linda Larsen

Adams Media
Avon, Massachusetts

To the memory of my grandmothers, Matha Mork and Clara Johnson, who were two of the best cooks in the world.

An Everything® Series Book.
Everything® and everything.com® are registered trademarks of F+W Publications, Inc.

Published by Adams Media, an F+W Publications Company
57 Littlefield Street, Avon, MA 02322 U.S.A.
www.adamsmedia.com

ISBN-10: 1-59869-533-9
ISBN-13: 978-1-59869-533-5

Printed in the United States of America.

J I H G F E D C B A

Library of Congress Cataloging-in-Publication Data
Larsen, Linda.
The everything no trans fat cookbook / Linda Larsen.
    p.   cm. — (Everything series)
Includes index.
ISBN-10: 1-59869-533-9 (pbk.)
ISBN-13: 978-1-59869-533-5 (pbk.)
1. Food—Fat content. 2. Low-fat diet—Recipes. 3. Trans fatty acids. I. Title.
TX553.L5L37 2007
613.2'84—dc22   2007010850

This book is available at quantity discounts for bulk purchases.
For information, please call 1-800-289-0963.

Contents

Acknowledgments

As always, my dear husband, Doug, has been a strong support during the research and writing of this book. And to the rest of my family, thank you so much for your love and support. My agent, Barb Doyen, deserves lots of thanks for her faith in me. And thanks to my editor, Kerry Smith, for her endless enthusiasm and help.

Introduction

EVERYONE IS CONCERNED about their health and eating healthy foods today. Many people have chronic diseases that are exacerbated by poor diet. With our busy lifestyles, we think it's much easier to patronize the drive-through window than to cook meals ourselves. But we're putting our collective and individual health at risk, losing time in the long run.

Trans fat is emerging as one of the greatest culprits in our health crisis. For years, we were encouraged to avoid saturated and animal fats and consume low- or no-cholesterol, polyunsaturated oils and hydrogenated fats like shortening and margarine. Scientists and nutritionists are now discovering that that advice was incorrect.

So what do we do now? Is there a way to eat a varied and balanced diet that doesn't include trans fat? Are the foods we enjoy going to lose their good taste and texture? And is it difficult to avoid consuming trans fat?

Yes, you can eat a diet that doesn't include trans fat. You'll learn about the latest research and the best ways to feed your family a nutritious, healthy, and delicious diet that won't leave them feeling deprived. You'll learn how to look for trans fats in foods—and which one of the two kinds of trans fats you should avoid.

The foods that you eat will actually taste better. Fresh foods, simply prepared with natural fats and oils and lots of spices, herbs, and seasonings, are what your body was meant to eat. After you've cooked for yourself, you'll find that the processed foods and fast foods you loved taste flat and artificial.

It's not difficult to avoid consuming trans fat. It just takes a little education and a little bit of work. Reading food labels will become second nature, and you'll be able to tell at a glance whether the food you're putting in your shopping cart is trans fat–free.

You'll find recipes for classic Real French Fries (page 238) along with baked Cheesy Home Fries (page 223) with less fat and fewer calories. You can choose from baked Glazed Raised Doughnuts (page 94) or classic Cake Doughnuts (page 87), cakes, pastries, and pies that are all more delicious than store-bought products and are better for you as well. And you'll nourish your family in emotional and psychological ways, too, by getting them involved in the cooking and meal-planning process.

Chapter 1

All about Trans Fat

Every time you turn on the news or open a newspaper these days there is a story about trans fat. New York City recently banned the use of this fat in restaurants, and fast food chains (like Wendy's, Taco Bell, and McDonald's) all over the country are changing their cooking techniques to eliminate trans fat from their products. Why is trans fat suddenly so newsworthy? Where did it come from? Why is it so bad for you, and how can you avoid it? Are there alternative fats that are safer? This chapter will help you learn more about these fats and your health.

What Is Trans Fat?

Trans fat is an artificial fat produced when liquid vegetable oil is treated with heat, chemicals, and hydrogen to transform it into a product that is semisolid at room temperature. The fat is inexpensive, performs beautifully in both baked and deep-fried applications, keeps food fresher longer, and provides a nice "mouthfeel" to many products. It is used instead of animal fats like butter or lard because it is easier to work with, doesn't become rancid, and can be used over and over again without breaking down or burning.

These fats are now ubiquitous in the processed food and restaurant industries. Products like fried chicken, potato chips, cookies, energy bars, and French fries all have artificial trans fat. And even products that you wouldn't associate with this fat, like cake mixes, canned soups, salad dressings, breakfast cereals, cookies, breads, and pies, all can contain substantial amounts of artificial trans fat. Restaurants use the fat to fry foods. Bakeries use it to make soft doughnuts, breads with a long shelf life, pastries with "snap," and tender cakes.

ALERT!

Even though the FDA required listing trans fat on processed food nutrition labels in January 2006, many companies have requested and have been granted waivers letting them delay this labeling for years, often to use up the old labels before they are forced to print new ones.

Trans fat was a godsend to the food industry. Fats are notoriously volatile. They become rancid quickly, are difficult to store, and can be very expensive. So when hydrogenated fat was invented it seemed like a quick and easy answer to food processors. But, as always with something that seems too good to be true, there was a catch. Trans fat is one of the few food ingredients that is truly bad for you.

Basic Food Science

The food science about trans fat is simple. Fats are simply chains of carbon molecules bonded with hydrogen molecules and attached to a glycerol molecule. There are three kinds of fat: saturated, monounsaturated, and polyunsaturated. These terms all define the type of bonds that the carbon molecules form with each other and with the hydrogen molecules.

Carbon molecules can bond with four other molecules in various formations. In saturated fats, all the carbon molecules are singly bonded to each other and bonded with two hydrogen molecules. In monounsaturated fats, one of the carbon-to-carbon bonds is a double bond without two hydrogen molecules. And in polyunsaturated fats, there are two or more double-bonded carbon molecules.

The Chemical Process

When hydrogen is introduced into a polyunsaturated fat, the hydrogen molecules begin to bond with the double-bonded carbon molecules. If they line up on the same side of the chain, the configuration is called *cis*. If they line up on the opposite sides of the chain, the configuration is called *trans*. Heat and pressure force the hydrogen molecules to line up in the trans configuration.

In the cis configuration, which is the natural form of mono- and polyunsaturated fats, the positioning of the hydrogen molecules makes a kink in the chain. This means they cannot pack closely together, so the fat will remain liquid at room temperature. In the trans configuration, the hydrogen molecules pair up on opposite sides of the carbon molecules. This straightens out the chain, so the molecules pack closely together, making a fat that is solid or semisolid at room temperature.

FACT

Fully hydrogenated oils are very solid at room temperature; in fact, they are so solid that they are basically unusable in food applications unless mixed with liquid oils. These types of fat do not contain any trans fat because all of the carbon molecules are bonded on both sides with hydrogen molecules.

The Bad Fat

The artificial trans fat that is causing all the uproar is made from partially hydrogenated polyunsaturated oil, usually soybean or cottonseed oil. To partially hydrogenate oil, the liquid oil is combined with a metal catalyst to speed up the chemical reaction. Hydrogen gas is bubbled through the mixture under high temperature and pressure, and the fat is then steam-cleaned and deodorized. All of these steps result in a highly processed, artificial food that is treated as a natural fat source by the body.

The Rise and Fall of Artificial Trans Fat

At the beginning of the twentieth century, the Procter & Gamble company needed a new product to increase their product line. A scientist had developed a means for making liquid cooking oils into a semisolid fat that was tasteless and odorless; the company hired the scientist and began perfecting the production of solid shortening.

When Procter & Gamble first introduced the fat as Crisco in 1911, it was hailed as a scientific breakthrough that revolutionized the food processing industry and consumer markets. A huge marketing campaign was conducted to introduce this fat to homemakers in the United States.

Entire advertising campaigns were built around this new product. Slogans like "for your heart's health," "rich, wholesome cream," "nutritious food oils," and "shortening is more digestible" were common.

FACT

The Twinkie mystery has been solved! Remember the experiment undertaken a few years ago by a college student who put a Twinkie on his windowsill for four days. Birds would not eat it, and the pastry's creamy filling remained intact through all sorts of weather. The culprit (or hero)? Trans fat! This is a prime example of how trans fat preserves food and extends shelf life.

The first cookbook promoting solid shortening was introduced in 1912. Companies held cooking classes for homemakers, teaching them how to use this new fat. And during World War II, consumers were urged to purchase and use this shortening and margarine so soldiers fighting overseas could have butter with their meals.

Butter and lard, which are high in saturated fats, were thought to be the culprit in the increasing number of cases of heart attack and cardiomyopathy occurring in the United States. Everyone from doctors to nutritionists urged consumers to avoid these natural saturated fats in favor of the cholesterol-free, low-saturated-fat margarines and shortenings. They were all wrong.

Questions Arise

In the 1960s and 1970s, a few researchers began to question the effect of trans fat on the body. Unfortunately, scientific research is never pure, and what the public finally hears from the government has had a lot of input from corporations, scientists, and lobbyists. Many of these research reports were minimized and diluted by those who stood to lose a lot if their favorite product was dethroned. Scientists, concerned about the purported effect of saturated fat on American health, endorsed the use of hydrogenated oils instead of animal fats.

In the 1970s, research started uncovering the truth about this fat. A report published in 1984 by Dr. Mary Enig showed that trans fat interferes with enzyme systems in the body. Studies showed that the fat tissues of people who had suffered heart attacks contained more trans fat than the fat tissues of healthy people. In the 1990s, more research was undertaken to study this fat, leading to a 2006 report in the *New England Journal of Medicine* that concluded that trans fat offers no nutritional benefit, but does considerable harm to your body and your health.

They're Everywhere!

Unless you are eating a strict vegan diet (no animal products of any kind), you are going to consume some naturally occurring and artificial trans fat. And even if you are a strict vegan, foods like cabbages, peas, and vegetable oils contain trans fat, too. Scientists estimate that the lowest amount of trans fat anyone can consume in a day is about 1 gram. Totally eliminating trans fat from your food means you would be eating such a restricted diet that you would miss out on other essential nutrients.

Any polyunsaturated oil is volatile under heat. Heating these oils produces a tiny amount of trans fat. Since most oils (except cold-pressed oils) are subjected to heat during the cleaning and deodorizing process, all of the polyunsaturated oils contain a small amount of artificial trans fat; most in negligible amounts that can still add up.

Table 1-1   Artificial Trans Fat in Fats and Oils*

Type of Fat	Amount of Trans Fat	Serving Size
Corn Oil	0.04 grams Artificial Trans Fat	One Tablespoon
Canola Oil	0.11 grams Artificial Trans Fat	One Tablespoon
Soybean Oil	0.09 grams Artificial Trans Fat	One Tablespoon
Solid Shortening	4.28 grams Artificial Trans Fat	One Tablespoon
Stick Margarine	2.70 grams Artificial Trans Fat	One Tablespoon
Nonfat Tub Margarine	0.03 grams Artificial Trans Fat	One Tablespoon
80% Fat Tub Margarine	1.10 grams Artificial Trans Fat	One Tablespoon

*Amounts were calculated using NutriBase Clinical version 7.0. When amounts were not available, all of the monounsaturated, polyunsaturated, and saturated fat numbers were added, then subtracted from the total number of fat grams. The remainder is a good approximation of the trans fat in each product.

Artificial trans fat is now found in almost 40 percent of the products available in grocery stores today. That means that out of the 100,000 products typically found in a large supermarket, 40,000 of them contain some amount of artificial trans fat. The transformation of processed foods to eliminate this fat (as much as is possible) is going to take some time, but it can be done.

Health Risks

Scientists and doctors estimate that the trans fat consumption in the United States causes about 30,000 deaths a year, perhaps as many as 100,000 deaths. That startling figure is what prompted the labeling changes and the call for banning trans fat in restaurants and processed foods.

Many laypeople consider scientific studies about food and health very confusing. It seems that the recommendations constantly change, and that foods considered good for your body are suddenly deemed bad, and vice versa. This is the nature of scientific research, which doesn't progress in a straight line, but changes as more sophisticated methods become standard and more questions are raised through research results.

Reliable Studies

Many studies that condemn trans fat use population and epidemiological studies as their methodology in addition to double-blind controlled studies. These studies have found that since the consumption of trans fat and processed foods increased in the United States, from next to nothing in the early 1900s to almost 45 percent of our diet today, heart disease rates have skyrocketed. At the same time, consumption of saturated fat, particularly butter and tropical oils, has plummeted. Many researchers have concluded that there is a connection.

Comparing populations that consume lots of saturated fat from natural sources to those that consume mainly oils and artificial fats shows an impressive difference in disease rates. People who eat natural saturated fats have lower rates of heart disease, diabetes, obesity, and cancer. Other studies have found that populations that have switched from a natural, plant- and animal-based diet to a "modern" diet of processed foods have undergone startling, detrimental changes to their health, including skyrocketing rates of diabetes, cancer, obesity, and heart disease.

How Trans Fat Affects Your Body:
- Changes hormone levels
- Increases LDL cholesterol levels
- Decreases HDL cholesterol levels
- Damages cell membranes, decreasing nutrient absorption
- Reduces flexibility of capillaries and arteries
- Increases the level of insulin in the bloodstream
- Contributes to weight gain, especially around the midsection
- Causes inflammation in cell walls and artery walls
- Increases the risk of cancer through free radicals

The Food Police?

As with any hot trend or new scientific fact, there is bound to be a backlash against regulation of trans fat. But most of those crusaders fail to recognize a crucial point. Americans didn't know they were consuming this fat, and didn't know what it did to their bodies. You can only have a choice when you are informed. You need to be informed about what the food you are eating does to your body, and you also need to know exactly what is in the food you are eating. Then, and only then, can you make the correct choices.

Trans Fat and Your Body

Artificial trans fat isn't recognized by your body as an artificial substance, so it is not discarded in the digestion process. Instead, it is used in chemical reactions as though it was a normal fatty acid. Trans fat is processed like the natural cis fatty acids. That means that in your cell membranes, in the lining of arteries and veins, and in your liver, brain, and kidneys, trans fat is fully incorporated, changing the functions and properties of your cells and of the enzymes that fuel your body. That's where the problems start.

Why You Need Fat

Fat is present in all of the cells of our body. It helps make cell walls permeable, it is metabolized into hormones, and is necessary for brain and heart health. The fat surrounding your heart is mostly saturated fat because it provides quick energy in times of stress. If you ate a totally fat-free diet you would quickly become sick. Substances called essential fatty acids cannot be made by your body, but must be consumed. Choosing the correct types of fats to eat is an important part of staying healthy.

Artificial trans fat, like other substances (including radioactive material), has a half-life of 51 days. In other words, it takes 51 days for your body to process half of the trans fat you eat. So, 51 days later, half of the remaining fat is processed. That means it takes 214 days, or more than seven months, to process 93 percent of this fat.

Fats help carry the fat-soluble vitamins (A, D, and E) throughout your body. Your brain, which is 60 percent fat, needs saturated fat to function properly. A low-fat or artificial-fat diet can increase the risk of osteoporosis. Fats perform important functions in your lungs, kidneys, and hormone production. But you have to avoid artificial trans fat, which interferes with all of these bodily functions.

Natural Trans Fat Is Different!

Naturally occurring trans fat is made when bacteria in the stomach of ruminant animals (cows and sheep) transform some of the fats found in plant material into the trans configuration. This means that products like milk, cheese, cream, beef, and lamb will have small amounts of naturally occurring trans fat.

These natural fats are actually good for you, unlike artificial trans fat. In your body they are transformed into CLA, or Conjugated Linoleic Acid, which has a positive effect on heart function. CLAs also help protect against free-radical damage to cells, which causes cancers to form, especially cancers of the breast and colon.

Table 1-2 Naturally Occurring Trans Fat in Dairy and Meat*

Food	Amount of Trans Fat	Serving Size
Butter	0.30 grams	One Tablespoon
Heavy cream	0.10 grams	One Tablespoon
Whole Milk (3.25% milk fat)	0.03 grams	One Cup
1% Milk	0.01 grams	One Cup
Sour Cream	0.04 grams	One Tablespoon
Hard Cheese	0.04 grams	One Tablespoon
Soft Cheese	0.08 grams	One Tablespoon
95% Lean Ground Beef	0.16 grams	3 Ounces
Sirloin Tip	0.11 grams	3 Ounces
Lamb Chop	0.79 grams	3 Ounces

*Amounts were calculated using NutriBase Clinical version 7.0. When amounts were not available, all of the monounsaturated, polyunsaturated, and saturated fat numbers were added, then subtracted from the total number of fat grams. The remainder is a good approximation of the trans fat in each product.

You'll notice that naturally occurring trans fat is found in very small quantities in these foods. At the current time, research indicates that these fats are not harmful, even in larger amounts. But you may still want to keep track of these naturally occurring fats, and the amounts per serving are listed in this book.

So, we've established that trans fat is bad for you in many ways. It's present in many of the foods you regularly consume. And it can hide in processed foods and doesn't yet have to be listed on all nutrition labels. What can you do?

A Little Bit Adds Up

Most Americans eat at least 5 to 6 grams of artificial trans fat per day. Some fast food meals used to be loaded with 8 grams of trans fat per serving! People who consume processed fats and solid shortening to avoid natural saturated animal and plant fats may be consuming 20 grams of trans fat per day.

The lowest amount of both naturally occurring and artificial trans fat that is possible to eat is about 1 to 2 grams. Trans fat occurs naturally in products from ruminant animals (cows and sheep), including butter, cream, and meats. And other foods, including cabbage and peas, have minute amounts. But we're concerned about artificial trans fat.

Why "Zero" Doesn't Mean "Zero"

The Food and Drug Administration now requires manufacturers to list the amount of trans fat present in each serving of processed food. The administration decided, under pressure from some in the food industry and their lobbyists, to set a standard of zero grams of trans fat if a serving offers less than 0.5 grams of trans fat. If a serving of potato chips, for instance, gives you 0.49 grams of trans fat, the label can claim zero trans fat.

But how often do you eat a recommended serving size? Most people eat far more than the recommended three cookies or fifteen potato chips in one sitting. Eat nine chocolate sandwich cookies with a trans fat amount of 0.40 grams per serving, and suddenly you have consumed 1.2 grams of artificial trans fat.

Canada has a stricter limit on labeling trans fat content. In that country, the food must have less than 0.2 grams of trans fat per serving to claim "zero trans fat" on the label. Some organizations, including *http://ban transfats.com,* are trying to get the U.S. government to follow suit.

The label requirements may change in the future, but for now, you need to know how to decipher the ingredient list on processed food labels to uncover the hidden artificial trans fat in foods.

How to Read a Label

Manufacturers are allowed to do one of two things if a food contains less than 0.5 grams of trans fat per serving. They can list "0 grams trans fat" under Fat Content in the nutrition labeling, or they can include the phrase "not a significant source of trans fat" under the nutrition label.

Why is there no daily value (DV) listed for trans fat?
There is no dietary or physical need for artificial trans fat in a healthy diet, and scientists cannot determine a safe upper limit of consumption. So there is no DV listed on food labels for trans fat. Take this as an extra warning to avoid consumption of this artificial fat when at all possible.

If the label has 0 grams of trans fat per serving, look at the ingredient list. If the words "partially hydrogenated," "margarine," or "shortening" appear in that list, the product does contain some artificial trans fat. Ingredients are listed in decreasing amounts, so if the hydrogenated fat or shortening appears toward the beginning of the list, there are probably close to 0.5 grams of trans fat per serving. If it appears toward the end of the list, there are probably close to 0 or 0.1 grams of trans fat per serving. If you purchase and eat processed foods, look for the phrase "No trans fat." In this labeling "zero" doesn't mean zero, but the word "No" means what it says.

Labels sometimes use "partially hydrogenated" and "hydrogenated" interchangeably, so avoid products that use either phrase. The words "ester-ification" or "esterified" are also a red light, indicating fats that have been manipulated with chemicals.

What You Can Do

After all that scary and discouraging information, we come to the solutions. And there are solutions! Now that you know about the dangers of trans fat and where to look for it, let's see how you can keep it out of your food and your body.

The Most Dangerous Aisle in the Supermarket

It's the bakery aisle! As long as food is produced on-site, bakeries are not required by the government to label their products with nutrition information. As we know, trans fat is commonly used in baked goods because it makes baked goods soft and flaky, contributes to a delicious flavor and mouthfeel, is inexpensive, and extends the shelf life of the product.

You can ask the bakery manager for nutrition information. If she doesn't have it, then ask to see the ingredient list for your favorite products. If that list includes the words "hydrogenated" or "shortening," then you know that the bread, cookie, or pastry contains artificial trans fat. If it doesn't, you can eat that product and not worry about it.

If you're interested in the glycemic Index, here's a relevant fact. Fats, especially saturated fats found in animal products, reduce the glycemic load of foods by slowing the rate at which they are processed by the body. So add a bit of butter to your baked potato or morning toast to reduce its glycemic index.

The snack foods aisle is almost as dangerous, but since those products have to (eventually) list nutrition information including trans fat content on their labels, at least you know a little about what is in the food. But you still have to be vigilant.

Reducing Your Risks

One of the best things you can do to reduce your family's exposure to trans fat is to start cooking more foods at home. Using natural fats like butter, cold-pressed olive oil, and coconut oil will ensure that even your baked and fried foods will have little or no artificial trans fat. Having control over the foods you put in your body is an important first step toward reclaiming your health.

You can substitute trans fat–free margarines specifically made for baking for the butter and coconut oil in this book if you'd like. And you can use egg substitutes and sugar substitutes, too, following the directions for converting recipes on their packages.

But remember, those products still have some artificial trans fat. And many scientists and nutritionists feel that we rely too much on synthetic foods in our diet—foods that our bodies were not made to use. You are also taking a chance that in the future these "foods" could turn out to be bad for your body.

Choose Good Fats

Medium-chain saturated fats, like those found in coconut oil and palm oil, need very little processing by the body to be absorbed and used. They are quickly metabolized in the liver and aren't stored in the body. They are a good source of quick energy and do not contribute to heart disease; in fact, they may protect against inflammation in the body. Medium-chain saturated fats also have antimicrobial properties.

Saturated fats, instead of being the villain in the cardiac heart disease epidemic gripping the country, may actually be healthy, according to the latest research. Your cell membranes, heart, brain, and liver require saturated fat for optimum performance.

Nut oils, including walnut oil, sesame oil, and almond oil, are rich-tasting and contain lots of monounsaturated fats that are important for heart health. They are mostly used as flavorings instead of the main oil or fat in a product.

And lard isn't as bad for you as previously thought. It's a natural fat, and has 66 percent of the saturated fats found in butter. If you want to use lard, render your own lard instead of purchasing processed lard. You can find instructions for this in *The Everything® Tex-Mex Cookbook*.

Is Butter Really Better?

Many researchers believe that natural fats, including those in butter and lard, are better for you than even "no trans fat" margarines. The types of saturated fat in these products include those heroes, CLAs, which may help protect the body against disease.

Butter, especially organic butter made from grass-fed cows, has high amounts of vitamins A and D and minerals like calcium and potassium that are necessary for good health. It also has lecithin, a natural emulsifier, omega-3 fatty acids, manganese, selenium, chromium, and iodine. Butter also protects against tumors and fungus infections. And remember, it's a natural food that has been nourishing populations for generations.

In Your Kitchen

The first step toward a trans fat–free life is to go through your pantry, fridge, and freezer and really look at the labels on the food stored there. Discard foods that include "shortening" and "hydrogenated" on the label. Only you can decide which foods you choose to keep or discard, and only after you have been informed and educated about nutrition.

Every time an oil is heated, small amounts of artificial trans fat are created. When you fry food in a polyunsaturated oil, use fresh oil each time to reduce this risk. And if you can find a cold-pressed oil to use in frying, you'll reduce the risk even more. Look for oils that contain the smallest amounts of artificial trans fat to use.

Base your diet on the color wheel. If you eat lots of brightly colored foods, like red bell peppers, strawberries, melons, tomatoes, blueberries, grapes, carrots, nuts, seeds, and legumes, you'll automatically improve your diet.

When you choose to fry or make a food that is higher in fat, use natural fats like butter, lard, and coconut oil. Cold-pressed peanut oil and canola oil are good choices for deep-frying. Smoothies made with coconut oil are delicious and healthy. An egg (especially eggs from organic, pasture-fed chickens) cooked in a little bit of butter is an excellent breakfast that satisfies you and holds back hunger until lunchtime.

Choosing Food

Whole foods, including meats and dairy products, whole grains, legumes, vegetables, and fruits, should form the bulk of your diet. Many scientists think that processed sugar is also bad for you; eat sugary foods like cookies, cakes, and pastries as an occasional treat. And make them at home! Baking with your family is not only a good way to teach them to feed themselves well, but it introduces concepts like math and physics to kids in a fun way.

Remember that totally banning any food group is going to eliminate some essential nutrients. The only really "bad" food is trans fat! In fact, nutritionists know that whole foods contain many vital micronutrients that haven't even been discovered. Eating processed foods and junk food and using a multivitamin to compensate isn't a viable option.

Other Fats to Choose

Palm oil, rice bran oil, avocado oil, flax seed oil, nut oils, grapeseed oil, and extra-virgin olive oil are all good choices. Browse through a natural-foods store or food co-op and really look at the oils lining their shelves. Read labels and browse the Internet for information about these fats and oils.

About This Book

No food in this book contains more than 0.49 grams of trans fat per serving—and that's natural trans fat. Artificial trans fat is limited to 0.08 grams per serving or less. If a recipe contains only natural trans fat, an asterisk (*) is added to the trans fat amount in the nutrition sidebar. If a recipe has both artificial and natural trans fat, as in Cilantro Chicken Tacos (page 156), only the artificial trans fat is listed.

Daily Values

Every one of these recipes includes nutrition information, calculated using NutriBase Clinical Version 7.0 (*www.dietsoftware.com*). In order to use this information, you have to know the recommended daily amounts of these nutrients.

Every day, an average healthy person should consume approximately 2,000 calories. Of that amount, 40 percent should be from carbohydrates, 30 percent from protein, and 30 percent from fats. That means that 800 calories should come from carbs, 600 calories from protein, and 600 calories from fat.

Try to keep trans fat consumption to less than 1 percent of your daily calories; that is about 2.0 grams. Saturated fat consumption should be around 20 to 30 grams per day. The total amount of cholesterol you should consume is around 200 to 300 mg.

Since the verdict is still out on saturated fat and fat in general, there are references in the book about reducing fat, even though some evidence indicates that natural fat is actually good for you. Some of these recipes were developed using oil, low-saturated fat foods, and fat replacements like fruit purees. Other recipes use butter and coconut oil, so you have a choice and can follow diets ordered by your doctor. This way you can choose which fats you want to eat while still enjoying a balanced diet, including desserts and sweets.

In these recipes, some sizes and types of food are standard. Eggs are large, milk is 2 percent fluid, ground beef is 95 percent fat-free, chicken breasts are skinless unless specified otherwise, and flour is all-purpose. Fruits and vegetables are medium-size, and beef is trimmed of most visible fat. For fried foods, it's assumed that 10 percent of the oil used in frying is absorbed into the food. That is calculated in the nutrition composition.

Let's Cook!

In this book you'll find ways that you can make your own Crisp and Healthy Fried Chicken (page 151) with less than 0.05 grams of artificial trans fat per serving. Or try Baked Fried Chicken (page 153), with 200 fewer calories per serving and no artificial trans fat. Make your own "Popped Tarts" pastries (page 91), and delicious yeast breads that will make your home smell like heaven.

You can make appetizers, desserts, pastries, potato chips, corn chips, entrees, soups, salads, and other snack foods that are artificial trans fat–free, or as close to it as possible. And you can feel confident feeding your family these wholesome foods, knowing you are cooking with natural ingredients and nourishing yourself, body and soul.

By starting to think differently about the foods that you buy and eat, you will improve your health and start to address chronic diseases. And the foods you eat and make to feed your family will be delicious and satisfying. Let's get started!

Chapter 2

Appetizers and Snacks

Yogurt Cheese Spinach Dip

SERVES 8

CALORIES	61.50
FAT	2.68 GRAMS
SATURATED FAT	0.85 GRAMS
TRANS FAT	0.0 GRAMS
CARBOHYDRATES	6.17 GRAMS
CHOLESTEROL	3.67 MG

Yogurt cheese is an excellent substitute for cream cheese in almost any recipe. Be sure you use the simplest yogurt, without gelatin or other thickening agents added.

2 cups plain low fat yogurt
½ cup finely chopped onion
2 cloves garlic, minced
1 tablespoon olive oil

2 cups fresh spinach
½ teaspoon salt
⅛ teaspoon cayenne pepper
2 tablespoons lemon juice

1. Place the yogurt in a strainer lined with cheesecloth. Rest the strainer over a bowl, cover with plastic wrap, and let stand in the refrigerator overnight.

2. The next day, remove the yogurt cheese from the strainer; save the whey for another use. In a heavy saucepan, cook onion and garlic in olive oil over medium heat until tender. Chop the spinach and add to the pan; cook and stir until spinach is wilted and water has evaporated, about 3 minutes. Remove from heat and sprinkle with salt, cayenne pepper, and lemon juice. Remove to a mixing bowl; let stand until cool, about 45 minutes. Blend in the yogurt cheese. Serve immediately or cover and chill for up to 3 days.

Herbed Potato Chips

YIELDS 16 CUPS

CALORIES	56.89
FAT	4.39 GRAMS
SATURATED FAT	0.41 GRAMS
TRANS FAT	0.03 GRAMS
CARBOHYDRATES	4.17 GRAMS
CHOLESTEROL	0.0 MG

Making your own potato chips is fun. You can sprinkle them with everything from dried herbs and spices to finely grated cheese.

Cold water
Ice cubes
2 lemons, juiced
1 russet potato (about 1 pound)

3 cups canola oil
1 tablespoon minced fresh dill weed
1 tablespoon minced thyme leaves
1 tablespoon salt, or to taste

1. Fill a bowl with cold water and add ice cubes and lemon juice, along with the lemon rinds. Peel potato and cut into thin chips using a food processor, a mandoline, or a vegetable peeler. Each chip should be almost translucent. Place chips into the water mixture as soon as they are formed.

2. In large heavy pan, heat canola oil to 375°F. Working with a handful of potato chips at a time, remove from water and drain on kitchen towels, then pat dry with paper towels. Drop chips into the oil; fry for 3 to 6 minutes, turning with slotted spoon, until chips are light golden brown. Remove and place on paper towels; sprinkle hot chips with a mixture of the herbs and salt. Repeat with remaining chips and salt mixture. Cool completely, then store in airtight container up to 3 days.

Cheesy Tomato Bruschetta

¼ cup tomato paste
2 tablespoons olive oil
1 (14-ounce) can diced Italian tomatoes, drained
3 cloves garlic, minced
1 teaspoon dried basil leaves
1 cup grated Parmesan cheese
16 (½-inch) slices Italian Loaf (page 46)

1. Preheat broiler in oven; set oven rack 6 inches from heat source.

2. In medium bowl, combine tomato paste and olive oil; blend well until smooth. Add remaining ingredients except for bread and mix gently.

3. Slice bread into 16 ½-inch slices and place on broiler pan. Broil bread slices until golden on one side, about 1 to 3 minutes. Turn and broil until light golden brown on second side. Remove from oven and top with tomato mixture. Return to oven and broil for 3 to 5 minutes or until tomato topping is bubbly and begins to brown. Serve immediately.

About Tomato Paste

Tomato paste is made by concentrating fresh tomatoes until almost all the water is evaporated. It is very flavorful, and can be found in seasoned varieties like Italian. If the recipe doesn't use a whole can, freeze the rest in 1-tablespoon amounts. To use, let stand at room temperature for 20 to 30 minutes until thawed.

SERVES 10

CALORIES	226.93
FAT	7.20 GRAMS
SATURATED FAT	2.60 GRAMS
TRANS FAT	0.06 GRAMS*
CARBOHYDRATES	30.79 GRAMS
CHOLESTEROL	20.93 MG

This flavorful tomato topping from your pantry can be used in other recipes, too. Fold some into mayonnaise for an appetizer dip, or use it to top broiled chicken or fish.

Red Pepper Almond Dip

SERVES 10

CALORIES	184.71
FAT	17.37 GRAMS
SATURATED FAT	3.01 GRAMS
TRANS FAT	0.03 GRAMS*
CARBOHYDRATES	4.75 GRAMS
CHOLESTEROL	18.77 MG

Two kinds of red peppers and two kinds of almonds make this beautiful little dip delicious. Serve with Sesame Corn Wafers (page 30) and Crisp Cheese Crackers (page 67).

1 (7-ounce) jar roasted red peppers
½ cup blanched almonds
½ cup Homemade Mayonnaise (page 31)
¼ cup sour cream
¼ cup grated Cotija cheese
1 red bell pepper
¼ cup chopped green onion
½ teaspoon salt
⅛ teaspoon cayenne pepper
½ cup sliced almonds, toasted

1. Drain roasted red peppers and place in food processor or blender along with blanched almonds, Mayonnaise, sour cream, and Cotija cheese. Process or blend until combined and smooth.

2. Seed and chop red bell pepper. Stir into sour cream mixture along with green onion, salt, and cayenne pepper. Arrange in serving bowl and sprinkle with sliced almonds. Serve immediately or cover and refrigerate up to 2 days before serving.

Basil Pesto

¼ cup pine nuts
¼ cup chopped walnuts
4 cloves garlic
1 teaspoon extra-virgin olive oil
3 cups packed fresh basil leaves
½ cup cubed Romano cheese
¼ cup cubed Parmesan cheese
½ teaspoon salt
⅛ teaspoon white pepper
¾ cup extra-virgin olive oil
2 tablespoons water

YIELDS 1-½ CUPS
(SERVING SIZE 1 TABLESPOON)

CALORIES	98.10
FAT	9.88 GRAMS
SATURATED FAT	1.81 GRAMS
TRANS FAT	0.02 GRAMS*
CARBOHYDRATES	0.87 GRAMS
CHOLESTEROL	4.37 MG

Pesto can be used as a dip on its own, mixed with some sour cream for another dip, or tossed with some hot pasta for an easy first course.

1. Preheat oven to 350°F. Spread pine nuts and walnuts on a small baking sheet. Sprinkle garlic with 1 teaspoon olive oil and add to baking sheet. Toast in oven for 5 to 8 minutes or until nuts smell fragrant and start to brown. Remove nuts and place on paper towel to cool. Continue roasting garlic for another 5 to 10 minutes or until it turns brown. Do not allow garlic to burn. Cool garlic and nuts completely.

2. Combine cooled nuts and garlic, basil leaves, cubed cheese, salt, and pepper in blender or food processor. Pulse until finely chopped. With the blender or food processor turned on, stream in ¾ cup olive oil until a thick sauce forms. Then add water and pulse until blended. Serve immediately or cover and refrigerate up to 3 days. Freeze for longer storage.

Preserving Pesto

Pesto will keep, well-covered, in the refrigerator for 3 to 4 days. Freeze this sauce for longer storage. Spoon the pesto into ice cube trays and freeze until solid. Then pop out the cubes and place them in a hard-sided freezer container or plastic freezer food-storage bag. Label and use within three months.

Spicy Empanadas

YIELDS 48 EMPANADAS

CALORIES	45.95
FAT	2.06 GRAMS
SATURATED FAT	1.00 GRAMS
TRANS FAT	0.04 GRAMS*
CARBOHYDRATES	5.40 GRAMS
CHOLESTEROL	4.47 MG

Read labels carefully! These products should be trans fat–free; be sure that no ingredient with the word "hydrogenated" is in the ingredient list.

1 tablespoon extra-virgin olive oil
½ cup finely chopped onion
2 teaspoons curry powder
1 cup frozen vegetarian burger crumbles, thawed
2 cups Garlic and Onion Smashed Potatoes (page 235)
1 teaspoon salt
⅛ teaspoon cayenne pepper
48 (3" to 4") won ton wrappers
Water
4 tablespoons butter, melted

1. Preheat oven to 375°F. In heavy saucepan, heat olive oil over medium heat. Add onion and curry powder; cook and stir for 4 to 5 minutes until onions are tender. Remove from heat and add crumbles, potatoes, salt, and pepper and stir together.

2. Place 6 won ton wrappers on work surface. Place 1 tablespoon filling in center of wrapper. Brush edges of wrapper with water. Fold wrapper over filling, forming a triangle. Press edges to seal. Place on ungreased cookie sheet and brush with butter. Repeat with remaining wrappers and filling, brushing each with butter. Bake for 8 to 12 minutes or until empanadas are light golden brown. Cool for 15 minutes, then serve.

Oil Retention
How much oil do fried foods absorb as they cook? The average "oil retention" amount for fried foods is about 10 percent; that means that 10 percent of the oil is absorbed. To keep this low percentage, the oil should be at the correct temperature so the food doesn't absorb oil before the surface seals. And the food should be cooked for the amount of time the recipe directs.

Eggplant Caviar

2 medium eggplants
⅓ cup olive oil
½ cup finely chopped onion
4 cloves garlic, minced
3 tablespoons lemon juice
1 teaspoon salt
⅛ teaspoon cayenne pepper
½ cup toasted pine nuts

1. Preheat oven to 375°F. Peel eggplants and slice into ½" rounds. Drizzle half of the olive oil on the bottom of a roasting pan and arrange eggplant in the oil. Drizzle remaining olive oil over eggplant. Roast for 20 minutes.

2. Remove pan from oven and sprinkle onion and garlic over eggplant. Return pan to oven and roast for 10 to 20 minutes longer or until eggplant is soft and onion and garlic are tender.

3. Place in medium mixing bowl and sprinkle with lemon juice, salt, and pepper. Using a fork, mash eggplant mixture until semi-smooth. Fold in pine nuts and serve immediately or omit nuts and cover and refrigerate up to 24 hours before serving. Fold in pine nuts just before serving.

Toasting Nuts

Toasting nuts brings out their flavor and makes a little go a long way. To toast nuts, preheat an oven (or the toaster oven) to 350°F. Spread nuts in a single layer on a baking sheet. Toast for 8 to 12 minutes, shaking sheet once during cooking time, until the nuts are fragrant and a bit darkened in color. Let cool completely before chopping.

SERVES 8

CALORIES	170.51
FAT	15.00 GRAMS
SATURATED FAT	1.70 GRAMS
TRANS FAT	0.0 GRAMS
CARBOHYDRATES	9.35 GRAMS
CHOLESTEROL	0.0 MG

Eggplant takes on a smoky taste when roasted; combined with onion and lemon juice it does taste a bit like caviar—only better for you!

Poppy Popcorn

**YIELDS 20 CUPS
(40 SERVINGS)**

CALORIES	165.61
FAT	9.41 GRAMS
SATURATED FAT	3.20 GRAMS
TRANS FAT	0.09 GRAMS*
CARBOHYDRATES	20.17 GRAMS
CHOLESTEROL	10.12 MG

This crunchy and crisp mixture makes a lot of sweetened popcorn and nuts. It's perfect for the holidays.

4 quarts air-popped popcorn
1 cup whole pecans
1 cup walnut pieces
1 cup sliced almonds
¾ cup butter
1-½ cups sugar
½ cup brown sugar
⅓ cup dark corn syrup
¼ cup honey
1 teaspoon salt
½ teaspoon baking soda
2 teaspoons vanilla
1 cup milk chocolate chips

1. Preheat oven to 350°F. Carefully remove any unpopped kernels from popcorn. Place remaining popcorn in two large baking pans. Spread pecans and walnuts on a cookie sheet. Toast for 8 minutes, stirring once during baking time. Add sliced almonds and toast 3 to 5 minutes longer until nuts are fragrant. Cool completely and mix with popcorn.

2. In large saucepan, combine butter, sugar, brown sugar, corn syrup, honey, and salt. Bring to a boil over high heat; reduce heat to medium and boil for 5 minutes, stirring frequently. Remove from heat and stir in baking soda; mixture will foam up. Stir in vanilla, then spoon mixture evenly over popcorn mixture. Toss to coat.

3. Reduce oven heat to 250°F. Bake popcorn mixture for 1 hour, stirring every 20 minutes during baking time. While mixture is baking, grind chocolate chips in blender or food processor. When popcorn mixture is golden, remove from oven and sprinkle ground chocolate evenly over both pans. Let stand for 10 minutes, then stir. Let cool completely, break into pieces, and place in airtight container.

Spinach Pesto Spread

1 cup frozen spinach, thawed
1 tablespoon lemon juice
½ cup Basil Pesto (page 23)
⅓ cup grated Parmesan cheese
¼ cup chopped walnuts
½ cup Homemade Mayonnaise (page 31)
¼ cup sour cream

SERVES 10	
CALORIES	215.23
FAT	21.33 GRAMS
SATURATED FAT	4.25 GRAMS
TRANS FAT	0.04 GRAMS*
CARBOHYDRATES	2.64 GRAMS
CHOLESTEROL	23.00 MG

Most recipes don't use a whole box or bag of frozen spinach, so the leftovers tend to collect in your freezer. Use them in this fabulous dip.

1. Squeeze the spinach over the sink to get rid of some of the water. Place spinach in a food processor and add lemon juice, Pesto, and Parmesan cheese. Process until well mixed.

2. Scrape into a medium bowl and add remaining ingredients; mix until blended. Serve immediately or cover and refrigerate for up to 2 days before serving.

Serve Your Dip with . . .

This dip is great with with sturdy crackers, chips, bread or baguette slices, and raw vegetables. Consider the flavor of the dip when you choose the dippers. A Tex-Mex dip, for instance, should be served with a variety of tortilla chips. Serve this pesto dip with carrot and celery sticks and some toasted sliced baguettes. Make sure the dippers are sturdy enough to carry the dip!

Easy Antipasto

SERVES 12

CALORIES	197.28
FAT	15.49 GRAMS
SATURATED FAT	5.42 GRAMS
TRANS FAT	0.16 GRAMS*
CARBOHYDRATES	5.84 GRAMS
CHOLESTEROL	34.61 MG

If you have a garden, this is a fabulous recipe to make in the summer when you have lots of fresh tomatoes, peppers, and zucchini on hand.

3 cups leftover Roasted Vegetables (page 226)
1 cup cubed Cheddar cheese
1 cup cubed Swiss cheese
2 (4-ounce) jars mushrooms, undrained
1 (8-ounce) package frozen artichoke hearts, thawed
¾ cup zesty Italian salad dressing
½ pound thinly sliced turkey salami

1. In bowl, combine vegetables, cheeses, mushrooms with their liquid, artichoke hearts, and salad dressing. Cover and chill for 12 to 24 hours.

2. Cut the salami slices in half. Roll each piece into a cone, using a toothpick if necessary, and place on serving platter. Using a slotted spoon, remove vegetables, cheeses, and mushrooms from the marinade and arrange around meat slices. Drizzle with any remaining marinade and serve.

Brown Sugar Glazed Salmon

SERVES 8

CALORIES	276.13
FAT	12.71 GRAMS
SATURATED FAT	3.53 GRAMS
TRANS FAT	0.08 GRAMS*
CARBOHYDRATES	15.06 GRAMS
CHOLESTEROL	77.93 MG

Brown sugar and ginger root add fabulous flavor to these little cubes of salmon. Serve with sour cream for dipping if you'd like.

2 (1-pound) salmon steaks
2 tablespoons butter
½ cup minced onion
3 cloves garlic, minced
½ cup brown sugar

2 tablespoons Dijon mustard
1 teaspoon grated ginger root
½ teaspoon salt
⅛ teaspoon cayenne pepper

1. Cut salmon steaks into 1-½" pieces. Thread onto metal skewers and place in glass baking dish. In small saucepan, melt butter over medium heat. Add onion and garlic; cook and stir until tender and onions begin to brown, about 6 to 7 minutes. Remove from heat and add brown sugar, mustard, ginger root, salt, and pepper and mix well. Pour mixture over salmon, turning to coat. Cover and refrigerate for 2 to 4 hours.

2. When ready to serve, prepare and preheat grill, or broiler. Cook salmon kebabs 6" from heat source (over medium coals, or under high broiler) for 4 to 7 minutes, turning once, until salmon is just done. Remove from skewers and arrange on serving plate.

Tex-Mex Popcorn

8 cups air-popped popcorn
½ cup butter
1 jalapeño pepper, minced
4 cloves garlic, minced
1 tablespoon chili powder
1 teaspoon cumin
1 teaspoon salt
⅛ teaspoon cayenne pepper
½ cup grated Cotija cheese

1. Preheat oven to 300°F. In large bowl, place popcorn. In small saucepan, heat butter over medium heat until melted. Stir in jalapeño; cook and stir for 1 minute. Then add garlic; cook and stir for 2 minutes longer until fragrant. Remove from heat and add chili powder and cumin. Drizzle over popcorn and toss to coat.

2. Sprinkle salt, cayenne pepper, and Cotija cheese over popcorn and toss to coat. Spread on large cookie sheet. Bake for 20 to 25 minutes, stirring once during baking time, until popcorn is glazed. Cool on paper towels. Store in airtight container at room temperature.

How to Pop Popcorn

You can pop popcorn with just a pan and a stove burner. Add a tablespoon of oil to the pan. Add about ½ cup of popcorn to make 10 cups of popped corn. Place the pan over high heat and add the popcorn. Gently shake the pan until the popcorn starts to pop, then put the cover on and keep shaking until the popping slows to 1 pop every 2 seconds.

YIELDS 8 CUPS

CALORIES	165.33
FAT	13.83 GRAMS
SATURATED FAT	8.45 GRAMS
TRANS FAT	0.34 GRAMS*
CARBOHYDRATES	7.60 GRAMS
CHOLESTEROL	36.00 MG

Popcorn is a great snack that you can dress up in infinite ways. If Tex-Mex isn't your favorite, use Italian spices, or try an Asian touch.

Sesame Corn Wafers

**YIELDS 8 CUPS;
(16 SERVINGS)**

CALORIES	89.09
FAT	6.50 GRAMS
SATURATED FAT	1.09 GRAMS
TRANS FAT	0.02 GRAMS
CARBOHYDRATES	6.82 GRAMS
CHOLESTEROL	1.91 GRAMS

These little wafers are a lot like commercial corn chips, but they're coated with sesame seeds for more flavor and crunch.

1 cup masa harina
2 tablespoons white cornmeal
1 teaspoon salt
½ cup boiling water
1 tablespoon butter
½ cup sesame seeds
2 cups canola oil
More salt, if desired

1. Combine masa harina, cornmeal, and salt in large bowl. Add boiling water and butter and stir until a soft dough forms. You may need to add another tablespoon or so of boiling water. Divide dough into 5 equal pieces. Roll out each piece to ⅛" thickness, about a 6" × 6" rectangle, between two sheets of plastic wrap. Remove the top sheet of plastic wrap, sprinkle with some of the sesame seeds and press seeds into the dough. Cut the dough into 1" × ½" pieces. Repeat with remaining dough.

2. Place oil in heavy saucepan and heat over medium high heat to 375°F. Remove dough pieces from plastic wrap and fry chips, about a fourth at a time, until light golden brown. Remove to paper towels, sprinkle with salt, and let cool. Store covered in airtight container.

3. These can also be baked. Add another 1-½ to 2 cups of boiling water to the masa harina mixture to make a batter. Drop by teaspoonfuls onto Silpat-lined cookie sheets and sprinkle with sesame seeds. Bake at 450°F for 11 to 14 minutes or until chips are golden brown. Calorie count per ½ cup of baked chips is 65.89, with 3.88 grams of fat and 0.02 grams of natural trans fat.

Masa Harina

Masa harina is not cornmeal; it is corn flour. You can find it in the ethnic foods aisle of most supermarkets, and in Mexican and Hispanic markets. It is very finely ground so the dough will hold together. There is no gluten in corn flour, so you can reroll scraps as long as you want to; they won't get tough.

Homemade Mayonnaise

1 pasteurized egg
1 pasteurized egg yolk
2 teaspoons Dijon mustard
¼ teaspoon garlic salt
2 tablespoons lemon juice
1-¼ cups extra-virgin olive oil
1 tablespoon boiling water

YIELDS 1-½ CUPS (SERVING SIZE 1 TABLESPOON)

CALORIES	105.39
FAT	11.66 GRAMS
SATURATED FAT	1.69 GRAMS
TRANS FAT	0.0 GRAMS
CARBOHYDRATES	0.18 GRAMS
CHOLESTEROL	17.55 MG

1. In blender or food processor, combine egg, egg yolk, mustard, garlic salt, and lemon juice. Blend or process until smooth. Remove cap from blender top, or remove feed tube cover from food processor. Very slowly, one drop at a time, begin adding the olive oil while the mixture is blending. Continue to add the oil as the mixture begins to emulsify.

2. Once the mixture looks like mayonnaise, you can add the oil in larger quantities, i.e., in a thin stream. Continue blending until all the oil is added. Then add 1 tablespoon boiling water and blend until combined. Store, covered, in the refrigerator for up to 4 days.

You can find pasteurized eggs in the dairy aisle of any large supermarket. Be sure to heed the expiration dates.

Emulsifying

Mayonnaise thickens and the sauce holds together because it is emulsified. That means that two ingredients that do not blend together are held in a stable form because of an emulsifier. In mayonnaise recipes, the two ingredients are egg yolk and oil; the emulsifier is the egg white and some type of mustard.

Creamy and Crunchy Hummus

**YIELDS 2 CUPS
(SERVING SIZE
2 TABLESPOONS)**

CALORIES	100.03
FAT	6.06 GRAMS
SATURATED FAT	0.92 GRAMS
TRANS FAT	0.01 GRAMS*
CARBOHYDRATES	9.42 GRAMS
CHOLESTEROL	1.19 MG

Sweet potato adds great color and nutrition to classic hummus. To make it easy, use canned sweet potatoes, drained and mashed.

1 tablespoon olive oil
5 cloves garlic, sliced
1 (15-ounce) can chickpeas
½ cup mashed sweet potato
¼ cup tahini
3 tablespoons lemon juice
½ teaspoon salt
⅛ teaspoon cayenne pepper
3 tablespoons sour cream
½ cup chopped walnuts

1. In small saucepan, heat olive oil over medium heat. Add sliced garlic; cook and stir until garlic turns light brown; do not let it burn. Remove from heat and cool until warm.

2. Combine with remaining ingredients except walnuts in blender or food processor; blend or process until smooth. Stir in walnuts and serve, or cover and chill before serving.

Pita Chips

Make your own pita chips to serve with Hummus and other dips. Start with Pita Bread (page 41), cut in half horizontally then cut into 8 wedges each. Drizzle with olive oil and sprinkle with salt and spices like cayenne pepper, garlic powder, and paprika. Bake at 400°F for 6 to 8 minutes until crisp, let cool slightly, and serve.

Spice and Honey Nuts

2 cups walnut halves
2 cups pecan halves
3 tablespoons butter
¼ cup honey
⅓ cup brown sugar
1 teaspoon cinnamon
1 teaspoon ginger
½ teaspoon cardamom
⅛ teaspoon cayenne pepper

1. Preheat oven to 375°F. Spread walnuts and pecans on large cookie sheet and toast for 8 to 12 minutes or until the nuts are fragrant, stirring once during cooking time. Set aside.

2. In small saucepan, combine butter, honey, and remaining ingredients over medium heat. Cook, stirring frequently, just until mixture comes to a boil. Drizzle over nuts, tossing to coat. Reduce oven temperature to 325°F. Bake nuts for 15 to 20 minutes, stirring every 5 minutes, until glazed. Cool completely, then break apart and store in airtight container.

Nut Nutrition

Some nuts are better than others! The types of nuts that may help reduce the risk of heart disease include almonds, peanuts, pecans, pistachio nuts, walnuts, and hazelnuts. They are a high-fat food, but the type of fat is monosaturated, which can help lower LDL cholesterol (the "bad" cholesterol).

SERVES 16

CALORIES	219.72
FAT	19.22 GRAMS
SATURATED FAT	2.90 GRAMS
TRANS FAT	0.06 GRAMS*
CARBOHYDRATES	12.26 GRAMS
CHOLESTEROL	5.72 MG

Watch the mixture carefully as it cooks; because it's high in sugar it can burn easily.

Cinnamon Curry Fruit Dip

SERVES 8

CALORIES	88.20
FAT	5.55 GRAMS
SATURATED FAT	3.47 GRAMS
TRANS FAT	0.08 GRAMS*
CARBOHYDRATES	8.79 GRAMS
CHOLESTEROL	17.59 MG

The sweet tartness of peaches combines beautifully with curry powder. This special dip can be served as dessert.

1 peach
1 teaspoon curry powder
½ teaspoon cinnamon
¼ cup brown sugar
½ cup low-fat sour cream
1 (3-ounce) package cream cheese, softened

1. Peel peach and remove stone; cut peach into slices. Place in food processor or blender along with curry powder, cinnamon, brown sugar, sour cream, and cream cheese and blend until smooth. Place in refrigerator and chill for at least 4 hours before serving. Serve with fruit and bread.

Cream and Cranberry Spread

SERVES 16

CALORIES	162.57
FAT	7.39 GRAMS
SATURATED FAT	2.98 GRAMS
TRANS FAT	0.06 GRAMS*
CARBOHYDRATES	21.50 GRAMS
CHOLESTEROL	15.69 MG

Serve this tart and creamy dip with crackers (trans fat–free!), slices of toasted French bread, and breadsticks for dipping.

1 (15-ounce) can whole-berry cranberry sauce
½ cup dried cranberries, chopped
1 teaspoon orange zest
2 tablespoons frozen orange juice concentrate
1 (8-ounce) package low-fat cream cheese
1 cup low-fat sour cream
2 tablespoons brown sugar
1 cup sliced almonds, toasted

1. In bowl, combine cranberry sauce with dried cranberries and orange zest; mix well and set aside. In large bowl, combine orange juice concentrate, cream cheese, sour cream, and brown sugar and beat until combined.

2. On large serving plate, spread cream cheese mixture into an even layer. Spoon cranberry mixture evenly over the cream cheese layer. Sprinkle with toasted almonds and serve immediately, or cover and chill for 4 to 6 hours before serving.

Gingerbread Fruit Dip

1 (8-ounce) package cream cheese, softened
½ cup low-fat sour cream
⅓ cup brown sugar
¼ cup maple syrup or light molasses
2 tablespoons chopped candied ginger
½ teaspoon ground ginger
½ teaspoon cinnamon
¼ teaspoon nutmeg

1. In medium bowl, beat cream cheese until light and fluffy. Gradually add sour cream, beating until smooth. Add sugar and beat well. Gradually add molasses and beat until smooth. Stir in remaining ingredients. Cover and chill for at least 3 hours before serving with fresh fruit.

Candied Ginger
Candied ginger is also known as crystallized ginger. It is made of pieces of ginger root simmered in a sugar syrup, then rolled in sugar. You can make your own by combining ¾ cup sugar with ¾ cup water and bringing to a simmer. Add ½ cup peeled and chopped fresh ginger root; simmer for 25 minutes. Drain, dry, then roll in sugar to coat.

**SERVES 12
(SERVING SIZE
2 TABLESPOONS)**

CALORIES	125.83
FAT	7.84 GRAMS
SATURATED FAT	4.94 GRAMS
TRANS FAT	0.12 GRAMS*
CARBOHYDRATES	12.55 GRAMS
CHOLESTEROL	25.94 MG

This dip is wonderful served with fresh fruits like apple and pear slices, banana slices, and strawberries.

Cheesy Filo Rolls

YIELDS 24 ROLLS

CALORIES	91.90
FAT	7.54 GRAMS
SATURATED FAT	3.48 GRAMS
TRANS FAT	0.11 GRAMS*
CARBOHYDRATES	3.77 GRAMS
CHOLESTEROL	14.52 MG

This savory little appetizer is perfect for special occasions. It's easy to make and is very impressive.

6 tablespoons Basil Pesto (page 23)
1 (3-ounce) package cream cheese, softened
¾ cup grated Parmesan cheese, divided
1 teaspoon dried Italian seasoning
8 (15" × 18") sheets filo dough, thawed
⅓ cup butter

1. Preheat oven to 375°F. In small bowl, make the filling by combining Pesto, cream cheese, and ¼ cup Parmesan cheese; mix well and refrigerate. In small bowl, combine ½ cup Parmesan cheese and seasoning and mix well. Work with one filo sheet at a time, keeping the rest covered. Place one sheet on work surface and brush with melted butter. Sprinkle with ¼ of the cheese mixture. Lay second filo sheet on top of first and brush with butter. Make three more stacks like this one.

2. Starting with 18" side, cut each stack into six 3" × 15" strips, making 24 strips in all. Place 2 teaspoons cheese filling at the 3" edge of each strip. Carefully roll up each filo stack strip, starting with 3" side. Place each roll seam-side down on Silpat-lined cookie sheets. Brush each with butter. Bake for 15 to 20 minutes or until pastries are golden brown. Cool for 15 minutes, then serve. Store leftovers in the refrigerator.

Chicken "Wings"

2 pounds chicken tenders
⅓ cup soy sauce
¼ cup apple-cider vinegar
2 tablespoons Dijon mustard
¼ cup honey
¼ cup brown sugar
1 teaspoon salt
1 teaspoon hot sauce
4 cloves garlic, minced
½ cup minced onion
1 cup low-fat sour cream
2 cups celery sticks

SERVES 10	
CALORIES	198.78
FAT	4.22 GRAMS
SATURATED FAT	2.14 GRAMS
TRANS FAT	0.05 GRAMS*
CARBOHYDRATES	17.03 GRAMS
CHOLESTEROL	62.06 MG

This spicy and savory sauce is perfect with tender chicken. Serve this appetizer with toothpicks for easy dipping.

1. Cut chicken tenders in half crosswise. In heavy-duty food-storage bag, combine remaining ingredients except sour cream and celery; mix well. Add chicken tenders and seal bag. Place bag in baking dish; refrigerate for at least 8 hours, up to 24 hours.

2. When ready to prepare, preheat oven to 400°F. Drain chicken tenders, reserving marinade. Arrange tenders in single layer in large pan. Drizzle with ½ cup of the reserved marinade. Bake for 20 to 25 minutes or until chicken is thoroughly cooked.

3. Meanwhile, place remaining marinade in small saucepan. Bring to a simmer over high heat, then reduce heat to low and cook for 10 to 15 minutes, stirring frequently, until mixture is syrupy. Combine with sour cream and serve as a dipping sauce for chicken along with celery.

Chicken Tenders
Chicken tenders are made from the strip of muscle underneath the breast. They are boneless, low in fat, and easy to use. There is a tough tendon running along them, but it usually becomes tender after the meat is cooked. You can use a knife to strip away that tendon before cooking.

Pesto Guacamole

SERVES 8

CALORIES	269.92
FAT	25.16 GRAMS
SATURATED FAT	4.05 GRAMS
TRANS FAT	0.0 GRAMS
CARBOHYDRATES	10.74 GRAMS
CHOLESTEROL	5.37 MG

By combining two fabulous dips, this recipe is creamy, flavorful, and spicy all at the same time.

1 tablespoon olive oil	¼ cup lemon juice
½ cup finely chopped onion	½ cup Basil Pesto (page 23)
3 garlic cloves, minced	¼ cup plain yogurt
4 ripe avocados	⅛ teaspoon cayenne pepper

1. In small saucepan, heat olive oil over medium heat. Add onion and garlic; cook and stir until tender, about 5 minutes. Remove from heat and cool completely.

2. When onion mixture is cool, peel and seed the avocados, sprinkling with some of the lemon juice as you work. Mash three of the avocados with remaining lemon juice, Pesto, yogurt, and cayenne pepper. Finely dice the remaining avocado and fold into the guacamole along with the onion mixture. Cover by placing plastic wrap directly on the surface of the dip, then chill for 2 to 3 hours before serving.

Fresh and Spicy Salsa

YIELDS 3 CUPS (SERVING SIZE ¼ CUP)

CALORIES	47.78
FAT	2.51 GRAMS
SATURATED FAT	0.37 GRAMS
TRANS FAT	0.0 GRAMS
CARBOHYDRATES	6.24 GRAMS
CHOLESTEROL	0.0 MG

Combining fresh and roasted tomatoes adds a great depth of flavor to this easy salsa recipe. Serve with Herbed Potato Chips (page 20) or Sesame Corn Wafers (page 30).

3 pounds tomatoes, divided	1 green bell pepper, chopped
4 cloves garlic, minced	½ cup chopped red onion
2 tablespoons olive oil	2 tablespoons lemon juice
½ teaspoon salt	⅛ teaspoon cayenne pepper
1 jalapeño pepper	

1. Preheat oven to 400°F. Cut 3 tomatoes in half; place cut-side up on cookie sheet. Top each tomato with some garlic. Drizzle with olive oil and sprinkle with salt. Roast for 15 to 25 minutes or until tomatoes have some brown spots. Remove from oven and cool.

2. Chop remaining tomatoes and place in bowl. Seed and mince jalapeño and add to chopped tomatoes along with green bell pepper and red onion.

3. Chop cooled roasted tomatoes and add to salsa. Sprinkle with lemon juice and cayenne pepper and stir gently. Cover and chill for 1 to 2 hours before serving.

Chapter 3

Yeast Breads

Cinnamon Batter Bread

YIELDS 1 LOAF (12 SLICES)

CALORIES	194.86
FAT	6.37 GRAMS
SATURATED FAT	3.57 GRAMS
TRANS FAT	0.13 GRAMS*
CARBOHYDRATES	30.00 GRAMS
CHOLESTEROL	48.81 MG

Oatmeal adds nutrition and great texture to this easy batter bread. Cinnamon sugar is layered in the bread to provide a sweet surprise.

1 (0.25-ounce) package active dry yeast
½ teaspoon sugar
⅓ cup warm water
½ cup sugar, divided
2 teaspoons cinnamon, divided
¼ teaspoon salt
⅓ cup butter, softened
2 eggs
⅓ cup oatmeal, ground
2 to 2-½ cups all-purpose flour

1. In small bowl, combine yeast, ½ teaspoon sugar, and warm water and set aside. In large bowl, combine ¼ cup sugar, 1 teaspoon cinnamon, salt, butter, and eggs and beat well. Add the yeast mixture and oatmeal along with 1 cup flour. Beat for 3 minutes. Then stir in enough remaining flour to form a stiff batter.

2. Cover and let rise for 30 minutes. Preheat oven to 375°F and grease a 9" × 5" loaf pan with unsalted butter.

3. In small bowl, combine ¼ cup sugar and 1 teaspoon cinnamon. Stir down batter and place half in prepared pan. Sprinkle with half of cinnamon sugar mixture. Repeat layers. Cover and let rise until batter expands to top of pan, about 30 minutes.

4. Bake for 25 to 35 minutes or until loaf is set and golden brown. Turn out onto wire rack to cool completely.

Batter Breads

Batter breads are a great way to learn how to make bread. They don't require any kneading, but you must beat the batter for as long as the recipe states. You also don't have to shape them; just spoon the batter into prepared pans. Any bread that calls for about 2 cups of flour can also be made into 12 individual muffin breads.

Pita Bread

1 (0.25-ounce) package active dry yeast
2 cups warm water
1 tablespoon honey
1-½ teaspoons salt
2 tablespoons olive oil
2 cups whole-wheat flour
3 to 4 cups bread flour

1. In large bowl, sprinkle yeast over water and let stand for 5 minutes. Add honey, salt, olive oil, and whole-wheat flour; beat for 3 minutes. Gradually stir in enough bread flour to form a stiff dough.

2. Knead on lightly floured surface for 8 to 10 minutes, until smooth and elastic. Place in greased bowl, turning to grease top. Let stand for 30 minutes.

3. Punch down dough and divide into thirds. Divide each third in half, then each half into fourths to make 24 balls. On floured surface, roll each ball to a 5" circle using a floured rolling pin. Cover with kitchen towel and let rise for 30 minutes.

4. Preheat oven to 475°F. Place a sheet of heavy-duty foil on the work surface and place 6 dough rounds on the foil. Carefully transfer the foil and dough to the oven and bake for 5 to 7 minutes. Bread should puff up immediately.

5. Bake until the tops of the pita breads begin to show brown spots. Remove and cool on wire racks. Repeat with remaining dough, using a fresh sheet of foil each time. To use, cut in half to expose pockets.

How to Knead
Kneading bread helps develop the gluten, or protein, in the flour. When dough is kneaded until it is elastic, the gluten has formed a web inside the dough that traps the CO_2 created by the yeast. That is what makes bread rise and gives it a fine texture. To knead, push the dough away from you with the heel of your hand, turn the dough, and repeat.

YIELDS 24 BREADS

CALORIES	119.49
FAT	1.66 GRAMS
SATURATED FAT	0.24 GRAMS
TRANS FAT	0.0 GRAMS
CARBOHYDRATES	22.58 GRAMS
CHOLESTEROL	0.0 MG

Pita breads are made from a firm dough that's baked at a very high temperature so the air inside literally explodes, creating a pocket. They're fun to watch in the oven.

Raisin Spice Swirl Bread

YIELDS 2 LOAVES (32 SLICES)

CALORIES	137.46
FAT	3.60 GRAMS
SATURATED FAT	2.07 GRAMS
TRANS FAT	0.08 GRAMS*
CARBOHYDRATES	23.78 GRAMS
CHOLESTEROL	21.45 MG

Putting raisins into the dough rather than just in the cinnamon swirl makes this bread easier to slice. It's fabulous toasted, or use it in any French toast recipe.

2 (0.25-ounce) packages active dry yeast	¼ teaspoon nutmeg
½ cup warm water	⅛ teaspoon ground cloves
¾ cup milk	1 cup raisins
⅓ cup butter	2 eggs
¾ cup brown sugar, divided	½ cup whole-wheat flour
½ teaspoon salt	4 to 5 cups all-purpose flour
2 teaspoons cinnamon, divided	3 tablespoons butter, softened

1. In large bowl, combine yeast and warm water; set aside. In large saucepan, combine milk, butter, ¼ cup brown sugar, salt, 1 teaspoon cinnamon, nutmeg, cloves, and raisins. Heat over medium heat until butter melts. Set aside to cool to lukewarm.

2. Add milk mixture to yeast mixture along with eggs; beat well. Beat in whole-wheat flour. Gradually add enough all-purpose flour to form a soft dough, beating well after each addition.

3. Turn dough onto floured surface and knead in enough remaining flour until dough is smooth and elastic. Place dough in greased bowl, turning to grease top. Cover and let rise until doubled, about 1 hour. Grease two 9" × 5" loaf pans with unsalted butter; set aside.

4. In small bowl, combine 3 tablespoons softened butter with ½ cup brown sugar and 1 teaspoon cinnamon. Punch down dough and divide into two parts. On lightly floured surface, roll out each part to a 7" × 12" rectangle. Spread each with the butter mixture. Roll up tightly, starting with 7" end. Pinch edges to seal. Place into prepared pans, cover, and let rise until doubled, about 30 minutes.

5. Preheat oven to 350°F. Bake bread for 30 to 45 minutes, or until bread is golden brown. Turn out onto wire racks to cool.

Oatmeal Bread

2 cups milk

2 (0.25-ounce) packages active
   dry yeast

1-¼ cups quick oatmeal, divided

1 cup regular oats

½ cup brown sugar

¼ cup honey

1 teaspoon salt

3 tablespoons butter,
   melted

1 egg yolk

5 to 5-½ cups all-purpose flour

1 egg white, slightly beaten

1. Place milk in large saucepan and heat over medium heat until steam rises. Remove and pour into large mixing bowl; let cool until lukewarm. Sprinkle yeast over milk and let stand for 10 minutes. Add 1 cup plus 2 tablespoons quick oatmeal, regular oats, brown sugar, honey, salt, butter, and egg yolk and beat well.

2. Gradually stir in all-purpose flour until a soft dough forms. Turn out onto floured surface and knead, adding additional flour if necessary, until dough is elastic, about 5 minutes. Place in greased bowl, turning to grease top; cover and let rise until double, about 1 hour.

3. Grease two 9" × 5" loaf pans with unsalted butter and set aside. Punch down dough and divide into two parts.

4. On floured surface, roll or pat each part into a 7" × 12" rectangle. Roll up tightly, starting with 7" side. Place in prepared loaf pans. Brush with egg white and sprinkle each with 1 tablespoon oatmeal. Cover with towel, and let rise until double, about 30 minutes. Preheat oven to 350°F.

5. Bake loaves for 35 to 45 minutes or until golden brown. Turn onto wire rack to cool completely.

About Oatmeal

There are four different types of oatmeal: groats, regular or rolled, quick-cooking, and steel-cut. Groats are the whole grain that has been cleaned and toasted. Rolled oats are steamed and pressed groats. Quick-cooking oats are rolled oats cut into thinner pieces. And steel-cut oats are made by cutting the groats into pieces, giving it the chewiest texture.

YIELDS 2 LOAVES (32 SLICES)

CALORIES	134.43
FAT	1.97 GRAMS
SATURATED FAT	0.94 GRAMS
TRANS FAT	0.03 GRAMS*
CARBOHYDRATES	25.29 GRAMS
CHOLESTEROL	10.03 MG

This bread is fabulous used in turkey stuffing and makes the world's best toast. It's also delicious when used to make French Toast (page 200).

White Bread

YIELDS 2 LOAVES (32 SLICES)

CALORIES	117.55
FAT	2.89 GRAMS
SATURATED FAT	1.70 GRAMS
TRANS FAT	0.06 GRAMS*
CARBOHYDRATES	19.85 GRAMS
CHOLESTEROL	7.78 MG

The small amount of heavy cream in this recipe adds moistness and makes a very fine crumb. It's an excellent toasting bread and great for sandwiches.

2 (0.25-ounce) packages dry yeast
2-½ cups warm water, divided
¼ cup sugar
½ cup buttermilk
¼ cup heavy cream
1 teaspoon salt
⅓ cup butter, melted
5-½ to 6-½ cups all-purpose flour

1. In large bowl, combine yeast, ½ cup warm water, and a pinch of the sugar and let stand for 10 minutes, until bubbly. Add remaining water, sugar, buttermilk, heavy cream, salt, butter, and 2 cups flour and beat for 3 minutes. Stir in enough remaining flour to make a soft dough.

2. Knead dough on lightly floured board until smooth and elastic, about 5 to 6 minutes. Place in greased bowl, turning to grease top. Cover and let rise in warm place until doubled, about 1 hour. Grease two 9" × 5" loaf pans with unsalted butter. Punch down dough and divide into two parts. Roll or pat each into a 7" × 12" rectangle. Tightly roll up, starting with 7" side, pinch edges to seal, and place into prepared pans.

3. Cover loaves with cloth and let rise until doubled, about 30 to 45 minutes. Preheat oven to 350°F. Bake bread for 25 to 35 minutes, or until bread is golden brown and loaves sound hollow when tapped with finger. Remove from pans, brush loaves with more melted butter, and let cool on wire racks.

Three-Grain Sourdough Bread

2 (0.25-ounce) packages dry yeast
1-½ cups warm water
1 tablespoon sugar
1 teaspoon salt
1 cup sour cream
1 tablespoon orange juice

2 tablespoons apple-cider vinegar
⅓ cup oat bran
1 cup whole-wheat flour
1 cup rye flour
2 to 3 cups bread flour
2 tablespoons butter, melted

1. In large bowl, combine yeast, warm water, and sugar and let stand for 10 minutes. Add salt, sour cream, orange juice, vinegar, oat bran, wheat flour, and rye flour and beat for 2 minutes. Stir in enough bread flour to make a firm dough.

2. On floured surface, knead dough until smooth and elastic, about 8 to 10 minutes. Place dough in greased bowl, turning to grease top. Cover dough and let rise for 1 hour, until doubled.

3. Grease two 9" × 5" loaf pans with unsalted butter and set aside. Punch down dough and divide into two pieces; let stand for 10 minutes. Roll or pat dough to 7" × 12" rectangles and roll up tightly, starting with 7" side. Pinch edges to seal; place in prepared pans. Cover and let rise for 30 to 40 minutes, until doubled.

4. Preheat oven to 375°F. Bake bread for 30 to 40 minutes or until loaves are deep golden brown and sound hollow when tapped with fingers. Turn out onto wire rack, and brush with more melted butter. Cool completely.

Why Bread Flour?

When a bread recipe calls for ingredients like whole-grain flours, whole grains like cracked wheat, or rolled oats, using bread flour will make a better bread. These extra ingredients "cut" the gluten as it forms, making a weaker structure. Bread flour contains more gluten so it will compensate for this effect, making nicely grained loaves that slice well.

YIELDS 2 LOAVES (32 SLICES)	
CALORIES	90.41
FAT	2.61 GRAMS
SATURATED FAT	1.45 GRAMS
TRANS FAT	0.04 GRAMS*
CARBOHYDRATES	14.61 GRAMS
CHOLESTEROL	5.07 MG

The sour cream, orange juice, and vinegar add a sour flavor to this hearty bread. Be sure to use bread flour for best results.

Italian Loaves

YIELDS 2 LOAVES (32 SLICES)

CALORIES	87.51
FAT	0.96 GRAMS
SATURATED FAT	0.30 GRAMS
TRANS FAT	0.0 GRAMS
CARBOHYDRATES	16.05 GRAMS
CHOLESTEROL	7.58 MG

A bit of wheat germ adds a tiny bit of crunch and more nutrition to these free-form loaves. The dry milk powder helps the dough rise even higher.

2 (0.25-ounce) packages active dry yeast
1-½ cups warm water
1 egg
1 tablespoon sugar
1 teaspoon salt
¼ cup dry milk powder
½ cup wheat germ
4 to 5 cups bread flour
1 tablespoon cornmeal

1. In large bowl, combine yeast with warm water and mix. Let stand for 15 minutes or until bubbly and creamy. Add egg, sugar, salt, dry milk powder, wheat germ, and 1 cup of the bread flour; beat for 1 minute. Cover and let stand for 1 hour.

2. Gradually add enough remaining bread flour to make a stiff dough. Knead on lightly floured surface for 8 minutes, until dough is smooth and elastic. Place dough in greased bowl, turning to grease top. Cover and let rise until doubled, about 1 hour.

3. Punch down dough and divide into two parts. Let stand for 10 minutes. Roll each part into a 12" × 12" rectangle. Roll up tightly, pinch edges to seal, and gently roll each cylinder on the countertop until it's about 2" in diameter.

4. Grease two 3" × 14" shapes side by side on a cookie sheet and sprinkle with cornmeal. Place one loaf on each greased area; slightly slash each loaf several times with a sharp knife (slashes should be ⅛" thick). Cover and let rise until almost doubled, about 30 minutes.

5. Preheat oven to 400°F. Spray each loaf with water and bake for 25 to 35 minutes or until loaves are golden brown. Cool on wire racks.

Almost Sourdough Rolls

3-½ to 4 cups all-purpose flour
1 cup whole-wheat flour
5 tablespoons wheat germ, divided
1 teaspoon salt
2 (0.25-ounce) packages instant
    blend dry yeast
1 tablespoon honey

1 cup buttermilk
½ cup sour cream
½ cup water
1 tablespoon apple-cider vinegar
1 egg white

YIELDS 24 ROLLS

CALORIES	106.67
FAT	1.55 GRAMS
SATURATED FAT	0.76 GRAMS
TRANS FAT	0.01 GRAMS*
CARBOHYDRATES	19.54 GRAMS
CHOLESTEROL	2.52 MG

The sour cream and vinegar give these rolls a slightly sour flavor. To make them even crisper, spray with some cold water halfway through the baking time.

1. In large bowl, combine 1 cup all-purpose flour, whole-wheat flour, 3 tablespoons wheat germ, salt, and yeast; stir until blended.

2. In small saucepan, combine honey, buttermilk, sour cream, and water and heat over low heat until warm to the touch. Add to flour mixture along with vinegar and beat for 2 minutes.

3. Stir in enough remaining all-purpose flour with a spoon until a soft dough forms. On floured surface, knead in enough remaining flour until the dough is elastic. Place dough in greased bowl, turning to grease top. Cover and let rise until doubled, about 1 hour.

4. Punch dough down and divide into 24 balls. Place balls on two greased cookie sheets. In small bowl, beat egg white until frothy and gently brush over rolls. Sprinkle with 2 tablespoons wheat germ, cover with a kitchen towel, and let rise for 30 to 40 minutes.

5. Place a 9" square pan with 1-½" of water on the bottom rack of oven. Preheat oven to 350°F. Bake rolls on cookie sheets for 15 to 25 minutes or until rolls are golden brown and sound hollow when tapped. Remove from cookie sheets and cool on wire rack.

Producing Crusty Rolls
To make rolls and breads with a crisp crust, there are two things you can do. One is to brush the dough with a slightly beaten egg white. Another is to create a moist environment in the oven. Place a pan with some water in the bottom rack of the oven, or spray the rolls with a bit of water before they bake and once during baking time.

Cinnamon Glazed Bagels

YIELDS 12 BAGELS

CALORIES	383.30
FAT	6.55 GRAMS
SATURATED FAT	1.83 GRAMS
TRANS FAT	0.05 GRAMS*
CARBOHYDRATES	72.24 GRAMS
CHOLESTEROL	6.10 MG

Your own homemade bagels are so delicious! These special treats are hearty and chewy, with a wonderful cinnamon flavor.

1 (0.25-ounce) package active dry yeast
½ cup warm water
1 cup milk
½ cup orange juice
2 tablespoons butter, melted
¾ cup sugar, divided
3 teaspoons cinnamon, divided
2 teaspoons salt, divided
1 cup whole-wheat flour
4-½ to 5-½ cups bread flour
1 cup raisins
½ cup chopped walnuts
⅓ cup sugar
1 teaspoon cinnamon
1 egg white, lightly beaten

1. In a large mixing bowl, combine yeast with ½ cup warm water. Stir and let stand for 10 minutes. Add milk, orange juice, melted butter, ¼ cup sugar, 2 teaspoons cinnamon, 1 teaspoon salt, and whole-wheat flour; beat for 1 minute. Gradually add 3 cups bread flour. Add raisins and walnuts.

2. Turn dough onto floured surface and knead in enough remaining bread flour until the dough is stiff, smooth, and elastic, about 10 minutes.

3. Place dough in greased bowl, turning to grease top. Cover and let rise until doubled, about 1 hour. Punch down and divide into four parts. Divide each part into three balls. Flatten balls until they are about 4" in diameter. Punch a hole in the center and gently stretch the rings until the hole is about 1-½" wide. Place on greased baking sheets and let rise until doubled, about 30 minutes.

4. Bring a large pot of water to a boil; add ½ cup sugar and 1 teaspoon salt. Drop three bagels at a time into the boiling water and let rise to the top. Boil for 1 minute, then remove with slotted spoon, drain briefly, and place on greased baking sheets.

5. Preheat oven to 425°F. Bake bagels until browned, about 15 minutes.

6. In small bowl, combine ⅓ cup sugar and 1 teaspoon cinnamon and mix well. Remove bagels from oven. Brush tops with egg white and sprinkle with cinnamon sugar. Return to oven and bake for 5 to 12 minutes longer until deep golden brown. Let cool on wire racks.

Homemade Pizza Crust

2 (0.25-ounce) packages active dry yeast
2 cups warm water, divided
2 tablespoons honey
6 tablespoons butter, divided
1 cup whole-wheat flour
4 to 4-½ cups all-purpose flour
3 tablespoons cornmeal

**YIELDS 3 CRUSTS
(24 SERVINGS)**

CALORIES	129.20
FAT	3.22 GRAMS
SATURATED FAT	1.88 GRAMS
TRANS FAT	0.08 GRAMS*
CARBOHYDRATES	22.03 GRAMS
CHOLESTEROL	7.63 MG

Making your own pizza crust is very easy; it's a good choice for beginning bakers. These crusts also freeze beautifully, so you can make pizza at a moment's notice.

1. In large bowl, combine yeast and ½ cup warm water and set aside. In heavy saucepan, combine remaining 1-½ cups water, honey, and 3 tablespoons butter; heat until butter melts. Let cool to lukewarm. Add to yeast mixture along with whole-wheat flour; beat for 1 minute. Gradually add enough all-purpose flour to form a soft dough. Turn onto floured surface and knead for 5 minutes.

2. Place dough in greased bowl, turning to grease top. Cover and let rise for 1 hour. Punch down dough and divide into thirds. Let rise while you grease three cookie sheets or pizza pans with remaining butter and dust with cornmeal. Sprinkle more cornmeal on work surface and roll out dough to 12" or 14" rounds. Place on prepared cookie sheets; cover and let rise for 15 minutes.

3. Preheat oven to 375°F. Bake pizza crusts for 10 to 13 minutes, or until set and very light golden brown. Remove from cookie sheets to wire racks. Let cool completely. Use the partially baked crusts in any pizza recipe. To freeze, wrap and freeze crusts up to 3 months. To use, just top with pizza toppings and bake as directed in recipe.

Your Own Pizza

Use your imagination when inventing your own pizzas. You can make crazy combinations, like pineapple with anchovy, or go classic, like Pepperoni Pizza (page 172). This crust is also good for making sweet pizzas; layer thinly sliced apples with brown sugar, ricotta cheese, and butter and bake until the apples caramelize.

Yeast Knot Rolls

YIELDS 20 ROLLS

CALORIES	134.75
FAT	4.02 GRAMS
SATURATED FAT	2.36 GRAMS
TRANS FAT	0.09 GRAMS*
CARBOHYDRATES	21.53 GRAMS
CHOLESTEROL	20.18 MG

It's fun to shape this velvety dough into knot shapes. Use this dough to make Glazed Honey Rolls (page 51) and Spicy Monkey Bread (page 87).

1 (0.25-ounce) package active dry yeast
¼ cup warm water
¾ cup milk
¼ cup sugar
2 tablespoons honey
¼ cup butter
1 egg
3 to 3-½ cups all-purpose flour
2 tablespoons butter, melted

1. In large bowl, combine yeast and warm water; set aside.

2. In heavy saucepan, combine milk, sugar, honey, and ¼ cup butter; heat until butter melts. Let cool to lukewarm. Add along with egg to yeast mixture; beat for 1 minute. Gradually add enough flour to form a soft dough. Turn onto floured surface and knead for 5 minutes.

3. Place dough in greased bowl, turning to grease top. Cover and let rise for 1 hour. Punch down dough and divide into fourths. Divide each fourth into five balls. Roll each ball to a 6" rope. Loosely tie a knot in each rope, and place on ungreased cookie sheets, tucking ends under roll. Cover and let rise until almost doubled, about 30 minutes.

4. Preheat oven to 375°F. Bake rolls for 15 to 25 minutes, or until golden brown. Remove from cookie sheets to wire racks and immediately brush with the melted butter. Let cool completely.

Freezing Bread

Bread freezes very well. Do not store bread in the refrigerator; that temperature actually hastens drying. Slice loaves before freezing, and make sure that all bread is completely cool. Package into freezer bags, allowing lots of extra room. Label bags and freeze bread up to 3 months.

Glazed Honey Rolls

1 recipe Yeast Knot Rolls (page 50)
1 egg white
¼ cup sugar

3 tablespoons honey
2 tablespoons butter, melted

1. Prepare Yeast Knot Roll dough; let rise once, then punch down. Divide into 20 balls; cover and let rest for 10 minutes. Grease two 9" round cake pans with unsalted butter. Place 10 rolls in each pan, arranging evenly.

2. In bowl, beat egg white until foamy. Add sugar, beating until the mixture turns white. Stir in honey and butter and mix well. Drizzle half of mixture over rolls in pans. Cover rolls and let rise until doubled, about 30 minutes.

3. Preheat oven to 375°F. Stir remaining honey mixture and drizzle over rolls. Bake for 15 to 25 minutes or until rolls are deep golden brown. Remove from pans immediately and let cool on wire rack. Serve warm.

YIELDS 20 ROLLS

CALORIES	165.04
FAT	5.17 GRAMS
SATURATED FAT	3.09 GRAMS
TRANS FAT	0.13 GRAMS*
CARBOHYDRATES	26.64 GRAMS
CHOLESTEROL	23.24 MG

Yes, these rolls are for dinner—they're not sweet rolls. The honey just adds a nice touch of flavor and adds color.

Cheesy Batter Bread

2 (0.25-ounce) packages active dry yeast
½ cup warm water
2 cups milk
¼ cup sugar
1 teaspoon salt

2 tablespoons butter, melted
5-¾ cups all-purpose flour
½ cup grated Cotija cheese
2 cups shredded sharp white Cheddar cheese
2 tablespoons grated Parmesan cheese

1. In large bowl, combine yeast and warm water; stir and let stand for 5 minutes. Stir in milk, sugar, salt, and melted butter. Then add flour, a cup at a time, beating for 30 seconds after each addition. When all the flour is added, beat 1 minute. Stir in Cotija and Cheddar cheeses. Cover and let rise until doubled, about 45 minutes.

2. Grease two 9" × 5" pans with unsalted butter. Stir down batter and beat for 1 minute. Spoon into prepared pans and sprinkle with Parmesan cheese. Cover and let rise for 20 to 30 minutes or until almost doubled. Preheat oven to 325°F. Bake for 40 to 50 minutes or until bread is firm and golden brown. Turn onto wire racks to cool.

YIELDS 2 LOAVES (24 SLICES)

CALORIES	184.99
FAT	5.34 GRAMS
SATURATED FAT	3.22 GRAMS
TRANS FAT	0.03 GRAMS*
CARBOHYDRATES	26.40 GRAMS
CHOLESTEROL	15.74 MG

This delicious bread is perfect to whip up at the last minute for a dinner party. Leftovers are great toasted and spread with butter for breakfast the next morning.

Norwegian Cardamom Bread

YIELDS 2 LOAVES (24 SLICES)

CALORIES	135.06
FAT	1.52 GRAMS
SATURATED FAT	0.73 GRAMS
TRANS FAT	0.03 GRAMS*
CARBOHYDRATES	26.54 GRAMS
CHOLESTEROL	11.48 MG

Just a small amount of whole-wheat flour adds body and texture to this fragrant bread. It's excellent made into French Toast (page 200).

2 (0.25-ounce) package dry yeast
½ cup warm water
½ cup brown sugar
1 teaspoon salt
2 tablespoons butter
½ teaspoon ground cardamom
2 tablespoons dry milk powder
1 cup boiling water
1 egg
1 cup whole-wheat flour
4 to 5 cups all-purpose flour

1. In small bowl, combine yeast and warm water; mix and set aside. In large bowl, place brown sugar, salt, butter, cardamom, and dry milk powder; add boiling water and stir. Let stand until lukewarm. Add yeast mixture and egg and beat well. Add whole-wheat flour and beat for 2 minutes. Then stir in enough of the all-purpose flour to make a soft dough.

2. On floured surface, knead dough until smooth and elastic, about 5 minutes. Place in greased bowl, turning to grease top. Cover and let rise until double, about 1 hour. Grease two 9" × 5" loaf pans with unsalted butter. Punch dough down and divide in half. Pat or roll to 7" × 12" rectangle, roll up tightly, starting with 7" side. Pinch edges to seal and place in prepared pans.

3. Cover and let rise until almost doubled, about 30 minutes. Preheat oven to 375°F. Bake bread for 25 to 30 minutes or until deep golden brown. Remove from pans and cool on wire racks.

Cardamom

Cardamom is a slightly orange flavored, intense spice that is commonly used in Scandinavian cooking. It's usually sold ground in small quantities. Be sure that your cardamom smells intensely flavorful and sweet; if the aroma is faint, buy a new bottle for cooking and baking. If you find the whole seeds, grind them finely in a spice grinder.

Yeast Biscotti

2 (0.25-ounce) packages dry yeast
½ cup warm water
½ cup butter
1 cup sugar, divided
1 teaspoon salt
2 teaspoons cinnamon, divided
2 cups boiling water
3 eggs
7 to 8 cups all-purpose flour

1. In small bowl, combine yeast with ½ cup water and set aside. In large bowl, combine butter, ¾ cup sugar, salt, and 1 teaspoon cinnamon. Pour boiling water over and stir until butter melts. Let stand until just warm. Beat in eggs and yeast mixture. Add 5 cups flour, a cup at a time, beating well after each addition.

2. Then stir in enough flour to make a firm dough. Knead on floured surface until smooth, about 5 minutes. Place in greased bowl, turning to grease top. Cover and let rise until doubled, about 1 hour. Punch down and divide into four balls. Grease two cookie sheets with unsalted butter. On prepared cookie sheets, roll out balls into 4" × 12" rectangles. Cover and let rise until doubled, about 30 minutes.

3. Preheat oven to 350°F. Bake loaves until light golden brown and set, about 25 to 35 minutes. Let cool on wire racks for 30 minutes.

4. Increase oven temperature to 400°F. Then cut loaves into 1" slices.

5. In small bowl, combine ¼ cup sugar with 1 teaspoon cinnamon. Dip both cut sides of slices into cinnamon sugar and return to cookie sheets. Bake again, turning once, until brown and crisp, about 5 minutes on each side. Cool completely on wire racks.

YIELDS 48 BISCOTTI

CALORIES	113.51
FAT	2.43
SATURATED FAT	1.34 GRAMS
TRANS FAT	0.05 GRAMS*
CARBOHYDRATES	20.09 GRAMS
CHOLESTEROL	18.30 MG

Flavor these little treats any way you'd like. A combination of orange zest and nutmeg instead of the cinnamon would be delicious, too.

Butterflake Rolls

YIELDS 30 ROLLS

CALORIES	147.69
FAT	7.78 GRAMS
SATURATED FAT	4.72 GRAMS
TRANS FAT	0.19 GRAMS*
CARBOHYDRATES	16.59 GRAMS
CHOLESTEROL	33.49 MG

It's kind of tricky to stack the
'ough, so make sure that the
lted butter is cooled but
ardened so it's not as
v.

2 (0.25-ounce) packages active
   dry yeast
½ cup warm water
4 to 5 cups all-purpose flour
¼ cup sugar
½ teaspoon salt
⅔ cup butter
1 cup milk
2 eggs
½ cup butter, melted and cooled

1. In small bowl, combine yeast and warm water; stir and set aside. In large
   bowl, combine 4 cups flour, sugar, and salt and mix well. Cut in ⅔ cup
   butter until particles are fine.

2. Pour milk into glass measuring cup. Microwave on 50 percent power for
   30 seconds or until warm. Add eggs and beat well. Stir into flour mixture
   along with yeast mixture until a dough forms. Add more flour if necessary to make a soft dough.

3. Cover dough and let rise for 1 hour, or until doubled. Punch down dough
   and divide into thirds.

4. On lightly floured surface, roll a third of the dough to ¼" thickness. Brush
   dough with some of the ½ cup melted butter. Cut into 1-½" strips. Stack
   5 strips on top of each other and cut into 1-½" squares. Place squares,
   cut-side down, into ungreased muffin tins.

5. Repeat with remaining dough. Cover and let rise until doubled, about 30
   minutes.

6. Preheat oven to 375°F. Bake rolls for 18 to 25 minutes or until they are
   deep golden brown. Remove to wire racks to cool.

Water Temperature

*When yeast is dissolved straight in water, the temperature of the water or
liquid should be about 100°F. When the yeast is mixed with flour, the temperature can be higher; in fact, it has to be, to offset the cool temperature
of the flour. Then the liquid temperature should be about 120°F. Measure
the temperature with a candy thermometer.*

Health Bread

5 to 6 cups all-purpose flour,
    divided

2 cups whole-wheat flour

¼ cup wheat germ

2 (0.25-ounce) packages active
    dry yeast

1-½ teaspoons salt

1 cup quick-cooking oatmeal

1-½ cups cottage cheese

2 cups water

¼ cup butter

½ cup milk

½ cup honey

1 cup bran cereal

2 eggs

1 cup raisins

1 tablespoon butter, melted

YIELDS 3 LOAVES (36 SLICES)

CALORIES	164.89
FAT	2.66 GRAMS
SATURATED FAT	1.30 GRAMS
TRANS FAT	0.04 GRAMS*
CARBOHYDRATES	30.85 GRAMS
CHOLESTEROL	16.64 MG

This super-hearty bread is so filling that one slice, toasted and spread with peanut butter, is enough for breakfast.

1. In a large mixer bowl, combine 2 cups all-purpose flour, whole-wheat flour, wheat germ, yeast, salt, and oatmeal and mix well.

2. In heavy saucepan, combine cottage cheese, water, ¼ cup butter, milk, honey, and bran cereal over medium heat and cook, stirring frequently, until butter melts. Remove from heat and let stand for 15 minutes to cool. Beat in eggs and stir into flour mixture. Add raisins and mix well. Then stir in enough remaining all-purpose flour to form a soft dough.

3. Turn dough out onto lightly floured surface and knead in enough remaining flour until dough is smooth and elastic, about 5 to 8 minutes. Place dough in greased bowl, turning to grease top. Cover with towel and let rise in warm place until double, about 1 hour.

4. Grease three 8" × 4" baking pans with unsalted butter and set aside. Punch down dough and turn out onto lightly all-purpose floured surface. Divide dough into three portions. Roll or pat each portion into a 12" × 7" rectangle. Roll up, starting with 7" side. Place each in a prepared pan. Cover and let rise until double, about 45 minutes.

5. Preheat oven to 375°F. Bake bread for 35 to 45 minutes or until loaves are dark golden brown and bread sounds hollow when tapped. Turn out onto wire racks, brush with melted butter, and let cool.

Orange Cracked-Wheat Bread

YIELDS 2 LOAVES (32 SLICES)

CALORIES	87.62
FAT	1.77 GRAMS
SATURATED FAT	0.96 GRAMS
TRANS FAT	0.04 GRAMS*
CARBOHYDRATES	15.79 GRAMS
CHOLESTEROL	3.81 MG

Orange juice adds a nice tang to this bread and helps offset the strong flavor some whole-wheat breads can have.

½ cup cracked wheat
1 cup boiling water
¼ cup butter
3 tablespoons honey
½ cup orange juice
1 teaspoon grated orange zest
½ teaspoon salt
1 cup whole-wheat flour
1 (0.25-ounce) package instant dry yeast
2-½ to 3-½ cups bread flour

1. Pour cracked wheat into large bowl. Pour boiling water over, stir, and let stand for 20 minutes. Add butter and stir until melted. Add honey, orange juice, orange zest, and salt and mix well. Stir in whole-wheat flour and instant dry yeast and beat for 2 minutes. Gradually stir in enough bread flour to make a medium-soft dough.

2. Turn dough onto floured surface and knead for 5 to 8 minutes or until elastic. Place in greased bowl, turning to grease top. Cover and let rise in warm place for 1 hour. Punch down dough, divide into two parts, cover with bowl, and let stand for 10 minutes.

3. Grease two 9" × 5" loaf pans with unsalted butter. On lightly floured surface, roll or pat dough to 7" × 12" rectangles. Roll up tightly, starting with 7" side; pinch ends and edges to seal. Place in prepared pans, cover, and let rise until bread fills pans, about 35 minutes.

4. Preheat oven to 350°F. Bake bread for 35 to 45 minutes, or until deep golden brown. Turn out onto wire racks to cool completely.

Regular Yeast or Instant?
If a recipe calls for dissolving the yeast in a small amount of warm water before adding to the remaining ingredients, you can use regular yeast or cake yeast. If the yeast is added to the ingredients along with the all-purpose flour, be sure to use instant yeast; it dissolves more easily in the smaller amount of liquid.

Focaccia

1 (0.25-ounce) package active
   dry yeast
¾ cup warm water, divided
5 tablespoons olive oil, divided
4 cloves garlic, minced
½ cup milk
1-½ cups bread flour
½ cup whole-wheat flour
6 tablespoons grated Parmesan
   cheese, divided

½ teaspoon dried thyme leaves
½ teaspoon dried oregano
   leaves
1 egg
1 to 2 cups all-purpose flour
2 tablespoons cornmeal
2 teaspoons chopped fresh
   rosemary leaves

SERVES 12

CALORIES	196.96
FAT	7.41 GRAMS
SATURATED FAT	1.49 GRAMS
TRANS FAT	0.02 GRAMS*
CARBOHYDRATES	26.49 GRAMS
CHOLESTEROL	20.33 MG

You could form this dough into 12 individual rolls; flatten, add toppings, and bake at 375°F for 12 to 15 minutes until golden brown.

1. In small bowl, combine yeast and ¼ cup warm water; set aside. In small saucepan, heat 2 tablespoons olive oil over medium heat. Cook garlic in the oil, stirring frequently, until light brown, about 2 to 3 minutes. Remove from heat, add ½ cup water and the milk, and set aside.

2. In large bowl, combine bread flour, whole-wheat flour, 3 tablespoons cheese, thyme, and oregano leaves and mix well. Add yeast mixture, garlic mixture, and egg to flour mixture and beat for 2 minutes at medium speed. Gradually stir in enough all-purpose flour to form a very soft dough. Turn dough out onto lightly floured surface and knead until smooth, about 5 minutes. Place in greased bowl, turning to grease top. Cover and let rise until double, about 45 minutes. Punch down dough and place on work surface.

3. Grease a large cookie sheet with some of the remaining olive oil and sprinkle with cornmeal. Place dough onto cookie sheet and pat or roll to 12" square or circle. Using fingertips, make even depressions over the dough. Drizzle with remaining olive oil, remaining Parmesan cheese, and fresh rosemary.

4. Cover dough and let rise for 30 minutes. Meanwhile, preheat oven to 375°F. Bake bread for 20 to 30 minutes or until focaccia is golden brown. Remove to wire rack to cool completely.

Easy Croissants

YIELDS 24 ROLLS

CALORIES	169.65
FAT	7.38 GRAMS
SATURATED FAT	4.35 GRAMS
TRANS FAT	0.18 GRAMS*
CARBOHYDRATES	21.59 GRAMS
CHOLESTEROL	43.89 MG

These aren't technically croissants, but rather butter crescent rolls. They taste so much better than the refrigerated-dough kind, you won't believe it!

4-½ to 5 cups all-purpose flour
2 tablespoons sugar
1 (0.25-ounce) package instant blend dry yeast
1 teaspoon salt
½ cup butter
1 cup milk, warmed
3 eggs
⅓ cup butter, softened

1. In large bowl, combine 3 cups flour, sugar, yeast, and salt and mix well. Cut in ½ cup butter until particles are fine. Stir in milk and eggs and beat well. Then stir in enough remaining flour until a soft dough forms; shape into a ball with hands. Place in greased bowl, turning to grease top. Cover and refrigerate overnight.

2. The next day, punch down dough if necessary and turn onto lightly floured surface. Divide into three parts. Roll each part into a 12" circle; spread each with one-third of the softened butter. Cut each into 8 wedges and roll up, starting with wide side. Place on ungreased cookie sheet, brush with more butter, and let rise for 1 hour (dough will not rise much).

3. Preheat oven to 350°F. Bake rolls for 13 to 17 minutes, or until set and golden brown. Store covered at room temperature.

Refrigerator Rising

Many yeast doughs can rise in the refrigerator overnight. Sometimes it's necessary to the recipe, as in the Easy Croissants (page 58) and Glazed Nut Twists (page 92). The yeast does rise in the cold refrigerator temperatures, but much more slowly. And it adds time to the whole process, giving the flavor of the wheat time to develop.

Caraway Breadsticks

1 (0.25-ounce) package active dry yeast
½ cup warm water
½ cup milk
2 tablespoons butter, melted
2 tablespoons sugar
1 teaspoon salt
½ cup whole-wheat flour
¼ cup wheat germ
1-¾ to 2 cups all-purpose flour
1 egg white
1 teaspoon caraway seeds
2 teaspoons sesame seeds

1. In large bowl, combine yeast and warm water; stir, and let stand for 10 minutes. Add milk, butter, sugar, and salt and beat well. Add whole-wheat flour, wheat germ, and ½ cup all-purpose flour and beat for 1 minute. Gradually add enough remaining flour to make a soft dough.

2. On lightly floured surface, knead dough for 5 minutes, or until smooth and elastic. Place in greased bowl, turning to grease top. Cover and let rise for about an hour, until doubled in size. Punch down dough and divide into four balls. Divide each ball into four parts. Roll each part on a lightly floured surface to an 8" rope; place 2" apart on ungreased cookie sheet.

3. In small bowl, beat egg white until foamy. Brush egg white over breadsticks and sprinkle with caraway and sesame seeds. Let rise until almost doubled, about 30 minutes.

4. Preheat oven to 400°F. Bake breadsticks for 15 to 25 minutes or until deep golden brown. Remove to wire racks to cool.

YIELDS 16 BREADSTICKS	
CALORIES	101.51
FAT	2.17 GRAMS
SATURATED FAT	1.07 GRAMS
TRANS FAT	0.04 GRAMS*
CARBOHYDRATES	17.27 GRAMS
CHOLESTEROL	4.12 MG

Breadsticks made with yeast have a wonderful chewy texture and crisp crust. Serve these with Cheese Vegetable Soup (page 105) for a hearty meal.

English Muffins

YIELDS 18 MUFFINS

CALORIES	150.56
FAT	3.05 GRAMS
SATURATED FAT	1.76 GRAMS
TRANS FAT	0.06 GRAMS*
CARBOHYDRATES	26.26 GRAMS
CHOLESTEROL	7.46 MG

Follow the directions carefully to form the large holes characteristic of English muffins. These freeze beautifully; split with a fork before freezing, then just toast to eat.

2 (0.25-ounce) packages active dry yeast
1 cup warm water, divided
1 cup milk
2 tablespoons butter, melted
1 teaspoon salt
1 tablespoon sugar
4 to 5 cups all-purpose flour
½ teaspoon baking soda
2 tablespoons cornmeal
Melted butter

1. In large bowl, combine yeast and ¾ cup warm water; set aside. In large saucepan, combine milk, melted butter, salt, and sugar and heat over low heat until warm. Add to bowl containing yeast mixture and stir.

2. Gradually add flour, beating for 30 seconds after each addition. When half of the flour has been added, dissolve baking soda in ¼ cup warm water and add to dough. Add remaining flour until a soft dough forms. Cover and let rise for 30 minutes.

3. Punch down dough and divide into 18 balls. Sprinkle cornmeal over a cookie sheet and place each ball in cornmeal, turning to coat. Flatten balls to ½" thickness. Cover and let rise for 20 minutes.

4. Heat a large griddle over medium heat. Carefully place muffins on ungreased griddle, six at a time, and cook until first side is golden brown, about 4 to 6 minutes. Turn when the sides start to look dry, and cook on the second side until the muffins are firm, about 4 minutes.

5. Repeat with remaining muffins. Cool on wire rack. To serve, split in half with fork, then toast and butter.

Baking Soda

Baking soda is a component of baking powder; it is also used as a gentle cleaner and deodorizes appliances. The box doesn't stay fresh forever, though. Replace the box that you use for baking at least once a year. And don't use the same box for freshening the fridge and baking and cooking.

Chapter 4

Quick Breads

Double-Apple Almond Bread

YIELDS 1 LOAF (12 SLICES)

CALORIES	298.95
FAT	9.06 GRAMS
SATURATED FAT	3.69 GRAMS
TRANS FAT	0.13 GRAMS*
CARBOHYDRATES	51.08 GRAMS
CHOLESTEROL	31.18 MG

Apple juice and apples add moistness and wonderful flavor to this delicious quick bread. And almond paste makes a velvety texture.

⅓ cup butter, softened
¼ cup almond paste
1 cup sugar, divided
½ cup brown sugar
1 egg
⅓ cup apple juice
1 cup peeled, chopped apples
2-½ cups flour
1 teaspoon baking soda
½ teaspoon cinnamon
¼ teaspoon nutmeg
½ cup sliced almonds, chopped
3 tablespoons apple juice

1. Preheat oven to 350°F. Grease a 9" × 5" loaf pan with unsalted butter and set aside. In large bowl, combine butter and almond paste and beat until combined. Add ½ cup sugar and brown sugar and beat until fluffy. Stir in egg until combined. Add ⅓ cup apple juice and chopped apples. Stir in flour, baking soda, cinnamon, and nutmeg until mixed, then add almonds.

2. Pour batter into prepared pan. Bake for 50 to 60 minutes or until bread is deep golden brown and a toothpick inserted in center comes out clean. In small bowl, combine 3 tablespoons apple juice and ½ cup sugar. Spoon over hot bread. Let bread stand in pan for 5 minutes, then turn out onto wire rack to cool.

What Kind of Almonds?

Almonds come in four varieties. Whole almonds are just the shelled almond. Blanched almonds have the brown skin removed. Slivered almonds are blanched almonds cut into little sticks. And sliced almonds are whole almonds, sliced, usually with the skin still attached. Slivered almonds are the easiest to chop.

Lemon Bread

2 lemons
5 to 6 tablespoons milk
6 tablespoons butter, softened
1-⅓ cups sugar, divided
2 eggs
1-¾ cups AP flour
1 teaspoon baking soda
½ cup ground cashews

YIELDS 1 LOAF (12 SLICES)

CALORIES	242.67
FAT	9.39 GRAMS
SATURATED FAT	4.43 GRAMS
TRANS FAT	0.15 GRAMS*
CARBOHYDRATES	36.97 GRAMS
CHOLESTEROL	50.76 MG

For lemon lovers. A whole pureed lemon adds fabulous flavor and moistness to this quick bread.

1. Preheat oven to 350°F. Grease a 9" × 5" loaf pan with unsalted butter and set aside. Remove 1 teaspoon zest from one lemon and squeeze the juice; reserve. Peel the second lemon, removing seeds and as much white pith as possible. Chop, place in food processor; process until smooth. Place in measuring cup and add enough milk to equal ½ cup.

2. In large bowl, beat butter with 1 cup sugar. Add eggs, one at a time, beating well after each addition. Stir in lemon zest. Alternately add lemon pulp mixture, flour, and baking soda, beating well after each addition. Stir in cashews.

3. Spoon batter into prepared pan. Bake for 55 to 65 minutes or until bread is deep golden brown and firm. Meanwhile, combine reserved lemon juice and ⅓ cup sugar in small bowl. Spoon over hot bread while it's still in the pan. Let cool for 10 minutes, then remove from pan and cool completely on wire rack.

Choosing Lemons
When purchasing lemons, look for fruit that is heavy for its size; that fruit will be full of juice. Make sure that the skins are smooth and shiny and quite thin, with bright color and an even texture. Store lemons in the refrigerator for up to 2 weeks. The yellow outer skin contains volatile oils that add lots of flavor to foods.

Rolled Cheese Biscuits

YIELDS 20 BISCUITS

CALORIES	116.50
FAT	6.32 GRAMS
SATURATED FAT	3.93 GRAMS
TRANS FAT	0.15 GRAMS*
CARBOHYDRATES	10.91 GRAMS
CHOLESTEROL	17.94 MG

Cotija cheese is a hard grated Mexican cheese that has a ton of flavor. It's similar to Parmesan cheese, but more intense.

2 cups flour
½ cup Cotija cheese
3 teaspoons baking powder
½ teaspoon salt
½ teaspoon cream of tartar
1 tablespoon sugar
6 tablespoons butter
⅔ cup milk
1 cup grated sharp Cheddar cheese

1. Preheat oven to 400°F. In large bowl, combine flour, Cotija cheese, baking powder, salt, cream of tartar, and sugar and mix well. Cut in butter until particles are fine. Stir in milk until a dough forms. On lightly floured surface, knead dough about eight times.

2. Roll dough to ¼" thickness (about 10" × 15" rectangle) and sprinkle with Cheddar cheese. Tightly roll up dough, starting with shorter side, and pinch edges to seal. Cut into ½" slices and place on parchment-paper-lined cookie sheets. Bake for 12 to 17 minutes or until biscuits are golden brown. Serve warm.

Honey Graham Crackers

YIELDS 24 CRACKERS (SERVING SIZE 1 CRACKER)

CALORIES	128.91
FAT	4.06 GRAMS
SATURATED FAT	2.47 GRAMS
TRANS FAT	0.10 GRAMS*
CARBOHYDRATES	22.09 GRAMS
CHOLESTEROL	10.25 MG

Your kids will adore these graham crackers. They're crisp yet tender, with a wonderful flavor from the honey, orange, and cinnamon.

1-½ cups all-purpose flour
1-½ cups whole-wheat flour
½ cup brown sugar
¼ cup sugar
1 teaspoon cinnamon
¼ teaspoon ginger
½ teaspoon salt
1 teaspoon baking soda
½ cup butter
⅓ cup honey
1 teaspoon vanilla
2 tablespoons orange juice
3 to 5 tablespoons milk

1. Preheat oven to 325°F. In bowl, combine the flours with the sugars, cinnamon, ginger, salt, and baking soda. Mix well. Cut in butter until particles are fine. Add honey, vanilla, juice, and 3 tablespoons milk; mix well until a dough forms. Add more milk (or flour) as necessary to form a firm dough.

2. On lightly floured surface, roll out dough to ⅛" thickness, about 18" × 24". Cut into 24 3" × 3" squares. Place squares on cookie sheet, about 1" apart, and prick with fork. Bake for 10 to 15 minutes or until crackers are golden brown and firm. Remove to wire racks to cool.

Big Bakery Muffins

2 cups flour
½ cup sugar
1 cup brown sugar, divided
1-½ teaspoons baking powder
1 teaspoon baking soda
¼ teaspoon salt
1 cup vanilla yogurt
½ cup butter, melted
2 eggs
2 teaspoons vanilla
1-¼ cups chopped walnuts, divided
3 tablespoons butter, softened

1. Preheat oven to 375°F. Spray 10 jumbo muffin cups with nonstick cooking spray containing flour and set aside. In large bowl, combine flour, sugar, ½ cup brown sugar, baking powder, baking soda, and salt. Add yogurt, melted butter, eggs, and vanilla and mix just until blended. Add ¾ cup of the walnuts.

2. Spoon batter into prepared pans. In small bowl, combine 3 tablespoons butter, ½ cup brown sugar, and ½ cup walnuts and mix until crumbly. Sprinkle over muffins and press in gently. Bake for 20 to 25 minutes or until muffins are set and golden brown. Cool in pans for 5 minutes, then remove to wire racks to cool.

Big, Jumbo, or Small Muffins?

If a muffin or quick bread recipe calls for about 2-½ cups flour, it will make 24 muffins, 10 to 12 jumbo muffins, or 48 mini muffins. The mini muffins use 1 tablespoon of batter. Regular muffin tins use 2 to 3 tablespoons, and the jumbo muffins use about ⅓ to ½ cup of batter. To make smaller muffins, just reduce the baking time (and you'll also reduce the fat and calories per serving!).

YIELDS 10 MUFFINS	
CALORIES	456.62
FAT	23.42 GRAMS
SATURATED FAT	9.09 GRAMS
TRANS FAT	0.33 GRAMS*
CARBOHYDRATES	55.50 GRAMS
CHOLESTEROL	77.08 MG

You can flavor these muffins just about any way you'd like. Fold in a cup of different types of chocolate chips, frozen or dried chopped fruit, or some mixed nuts.

Oatmeal Streusel Muffins

YIELDS 12 MUFFINS

CALORIES	237.16
FAT	8.49 GRAMS
SATURATED FAT	4.42 GRAMS
TRANS FAT	0.15 GRAMS*
CARBOHYDRATES	34.25 GRAMS
CHOLESTEROL	52.15 MG

Oatmeal muffins with a brown sugar oatmeal streusel topping are perfect for breakfast on the run.

1 cup flour
¼ cup whole-wheat flour
¾ cup ground quick oatmeal
¼ cup brown sugar
¼ teaspoon salt
1 teaspoon baking powder
½ teaspoon baking soda
1 cup buttermilk
2 eggs, beaten
¼ cup butter, melted

2 tablespoons butter
⅓ cup brown sugar
½ cup quick oatmeal
½ teaspoon cinnamon

1. Preheat oven to 400°F. Line 12 muffin cups with paper liners and set aside. In large bowl, combine flour, whole-wheat flour, ground oatmeal, ¼ cup brown sugar, salt, baking powder, and baking soda and mix well. Stir in buttermilk, eggs, and ¼ cup melted butter.

2. In small bowl, combine 2 tablespoons butter, ⅓ cup brown sugar, ½ cup oatmeal, and cinnamon and mix until crumbly. Divide batter among prepared muffin cups and sprinkle with cinnamon mixture. Bake for 15 to 25 minutes or until muffins are golden brown and set. Cool on wire racks.

About Streusel

The word "streusel" comes from the German word ströusel, which means "strewn," or ströuwen, which means "to sprinkle." Streusels are usually made with a combination of butter, sugar, flour, and another ingredient like chopped nuts, oatmeal, or dried fruits. The sugars in the streusel caramelize as the product bakes, forming a crunchy topping.

Crisp Cheese Crackers

1 cup all-purpose flour
1 cup whole-wheat flour
½ cup wheat germ
½ teaspoon baking powder
Dash cayenne pepper
¼ teaspoon dry mustard powder
2 teaspoons salt, divided
½ cup butter
1 cup grated Parmesan or Cotija cheese
1 cup grated sharp Cheddar cheese
¼ to ½ cup water

YIELDS 56 CRACKERS (SERVING SIZE 2 CRACKERS)

CALORIES	99.01
FAT	5.97 GRAMS
SATURATED FAT	3.60 GRAMS
TRANS FAT	0.14 GRAMS*
CARBOHYDRATES	7.74 GRAMS
CHOLESTEROL	15.89 MG

The amount of water varies in this recipe because the amount you need to make the dough will vary with the flour and cheese you use.

1. In large bowl, combine flours, wheat germ, baking powder, cayenne pepper, mustard powder, and 1 teaspoon salt. Cut in butter until particles are fine. Add cheeses to dough, then work in enough water to form a firm but pliable dough. Cover and refrigerate for at least two hours.

2. When ready to bake, preheat oven to 350°F. Remove half of dough from fridge and roll out directly on a cookie sheet to 12" × 14" rectangle, about ⅛" thick. Cut into 28 squares, rectangles, or triangles as desired, but do not separate. Sprinkle with more salt and prick crackers thoroughly with fork.

3. Bake for 15 to 20 minutes, watching carefully for the last 5 minutes, until crackers are light golden brown and crisp. Cool on cookie sheet for 5 minutes, then carefully break crackers apart along cut lines and cool on wire rack. Repeat with remaining dough, making 56 crackers in all.

Fluffy Waffles

YIELDS 6 WAFFLES

CALORIES	328.41
FAT	17.36 GRAMS
SATURATED FAT	9.96 GRAMS
TRANS FAT	0.15 GRAMS*
CARBOHYDRATES	33.96 GRAMS
CHOLESTEROL	141.13 MG

You can add many things to waffles to vary the flavor. Add ⅓ cup finely chopped toasted nuts, dried fruits like blueberries or raisins, fresh fruit, or 1/4 cup melted chocolate or 2 tablespoons cocoa powder.

3 eggs, separated
3 tablespoons butter, melted
3 tablespoons sugar
1 cup milk
1 cup sour cream
1 teaspoon baking powder
½ teaspoon baking soda
1-½ cups flour
Butter

1. In large mixing bowl, combine egg yolks, butter, and sugar and beat until the mixture turns light yellow. Stir in milk and sour cream, then add baking powder, baking soda, and flour; mix just until blended. In small mixing bowl, beat egg whites until fluffy. Fold into the batter. Let stand at room temperature for 30 minutes.

2. Preheat waffle iron. Brush lightly with unsalted butter. Pour batter into waffle iron, using about ½ cup at a time. Close waffle iron and cook according to directions until steaming stops. Carefully open the iron and, using a fork, gently pry the waffle off of the iron. Serve immediately.

Waffles

Waffles are easy, once you learn a few rules. Let the batter stand for 30 minutes before cooking so the gluten in the flour can form. Preheat the waffle iron before you begin; grease it lightly but thoroughly with unsalted butter. The first waffle almost always sticks; just keep on going. And cook the waffles just until the steaming stops.

Currant Spice Oatmeal Bread

¾ cup applesauce
¼ cup honey
¼ cup butter
1 cup dried currants
1 cup quick-cooking oatmeal
¼ cup sugar
¼ cup brown sugar
½ teaspoon cinnamon
¼ teaspoon allspice
¼ teaspoon cardamom
2 eggs
1-½ cups all-purpose flour
¼ cup whole-wheat flour
½ teaspoon baking powder
½ teaspoon baking soda

YIELDS 1 LOAF (12 SLICES)

CALORIES	217.62
FAT	5.08 GRAMS
SATURATED FAT	2.75 GRAMS
TRANS FAT	0.10 GRAMS*
CARBOHYDRATES	40.73 GRAMS
CHOLESTEROL	45.42 MG

Currants are—well, dried currants! They look a lot like raisins, but are smaller and sweeter.

1. Preheat oven to 350°F. Spray a 9" × 5" loaf pan with nonstick baking spray containing flour and set aside. In heavy saucepan, combine applesauce, honey, butter, and currants. Bring to a simmer, then remove from heat, cover, and let stand for 20 minutes.

2. Add oatmeal, sugar, brown sugar, cinnamon, allspice, and cardamom and mix well. Beat in eggs. Stir in flour, whole-wheat flour, baking powder, and baking soda just until combined. Pour into prepared pan. Bake for 50 to 60 minutes or until bread is deep golden brown and sounds hollow when tapped with fingers. Turn out onto wire rack to cool.

Raspberry Cinnamon Muffins

YIELDS 18 MUFFINS

CALORIES	255.00
FAT	11.05 GRAMS
SATURATED FAT	5.31 GRAMS
TRANS FAT	0.15 GRAMS*
CARBOHYDRATES	35.67 GRAMS
CHOLESTEROL	68.42 MG

Fresh raspberries work best in these tender little muffins. If you can only find frozen berries, add them to the batter when still frozen.

½ cup butter, softened
1-¼ cups sugar, divided
½ cup brown sugar
4 eggs
1-½ cups light sour cream
2-½ cups flour
1 teaspoon baking soda
1 teaspoon cinnamon, divided
¼ teaspoon nutmeg
½ cup chopped pecans
1-½ cups fresh raspberries

1. Preheat oven to 400°F. In large bowl, beat butter until fluffy. Add 1 cup sugar gradually, then add brown sugar and beat until light and fluffy. Add eggs, one at a time, beating after each addition until incorporated. Place flour, baking soda, ½ teaspoon cinnamon, and nutmeg in sifter. Add flour mixture alternately with sour cream to butter mixture, stirring well after each addition. Fold in pecans, then carefully fold in raspberries.

2. In small bowl, combine ¼ cup sugar and ½ teaspoon cinnamon and mix well. Spoon batter into prepared muffin cups and sprinkle with sugar mixture. Bake for 12 to 18 minutes or until muffins are golden brown and firm. Cool on wire racks for 30 minutes, then serve.

Sour Cream in Baking
Unlike butter and margarines, light or low-fat sour cream will work well in baking recipes. The sour cream has added stabilizers and thickeners that substitute for the fat that has been removed. Whether you use full fat or low-fat, be sure to heed the expiration date on the carton.

Triple-Cheese Muffins

1-¾ cups flour
¼ cup oat bran
½ teaspoon dried basil leaves
½ teaspoon dried thyme leaves
½ cup grated Parmesan cheese, divided
1 tablespoon sugar
1 tablespoon baking powder
½ teaspoon salt
¼ cup butter
1 egg
½ cup milk
½ cup part-skim ricotta cheese
1 cup finely cubed Cheddar cheese

YIELDS 12 MUFFINS

CALORIES	196.05
FAT	10.32 GRAMS
SATURATED FAT	6.23 GRAMS
TRANS FAT	0.21 GRAMS*
CARBOHYDRATES	17.63 GRAMS
CHOLESTEROL	46.72 MG

Whip up these cheesy little muffins for a nice addition to a grilled steak dinner. They're also great for breakfast on the run.

1. Preheat oven to 375°F. Line 12 muffin cups with paper liners and set aside. In large bowl, combine flour, oat bran, basil, thyme, ¼ cup Parmesan cheese, sugar, baking powder, and salt and mix well. Cut in butter until particles are fine. In small bowl combine egg, milk, and ricotta cheese and stir until combined. Stir into flour mixture, then fold in Cheddar cheese.

2. Divide dough among prepared muffin cups. Sprinkle with remaining Parmesan cheese. Bake for 20 to 25 minutes or until muffins are light golden brown and firm. Cool on wire racks for 20 minutes, then serve.

Substituting Cheeses
Most cheeses can be substituted for each other, as long as you make sure to keep the texture and moisture of the cheeses consistent. For example, any hard grating cheese (Romano, Parmesan, Cotija) can be substituted for another. And semi firm cheeses (Cheddar, Swiss, Edam, Gruyère, and fontina) can be substituted for each other.

Cranberry Corn Bread

SERVES 9

CALORIES	307.78
FAT	12.10 GRAMS
SATURATED FAT	7.02 GRAMS
TRANS FAT	0.27 GRAMS*
CARBOHYDRATES	44.68 GRAMS
CHOLESTEROL	75.13 MG

Corn bread is dense and moist when made with whole-wheat flour, brown sugar, and some orange juice. And the cranberries add a delicious sweet tart flavor.

1 cup cornmeal
1 cup all-purpose flour
⅓ cup whole-wheat flour
¼ cup sugar
¼ cup brown sugar
½ teaspoon salt
½ cup butter
2 eggs
¼ cup orange juice
¾ cup milk
½ cup cranberries, chopped
¼ cup dried sweetened cranberries

1. Preheat oven to 375°F. Grease a 9" × 9" pan with unsalted butter and set aside. In large bowl, combine cornmeal, all-purpose flour, whole-wheat flour, sugar, brown sugar, and salt and mix well. Cut in butter until particles are fine. Add eggs, orange juice, and milk and stir just until combined. Stir in cranberries and dried cranberries.

2. Pour batter into prepared pan. Bake for 30 to 40 minutes or until corn bread is deep golden brown around edges and firm to the touch. Let cool on wire rack for about 15 minutes; cut into squares and serve hot.

Pumpkin Pear Bread

¾ cup butter, softened
1 cup sugar
1 cup brown sugar
1 (15-ounce) can solid-pack pumpkin
1 (6-ounce) jar puréed pears
4 eggs
3-½ cups flour
2 teaspoons baking soda
1 teaspoon cinnamon
½ teaspoon nutmeg
¼ teaspoon cardamom
1-½ cups chopped pecans

YIELDS 2 LOAVES (24 SLICES)

CALORIES	239.58
FAT	11.73 GRAMS
SATURATED FAT	4.38 GRAMS
TRANS FAT	0.15 GRAMS*
CARBOHYDRATES	31.17 GRAMS
CHOLESTEROL	50.50 MG

Pears add moisture and flavor to these loaves, and help reduce fat, too. This bread tastes even better the next day.

1. Preheat oven to 350°F. Grease two 9" × 5" loaf pans with unsalted butter and set aside. In large bowl, combine butter and sugars and beat until light and fluffy. Add pumpkin and beat well. Then add pears and mix until combined. Add eggs, one at a time, beating well after each addition. Add flour, baking soda, cinnamon, nutmeg, and cardamom and mix just until blended. Stir in pecans.

2. Pour batter into prepared pans. Bake for 55 to 65 minutes or until bread is golden brown and pulls away from sides of pan, and a toothpick inserted in center comes out clean. Cool in pans for 5 minutes, then turn out onto wire racks to cool completely.

Puréed Pears
The puréed pears sold in the store are usually baby food! This is an excellent ingredient to use in baking to help reduce fat and add moisture and flavor. You can purée canned, drained pears instead. About 1-½ pears will equal ¾ cup puréed pears, which is equivalent to a 6-ounce jar.

Chocolate Date Muffins

YIELDS 12 MUFFINS

CALORIES	396.71
FAT	19.80 GRAMS
SATURATED FAT	8.25 GRAMS
TRANS FAT	0.10 GRAMS*
CARBOHYDRATES	54.93 GRAMS
CHOLESTEROL	28.41 MG

Melted chocolate in the batter and chocolate chips stirred in with nuts add fabulous flavor and texture to these rich little muffins. They could even be served as dessert!

1 cup chopped dates
¾ cup boiling water
1 (12-ounce) package semisweet chocolate chips, divided
⅓ cup brown sugar
¼ cup butter
2 cups flour
½ cup oatmeal
1 teaspoon baking soda
1 teaspoon baking powder
2 tablespoons sugar
1 cup chopped pecans
¾ cup buttermilk
1 egg
1 teaspoon vanilla

1. Preheat oven to 350°F. Line 12 muffin cups with paper liners and set aside. Put dates in a small bowl. Pour over boiling water. Add 1 cup chocolate chips, brown sugar, and butter and set aside. In large bowl, combine flour, oatmeal, baking soda, baking powder, and sugar and mix well.

2. Stir date mixture and add to flour mixture along with buttermilk, egg, and vanilla. Stir just until combined. Stir in 1 cup chocolate chips and pecans. Fill prepared muffin cups three-quarters full. Bake for 15 to 23 minutes or until muffins are firm. Cool in muffin tins for 3 minutes, then remove to wire racks to cool completely.

Banana Bread

1-½ cups flour
¼ cup whole-wheat flour
⅓ cup sugar
⅓ cup brown sugar
2 teaspoons baking powder
1 teaspoon baking soda
⅓ cup butter
1 cup mashed bananas
2 eggs
½ cup chopped pecans
½ cup coconut
½ cup dried currants

YIELDS 1 LOAF (12 SLICES)	
CALORIES	246.61
FAT	10.51 GRAMS
SATURATED FAT	4.73 GRAMS
TRANS FAT	0.15 GRAMS*
CARBOHYDRATES	35.98 GRAMS
CHOLESTEROL	48.81 MG

Banana bread has a velvety texture when made this way. If you'd like, you could use all pecans or all coconut in place of the fruit and nut mixture.

1. Preheat oven to 350°F. Grease a 9" × 5" pan with unsalted butter and set aside. In large bowl, combine flour, whole-wheat flour, sugar, brown sugar, baking powder, and baking soda and mix well. Cut in butter until particles are fine. Add bananas and eggs and beat until combined. Stir in pecans, coconut, and currants.

2. Pour batter into prepared pan. Bake for 55 to 65 minutes or until bread is dark golden brown and begins to pull away from sides of pan. Cool in pan for 5 minutes, then turn out onto wire racks to cool completely.

About Quick Breads

Quick breads are easy to make if you follow a few rules. First, mix the batter as the recipe directs. You may be making a smooth cake batter or a traditional quick bread where the ingredients are mixed just until combined. Make sure the oven is preheated, and watch the breads carefully for the last 5 to 10 minutes. Remove from pans immediately and cool on wire racks.

Gingerbread Banana Muffins

YIELDS 12 MUFFINS

CALORIES	245.12
FAT	6.00 GRAMS
SATURATED FAT	3.46 GRAMS
TRANS FAT	0.13 GRAMS*
CARBOHYDRATES	45.70 GRAMS
CHOLESTEROL	31.18 MG

Gingerbread and banana are natural partners in these wonderful muffins. And they're glazed with a lemon icing. Yum!

⅓ cup butter, softened
⅓ cup brown sugar
2 tablespoons sugar
⅓ cup light molasses
1 cup mashed bananas
1 egg
1-¾ cups flour
½ cup quick oatmeal
1 teaspoon baking soda
1 teaspoon ground ginger
½ teaspoon cinnamon
½ teaspoon salt
1 cup powdered sugar
2 tablespoons lemon juice

1. Preheat oven to 400°F. Line 12 muffin cups with paper liners and set aside. In large bowl, combine butter and sugars and beat well until fluffy. Add molasses and bananas and beat until combined. Then add egg and beat well. Stir in flour, oatmeal, baking soda, ginger, cinnamon, and salt just until mixed.

2. Divide batter among prepared muffin cups. Bake for 15 to 20 minutes, or until muffins are set and toothpick inserted in center comes out clean. Let cool in muffin tins on wire racks for 10 minutes. In small bowl, combine powdered sugar and lemon juice and mix well. Drizzle over muffins and remove from tin; serve warm.

Apple Pancakes

2 eggs, separated
3 tablespoons sugar, divided
2 cups milk
2 tablespoons butter, melted
1 cup grated apple
2 cups flour
4 teaspoons baking powder
½ teaspoon salt
More melted butter

1. Place egg yolks in large bowl with 2 tablespoons sugar; beat well. Stir in milk and 2 tablespoons melted butter. Stir in apple. Add flour, baking powder, and salt and stir just until combined.

2. In small bowl, combine egg whites with 1 tablespoon sugar and beat until stiff peaks form. Fold into apple mixture. Heat griddle over medium heat and brush with melted butter. Pour batter onto skillet in ¼-cup portions. Cook until bubbles form and start to break on pancakes; carefully flip and cook for 2 to 3 minutes on second side. Repeat with remaining batter, adding more butter to skillet if necessary. Serve immediately.

Apples for Cooking

Almost any apple can be used in cooking and baking, but there are some that are better choices. If you want to add tartness, McIntosh and Haralson apples are good. For sweetness and juiciness, Red and Golden Delicious apples are an excellent choice. When a recipe calls for grated apples, peel the apple before grating on a box grater.

SERVES 6–8

CALORIES	247.03
FAT	8.55 GRAMS
SATURATED FAT	4.86 GRAMS
TRANS FAT	0.15 GRAMS*
CARBOHYDRATES	35.57 GRAMS
CHOLESTEROL	73.02 MG

Grated apple adds wonderful flavor and moist texture to these simple pancakes. Top the hot cakes with butter and cinnamon sugar, or warmed maple syrup.

Chocolate Chip Oatmeal Scones

YIELDS 16 SCONES

CALORIES	208.76
FAT	9.77 GRAMS
SATURATED FAT	5.73 GRAMS
TRANS FAT	0.15 GRAMS*
CARBOHYDRATES	28.81 GRAMS
CHOLESTEROL	28.78 MG

Scones are a wonderful quick bread to make for breakfast on the run. They're good fresh from the oven, reheated in the microwave, or eaten cold.

1 egg
½ cup buttermilk
1 teaspoon vanilla
½ cup quick-cooking oatmeal
1 cup semisweet chocolate chips
1-½ cups flour
¼ cup whole-wheat flour
1 teaspoon baking powder
½ teaspoon baking soda
¼ teaspoon salt
½ cup brown sugar
½ cup butter
2 tablespoons sugar

1. Preheat oven to 400°F. In medium bowl, combine egg, buttermilk, vanilla, and oatmeal and mix well; set aside. Coarsely chop chocolate chips; set aside.

2. In large bowl, combine flour, whole-wheat flour, baking powder, baking soda, salt, and brown sugar and mix well until blended. Using a pastry blender or two knives, cut in butter until particles are fine. Stir in oatmeal mixture just until blended, then add chopped chocolate chips.

3. Compact dough with hands, remove it from bowl, and divide it into four pieces. Divide each piece into four balls, making 16 balls. Place on ungreased cookie sheet and flatten each with palm of hand. Sprinkle each with sugar. Bake for 15 to 23 minutes or until scones are set and crisp around edges. Remove to wire rack to cool; serve warm.

Irish Soda Biscuits

3 cups flour
3 tablespoons oat bran
⅓ cup sugar
1 teaspoon baking powder
1 teaspoon baking soda
½ teaspoon salt
1 teaspoon caraway seeds
¼ teaspoon ground ginger
1 cup buttermilk
1 (3-ounce) package cream cheese
2 eggs, beaten
1 cup raisins

YIELDS 24 BISCUITS

CALORIES	110.07
FAT	1.97 GRAMS
SATURATED FAT	1.00 GRAMS
TRANS FAT	0.02 GRAMS*
CARBOHYDRATES	20.59 GRAMS
CHOLESTEROL	21.93 MG

These little biscuits are perfect for any everyday meal and are especially good for a St. Patrick's Day feast. The cream cheese adds great flavor and texture.

1. Preheat oven to 350°F. In large bowl, combine flour, oat bran, sugar, baking powder, baking soda, salt, caraway seeds, and ginger and mix well. In small saucepan, combine buttermilk and cream cheese, and heat over low heat until cream cheese melts. Remove from heat.

2. In small bowl, beat eggs; reserve 1 tablespoon. Add remaining eggs to buttermilk mixture along with raisins. Add to flour mixture and stir just until a dough forms. On lightly floured surface, knead dough ten times.

3. Divide dough into four parts; divide each part into three parts, then each into two balls, for a total of 24 balls. Place on ungreased cookie sheet; flatten slightly with palm. Brush lightly with reserved beaten egg. Bake for 15 to 25 minutes or until rolls are crusty and golden brown around edges. Serve warm.

Freezing Biscuit Dough
You can make this dough and freeze it. Shape the dough into balls, flatten slightly, then freeze on wax-paper-lined cookie sheets until frozen solid. Remove from sheets and package into freezer bags and label; freeze up to 6 months. To thaw and bake, place frozen balls on cookie sheets. Brush with some beaten egg and bake for 20 to 35 minutes until rolls are crusty and baked through.

Toasted Cornmeal Pancakes

YIELDS 12 PANCAKES

CALORIES	157.48
FAT	6.00 GRAMS
SATURATED FAT	3.38 GRAMS
TRANS FAT	0.10 GRAMS*
CARBOHYDRATES	22.15 GRAMS
CHOLESTEROL	48.23 MG

Toasting the cornmeal intensifies the flavor and adds a wonderful nutty undertone. Serve these pancakes with melted butter and warmed maple syrup or pancake syrup.

1 cup cornmeal
½ teaspoon salt
2 tablespoons honey
1 cup boiling water
2 eggs
⅓ cup buttermilk
4 to 5 tablespoons butter, melted, divided
1-¼ cups flour
1-½ teaspoons baking powder
½ teaspoon baking soda

1. Place cornmeal in heavy skillet (not nonstick) over medium heat. Toast the cornmeal, stirring frequently, until fragrant. Pour into a medium mixing bowl and add the salt, honey, and boiling water. Cover and let stand for 5 minutes.

2. In a small bowl, combine eggs, buttermilk, and 3 tablespoons melted butter and beat well. Stir into the cornmeal mixture along with the flour, baking powder, and baking soda just until combined.

3. Heat a large skillet over medium heat or heat an electric skillet to 375°F. Brush skillet with melted butter. Pour batter onto skillet by scant ¼ cup portions. Cook until bubbles form and start to break on pancakes, carefully flip and cook for 2 to 3 minutes on second side. Repeat with remaining batter, adding more butter to skillet if necessary. Serve immediately.

Chapter 5

Sweet Breads and Coffeecakes

Lemon Coconut Coffeecake

SERVES 16

CALORIES	284.68
FAT	11.58 GRAMS
SATURATED FAT	7.16 GRAMS
TRANS FAT	0.23 GRAMS*
CARBOHYDRATES	42.22 GRAMS
CHOLESTEROL	62.53 MG

This light and tender coffeecake has a wonderful lemon flavor. The streusel topping has both coconut and oatmeal for a nice crunch.

¾ cup butter, softened, divided
1 cup sugar
3 eggs
1 (16-ounce) can pears, drained
⅓ cup lemon juice
2-¼ cups flour
1 teaspoon baking powder
½ teaspoon baking soda
1 cup coconut, divided
½ cup brown sugar
1 teaspoon lemon zest
¼ teaspoon ground cardamom
½ cup quick-cooking oatmeal

1. Preheat oven to 350°F. Grease a 13" × 9" baking pan with unsalted butter and set aside. In large bowl, combine ½ cup softened butter with 1 cup sugar and beat until light and fluffy. Add eggs, one at a time, beating well after each addition. Drain pears, discarding juice. Purée pears in blender or food processor. Add lemon juice to pears and mix well.

2. Place flour, baking powder, and baking soda in sifter. Sift and add alternately with pear mixture to butter mixture, beating well after each addition. Stir in ½ cup coconut and spoon batter into prepared pan.

3. In small bowl, combine brown sugar, lemon zest, cardamom, and ¼ cup softened butter and mix well. Stir in ½ cup coconut and oatmeal. Sprinkle over batter. Bake for 30 to 40 minutes, or until coffeecake is firm and edges begin to pull away from sides of pan. Cool completely on wire rack.

Mocha Nut Muffins

½ cup brewed coffee
¼ cup butter, melted
1 cup brown sugar
2 eggs
1 teaspoon vanilla
1-¾ cups flour
2 tablespoons cocoa powder
½ teaspoon baking powder
½ teaspoon baking soda
¼ teaspoon salt
½ cup chopped toasted walnuts
2 tablespoons sugar
½ teaspoon cinnamon

YIELDS 12 MUFFINS

CALORIES	223.88
FAT	8.03 GRAMS
SATURATED FAT	2.96 GRAMS
TRANS FAT	0.10 GRAMS*
CARBOHYDRATES	34.91 GRAMS
CHOLESTEROL	45.42 MG

Coffee and chocolate make a wonderful flavor combination in these special little muffins.

1. Preheat oven to 375°F. Line 12 muffins cups with paper liners and set aside. In large bowl, combine coffee, melted butter, brown sugar, eggs, and vanilla and beat until blended. In sifter or large strainer, place flour, cocoa powder, baking powder, baking soda, and salt. Sift into coffee mixture, then stir just until blended. Stir in walnuts.

2. Spoon batter into each of the prepared muffin cups. In small bowl, combine sugar and cinnamon and mix well. Sprinkle sugar mixture over each muffin. Bake for 17 to 22 minutes or until muffins are firm. Cool in pan 4 minutes, then remove to wire racks to cool. Serve warm.

Unsweetened Cocoa Powder

Cocoa powder is not only less expensive than baking chocolate or semi-sweet chocolate, it's also better for you. Cocoa powder only contains about 10 percent cocoa butter, while dark chocolate contains 50 percent. Using cocoa powder instead of chocolate also makes cakes and breads that are more velvety, since the "finely divided solids" enhance the mouthfeel.

Chocolate Glazed Doughnuts

YIELDS 24 DOUGHNUTS

CALORIES	207.01
FAT	8.41 GRAMS
SATURATED FAT	4.97 GRAMS
TRANS FAT	0.13 GRAMS*
CARBOHYDRATES	31.48 GRAMS
CHOLESTEROL	41.41 MG

Baking this batter in mini Bundt pans (1-cup capacity each) and using a lower temperature are the secrets to making these little cakes taste just like doughnuts.

½ cup butter, softened
1 cup brown sugar
1 cup sugar
½ cup sour cream
3 eggs
2 teaspoons vanilla
2-¼ cups flour
1 teaspoon baking powder
½ teaspoon baking soda
1 cup milk
1 cup semisweet chocolate chips
⅓ cup heavy cream

1. Preheat oven to 325°F. Spray twelve 1-cup mini Bundt pans with cooking spray containing flour and set aside. In large bowl, beat butter until fluffy. Add brown sugar gradually, beating until fluffy. Add sugar and sour cream and beat for 1 minute. Then beat in eggs, one at a time, beating well after each addition. Stir in vanilla.

2. Put flour, baking powder, and baking soda in a sifter. Sift and add flour mixture alternately with milk to butter mixture, beating well after each addition. When everything has been added, beat batter for 1 minute.

3. Place half of batter into prepared pans, using a scant ¼ cup batter per pan. Refrigerate remaining batter while doughnuts are baking. Bake for 13 to 18 minutes or until crust is deep golden brown and doughnuts are set when tapped with a finger. Invert onto cooling racks and let cool for 30 minutes. Re-spray cups and bake remaining batter.

4. In small microwave-safe bowl, combine 1 cup chocolate chips with ⅓ cup heavy cream; microwave on 50 percent power for 2 minutes, then stir until smooth. Spoon mixture over doughnuts and let stand until firm.

Pineapple Hawaiian Coffeecake

1-½ cups sugar, divided
¼ cup brown sugar
1 teaspoon cinnamon
1 cup coconut
½ cup chopped macadamia nuts
⅓ cup butter, softened
2 eggs
1 (6-ounce) container coconut yogurt
1 (5-ounce) can crushed pineapple, drained
2 tablespoons butter, melted
2-½ cups flour
2 teaspoons baking powder
1 teaspoon baking soda

YIELDS 18 PIECES

CALORIES	264.48
FAT	11.52 GRAMS
SATURATED FAT	5.47 GRAMS
TRANS FAT	0.12 GRAMS*
CARBOHYDRATES	38.16 GRAMS
CHOLESTEROL	36.12 MG

This delicious and easy coffeecake has double the coconut flavor and the sweet tang of pineapple. Serve it warm with some scrambled eggs for a great brunch.

1. Preheat oven to 375°F. Grease a 9" × 13" pan with unsalted butter and set aside. In small bowl, combine ½ cup sugar, ¼ cup brown sugar, cinnamon, coconut, and macadamia nuts and mix well. Mix in ⅓ cup butter until crumbly; set aside.

2. In large bowl, beat eggs with the yogurt until blended. Stir in drained pineapple, 1 cup sugar, and 2 tablespoons melted butter. Add flour, baking powder, and baking soda and mix until mixture is just combined. Pour into prepared pan and sprinkle with coconut mixture. Bake for 25 to 35 minutes or until coffeecake is deep golden brown. Cool on wire rack for 30 minutes, then serve.

Flaked or Grated Coconut?

It all depends on your taste! Flaked coconut is made of slightly thicker and shorter strands. Grated coconut has longer and thinner strands. And shredded coconut is usually the thinnest of all; it can dry out within a couple of weeks. If it does become dry, you can soak it, or any of these prepared coconut forms, in milk for 30 minutes; squeeze dry and use immediately.

Mini Cinnamon Rolls

YIELDS 36 ROLLS

CALORIES	153.80
FAT	6.25 GRAMS
SATURATED FAT	3.84 GRAMS
TRANS FAT	0.09 GRAMS*
CARBOHYDRATES	22.97 GRAMS
CHOLESTEROL	22.58 MG

Tiny cinnamon rolls are fun to make and eat. The cream cheese frosting adds a nice depth of flavor. Your kids will love them.

1 recipe Yeast Knot Rolls (page 50)
9 tablespoons butter, softened, divided
¾ cup brown sugar
1 teaspoon cinnamon
½ cup dried currants
1 (3-ounce) package cream cheese
1-½ cups powdered sugar
1 to 3 tablespoons heavy cream

1. Grease one large cookie sheet with unsalted butter and set aside. Prepare Yeast Knot Roll dough. After first rising, punch down dough. Divide in half; roll each half to an 18" × 6" rectangle. Spread each with 3 tablespoons softened butter. In small bowl, combine ¾ cup brown sugar and 1 teaspoon cinnamon. Sprinkle evenly over rectangles. Sprinkle with currants. Roll up tightly, starting with 18" side. Cut each roll into eighteen 1" slices and place, cut-side down, on prepared cookie sheet.

2. Cover and let rise for 30 minutes or until doubled. Preheat oven to 350°F. Bake rolls for 15 to 25 minutes or until golden brown. Cool for 5 minutes, then remove to wire racks to cool. In small saucepan, combine cream cheese and 3 tablespoons butter over low heat and melt together. When melted and smooth, remove from heat and stir in powdered sugar, then enough heavy cream to make a spreadable frosting. Spread frosting over warm rolls.

Spicy Monkey Bread

1 Recipe Yeast Knot Rolls (page 50)
¾ cup sugar
2 teaspoons ground cinnamon
½ teaspoon ground nutmeg
¼ teaspoon ground cardamom

1 cup chopped pecans
¾ cup brown sugar
⅓ cup butter
¼ cup maple syrup
2 tablespoons heavy cream

1. Preheat oven to 350°F. Spray a 12-cup fluted tube pan with nonstick cooking spray containing flour and set aside. Divide dough into 1" pieces and roll each piece into a smooth ball. Combine sugar with cinnamon, nutmeg, and cardamom on a shallow plate. Roll dough balls in this mixture and place in prepared pan, sprinkling each layer with pecans.

2. In saucepan, combine brown sugar, butter, maple syrup, and cream; bring to a boil. Pour over dough. Bake 30 minutes or until bread is deep golden brown. Invert onto a serving plate and let cool for 20 minutes, then serve.

SERVES 18

CALORIES	294.16
FAT	12.86 GRAMS
SATURATED FAT	5.54 GRAMS
TRANS FAT	0.20 GRAMS*
CARBOHYDRATES	42.03 GRAMS
CHOLESTEROL	33.75 MG

The cream in the brown sugar syrup adds a rich moistness to this coffeecake. Be sure to let it cool a bit before serving; the sticky coating is very hot!

Cake Doughnuts

3 eggs
¾ cup sugar
¼ cup brown sugar
1 cup buttermilk
1 teaspoon vanilla
¼ cup butter, melted

3 to 3-½ cups flour
¼ teaspoon salt
1 teaspoon baking powder
1 teaspoon baking soda
½ teaspoon ground nutmeg
3 cups corn oil

1. In bowl, beat eggs until light. Gradually add sugars, beating until light and fluffy. Add buttermilk, vanilla, and melted butter and mix well. In sifter, combine 3 cups flour, salt, baking powder, baking soda, and nutmeg, and sift over batter; stir in. You may need to add more flour to make a soft dough.

2. On floured surface, roll out dough ⅓" thick. Cut with doughnut cutters. In large skillet, heat oil to 375°F (use a thermometer for best results). Carefully add four doughnuts; fry on both sides, turning once, until golden brown, about 3 to 4 minutes for each side. Repeat with remaining dough. Fry doughnut holes for 1 to 2 minutes on each side.

YIELDS 18 DOUGHNUTS

CALORIES	193.30
FAT	7.49 GRAMS
SATURATED FAT	2.47 GRAMS
TRANS FAT	0.08 GRAMS
CARBOHYDRATES	27.92 GRAMS
CHOLESTEROL	42.57 MG

For baked doughnuts, please see Glazed Raised Doughnuts (page 94). You can glaze or frost these doughnuts, or dip them in cinnamon sugar while they're hot.

Triple-Chocolate Bread

YIELDS 2 LOAVES (24 SLICES)

CALORIES	266.76
FAT	13.83 GRAMS
SATURATED FAT	5.96 GRAMS
TRANS FAT	0.10 GRAMS*
CARBOHYDRATES	35.31 GRAMS
CHOLESTEROL	37.58 MG

A mashed avocado is the secret ingredient in this bread. Remember, the oil in avocado is very good for you. This bread is very chocolaty and rich.

½ cup butter, softened
1 peeled, mashed avocado
1 cup sugar
½ cup brown sugar
3 eggs
½ cup chocolate milk
1 cup milk
1 teaspoon vanilla
2-½ cups flour
½ cup cocoa powder
1 teaspoon baking powder
1 teaspoon baking soda
1 cup semisweet chocolate chips
1 cup white chocolate chips
1 cup chopped pecans

1. Preheat oven to 350°F. Grease two 9" × 5" loaf pans with unsalted butter and set aside. In large bowl, combine butter and avocado and beat until fluffy. Add sugar and brown sugar and beat until light. Beat in eggs, one at a time, beating after each addition.

2. Add chocolate milk, milk, and vanilla and beat until smooth. Add flour, cocoa powder, baking powder, and baking soda and mix just until ingredients are combined. Stir in chips and pecans. Spoon batter into prepared pans. Bake for 55 to 65 minutes or until bread pulls away from sides of pan and is firm to the touch. Cool in pans for 5 minutes, then remove to wire racks to cool completely.

Peach Cranberry Spice Turnovers

2 ripe peaches, peeled and chopped
⅓ cup dried sweetened cranberries
2 teaspoons lemon juice
1 tablespoon flour
5 tablespoons sugar, divided
1-½ teaspoons cinnamon, divided
¼ teaspoon cardamom

8 (15" × 18") sheets frozen filo
    dough, thawed
½ cup finely chopped pecans
¼ cup sugar
½ cup butter, melted

YIELDS 12 TURNOVERS

CALORIES	212.83
FAT	11.86 GRAMS
SATURATED FAT	5.33 GRAMS
TRANS FAT	0.20 GRAMS*
CARBOHYDRATES	26.14 GRAMS
CHOLESTEROL	20.34 GRAMS

These little turnovers are like a cross between baklava and peach strudel. They're delicious for a special brunch; make them for Christmas breakfast!

1. In medium bowl, combine peaches, cranberries, lemon juice, flour, 3 tablespoons sugar, 1 teaspoon cinnamon, and cardamom and mix well; set aside. Place thawed filo dough on work surface and cover with a damp kitchen towel to prevent drying. Work with one sheet at a time. In small bowl, combine pecans and ¼ cup sugar.

2. Lay one sheet filo on work surface; brush with melted butter. Sprinkle with 2 tablespoons of the pecan mixture. Place another sheet of filo on top, brush with butter, and sprinkle with 1 tablespoon of the pecan mixture. Cut into three 5" × 18" strips. Using a slotted spoon, place 2 tablespoons of the peach filling at one end of dough strips, leaving about a ½" border. Fold a corner of the short end of the dough over the filling at a 45-degree angle so edges match, making a triangle at the base of the strip, then continue folding that triangle, folding up the dough as you would fold a flag. Place on ungreased cookie sheets and brush with more butter. Repeat with remaining strips. Repeat with remaining filo, butter, and filling.

3. Preheat oven to 375°F. In small bowl, combine 2 tablespoons sugar and ½ teaspoon cinnamon and mix well. Sprinkle over turnovers. Bake for 20 to 30 minutes or until pastries are golden brown and crisp. Remove to wire racks to cool.

Filo Dough

Filo (also known as phyllo or fillo dough) is made of paper-thin layers of dough. You can find it in the frozen aisle of your supermarket. Follow the thawing instructions on the box carefully. It dries out very quickly, so be sure that the dough you aren't working with is covered with a damp towel or plastic wrap.

Lemon Meringue Coffeecake

This no-knead coffeecake has the flavors and texture of lemon meringue pie!

3-½ to 4 cups all-purpose flour
2 (0.25-ounce) packages instant blend yeast
1 cup sugar, divided
½ teaspoon salt
2 teaspoons lemon zest, divided
½ cup milk
⅓ cup water
2 tablespoons lemon juice
½ cup butter
3 eggs, separated
½ cup Honey Graham Crackers (page 64), crushed
½ cup chopped pecans
2 cups powdered sugar
¼ cup lemon juice

1. In large bowl, combine 1 cup flour, yeast, ¼ cup sugar, salt, and 1 teaspoon lemon zest and mix well. In glass measuring cup, combine milk, water, 2 tablespoons lemon juice, and butter. Microwave on high power for 1 minute until hot. Let cool to 120°F. Add to flour mixture along with egg yolks and beat for 1 minute. Gradually add enough remaining flour to make a soft dough. Cover and let rise until double, about 1 hour.

2. In small bowl, combine graham cracker crumbs and nuts and set aside. Punch down dough. On floured surface, roll dough to a 12" × 15" rectangle. In small bowl, beat egg whites until foamy. Gradually beat in ¾ cup sugar until stiff peaks form. Fold in 1 teaspoon lemon zest. Spread meringue mixture over dough, then sprinkle with nut mixture. Roll up dough, starting with 15" side, and seal edges.

3. Cut dough into six 2-½" pieces. Grease a 10-inch tube pan with removable bottom with unsalted butter. Place pieces, cut-side up, in pan. Cover and let rise for 30 minutes. Preheat oven to 350°F. Bake for 45 to 55 minutes until golden brown. Cool in pan for 5 minutes, then remove from pan. In small bowl combine powdered sugar and lemon juice. Drizzle over coffeecake; cool completely.

Popped Tarts

2-¼ cups flour
¼ cup brown sugar
¼ teaspoon salt
½ cup butter
¼ cup coconut oil
1 egg
1 teaspoon lemon juice

¼ cup milk
¼ cup butter, softened
⅓ cup brown sugar
½ cup chopped pecans
1 cup powdered sugar
1 tablespoon cream

YIELDS 10 PASTRIES

CALORIES	419.62
FAT	24.59 GRAMS
SATURATED FAT	14.39 GRAMS
TRANS FAT	0.36 GRAMS*
CARBOHYDRATES	47.09 GRAMS
CHOLESTEROL	60.05 MG

Yes, your own homemade Pop-Tarts! These little sweet treats are fun to make, too.

1. In a large bowl, combine flour, ¼ cup brown sugar, and salt and mix well. Cut in ½ cup butter and coconut oil until particles are fine. In small bowl, combine egg, lemon juice, and ¼ cup milk and beat well. Add to flour mixture and stir until a dough forms. Cover and chill for at least 2 hours.

2. When ready to bake, preheat oven to 350°F. In small bowl, combine ¼ cup butter, ⅓ cup brown sugar, and pecans and mix well. On lightly floured surface, roll out dough to a 20" × 12" rectangle, ⅛" thick. Cut into twenty 4" × 3" rectangles (four 3"-wide columns and five 4"-tall rows). Spread half of the rectangles with the pecan mixture, leaving a ⅓" border on all sides. Cover with plain rectangles and seal edges with fork; prick tops with fork.

3. Place pastries on ungreased cookie sheets. Bake for 12 to 16 minutes or until pastries are golden brown. Cool on wire racks. In small bowl, combine powdered sugar with cream and mix well. Drizzle over pastries and serve.

What Does "Cut In" Mean?

When a recipe calls for you to "cut in" fat into a flour mixture, it means that you should cut the fat into small pieces and work it into the flour using two knives, your fingertips, or a pastry blender. This makes a flaky pastry, because the butter coats the flour particles, and when it melts in baking, it forms layers of dough.

Glazed Nut Twists

YIELDS 32 ROLLS

CALORIES	156.96
FAT	9.02 GRAMS
SATURATED FAT	4.58 GRAMS
TRANS FAT	0.11 GRAMS*
CARBOHYDRATES	17.48 GRAMS
CHOLESTEROL	24.89 MG

These little twists rival the best your bakery has to offer. The dough is made like pie dough, and then rolled into layers with sugar and ground pecans. Yum!

1 (0.25-ounce) package active dry yeast
¾ cup buttermilk, divided
3-¼ cups flour
¼ cup oat bran
1 teaspoon salt
1 cup sugar, divided
¾ cup butter
¼ cup coconut oil
¼ cup orange juice
1 teaspoon vanilla
2 eggs
¾ cup finely ground pecans
2 teaspoons cinnamon

1. In medium bowl, combine yeast and ¼ cup buttermilk and set aside. In large bowl, combine flour, oat bran, salt, and ½ cup sugar and mix well. Cut butter into small pieces and add along with coconut oil to flour mixture. Work with pastry blender until fine crumbs form. Add remaining ½ cup buttermilk, orange juice, vanilla, and eggs to yeast mixture and beat well. Stir into flour mixture until blended.

2. Cover dough and refrigerate overnight. When ready to bake, preheat oven to 375°F. In small bowl, combine ½ cup sugar, pecans, and cinnamon and mix well. Divide sugar mixture in half; sprinkle some of one half on work surface.

3. Divide dough in half and roll out each half on sugar mixture to a 15" × 7" rectangle. Sprinkle with sugar mixture and fold dough into thirds, sprinkling each new layer with sugar mixture. Repeat with second half of dough and second half of sugar mixture. Roll each half out to a 16" × 6" rectangle and cut into sixteen 1" × 6" strips. Twist each strip and place 2" apart on two silicone-lined baking sheets. Sprinkle with any remaining sugar mixture.

4. Bake twists for 12 to 18 minutes or until light golden brown and puffed, reversing cookie sheets once during baking time. Remove from cookie sheets as soon as the twists are done. Cool on wire racks.

Caramel Pull-Apart Rolls

2-½ to 3 cups all-purpose flour
½ cup whole-wheat flour
¼ cup sugar
1 (0.25-ounce) package instant blend yeast
½ cup milk
¼ cup orange juice
½ cup butter, divided

1 egg
1 teaspoon vanilla
1-½ cups brown sugar, divided
1 teaspoon cinnamon
3 tablespoons maple syrup
½ cup chopped pecans
2 tablespoons butter, melted

SERVES 12	
CALORIES	394.10
FAT	13.82 GRAMS
SATURATED FAT	6.62 GRAMS
TRANS FAT	0.25 GRAMS*
CARBOHYDRATES	63.68 GRAMS
CHOLESTEROL	43.55 MG

These superb rolls taste better than anything you'll get at the bakery!

1. In bowl, combine 1 cup all-purpose flour, whole-wheat flour, sugar, and yeast and mix well. In saucepan, combine milk, orange juice, and ¼ cup butter and heat over low heat until warm (about 120°F). Remove from heat and beat in egg and vanilla. Add to flour mixture and beat for 2 minutes.

2. Gradually add enough remaining flour to form a firm dough. Knead on floured surface until smooth and elastic, about 5 minutes. Place in greased bowl, turning to grease top. Cover and let rise until doubled, about 1 hour. In small bowl, combine 1 cup brown sugar and cinnamon and mix well. In small saucepan, combine ¼ cup butter, ½ cup brown sugar, maple syrup, and pecans. Cook and stir over low heat until blended. Place pecan mixture in 13" × 9" baking pan and spread evenly.

3. Punch down dough and divide into four parts. On lightly floured surface, roll each part into a 12" × 6" rectangle. Spread each with one-fourth of the 2 tablespoons melted butter and sprinkle with cinnamon mixture. Roll up, starting with 12" side. Place rolls on pecan mixture in pan. Starting on the same side of each roll, cut slashes 1" apart, going almost through roll. Turn the cut pieces on their sides, twisting to expose filling. Cover and let rise until light, about 30 minutes. Preheat oven to 375°F. Bake for 25 minutes or until rolls are deep golden brown. Invert onto foil-covered rack to cool.

Maple Syrup

When a recipe calls for real maple syrup, don't substitute pancake syrup! The taste will be different. The former has a special flavor and texture. It is made from sap from the maple tree, harvested in the early spring. It takes more than 43 gallons of sap to produce one gallon of maple syrup.

Glazed Raised Doughnuts

YIELDS 36 DOUGHNUTS

CALORIES	133.35
FAT	3.90 GRAMS
SATURATED FAT	2.28 GRAMS
TRANS FAT	0.07 GRAMS*
CARBOHYDRATES	22.24 GRAMS
CHOLESTEROL	20.61 MG

These doughnuts are baked, not fried, for a lower fat and calorie content. For classic fried doughnuts, take a look at Cake Doughnuts (page 87).

2 (0.25-ounce) packages active dry yeast
½ cup warm water
1 cup whole milk, divided
½ cup butter, divided
¾ cup sugar, divided
½ teaspoon salt
¾ teaspoon nutmeg, divided
2 eggs
½ cup sour cream
4 to 5 cups all-purpose flour
2 cups powdered sugar
1 teaspoon vanilla

1. In small bowl, combine yeast and ½ cup warm water; mix and set aside. In heavy saucepan, heat ¾ cup milk until steam rises. Pour milk into large bowl; add ¼ cup butter, ½ cup sugar, salt, and ½ teaspoon nutmeg and stir until butter melts. Let stand until lukewarm. Then add eggs and yeast mixture; beat until combined.

2. Stir in sour cream and 1 cup flour; beat for 1 minute. Then gradually add enough remaining flour to make a soft dough. Grease top of dough with some soft butter, cover, and let rise for 1 hour. Punch down dough, cover with plastic wrap, and refrigerate overnight.

3. When ready to bake, punch down dough. Roll on lightly floured surface to ½" thickness. Cut with a 2-½" doughnut cutter. Place doughnuts on parchment-paper-lined cookie sheets and brush with 2 tablespoons melted butter. Let rise until almost doubled, about 1 hour.

4. Preheat oven to 425°F. In heavy saucepan, combine ¼ cup milk, ¼ cup sugar, and 2 tablespoons butter over medium heat. Cook and stir until butter melts and sugar dissolves. Remove from heat and stir in powdered sugar, ¼ teaspoon nutmeg, and vanilla to make a glaze.

5. Bake doughnuts for 20 to 25 minutes, or until light, puffy, and light golden brown. Bake doughnut holes in one batch for 8 to 12 minutes or until light golden brown. Remove to wire racks and immediately spoon glaze over each doughnut. Cool completely.

Applesauce Honey Rolls

5 to 6 cups flour
2 (0.25-ounce) packages instant blend dry yeast
1-¼ cups brown sugar, divided
1 teaspoon salt
1-½ cups milk
1 cup applesauce, divided
¾ cup butter, softened, divided
2 eggs
⅔ cup honey
2 teaspoons cinnamon

YIELDS 24 ROLLS

CALORIES	246.76
FAT	6.98 GRAMS
SATURATED FAT	4.15 GRAMS
TRANS FAT	0.15 GRAMS*
CARBOHYDRATES	42.64 GRAMS
CHOLESTEROL	35.01 MG

Applesauce and honey combine for wonderful flavor in these light sweet rolls. Serve them for a special breakfast or brunch.

1. In large bowl, combine 2 cups flour, yeast, ½ cup brown sugar, and salt and mix well. In large saucepan, combine milk, ½ cup applesauce, and ¼ cup butter over medium heat; cook and stir until mixture is warm. Add to flour mixture along with eggs and beat well. Gradually stir in enough remaining flour to make a soft dough.

2. Knead dough on floured surface until smooth and elastic, about 5 minutes. Place in greased bowl, turning to grease top. Cover and let rise until doubled, about 1 hour. In small bowl combine ½ cup brown sugar, honey, and ¼ cup butter. Divide between two 9" × 13" pans, spread evenly, and set aside. In medium bowl, combine ¼ cup butter, ½ cup applesauce, ¼ cup brown sugar, and cinnamon and mix well.

3. Punch down dough and divide in half. Roll to two 9" × 12" rectangles. Spread each with half of applesauce mixture. Roll up, starting with 12" side; pinch edges to seal. Cut each into 1" slices; place, cut-side down, over honey mixture in pans. Cover and let rise until double, about 40 minutes. Preheat oven to 375°F. Bake for 25 to 35 minutes or until rolls are deep golden brown. Immediately invert onto racks to cool.

Honey Lore

Did you know that if you eat honey that has been harvested from the county where you live, it can help reduce allergic reactions? Honey will have different flavor and aroma depending on what flowers the bees used to gather nectar.

Mocha Puff-Pastry Rounds

SERVES 12

CALORIES	358.78
FAT	20.44 GRAMS
SATURATED FAT	12.40 GRAMS
TRANS FAT	0.48 GRAMS*
CARBOHYDRATES	40.50 GRAMS
CHOLESTEROL	102.88 MG

This variation on a classic recipe adds coffee and chocolate to make a mocha flavor, and divides a large coffeecake into individual pastries. They're cute, delicious, and fun to make.

2-½ cups flour, divided
2 tablespoons sugar
¼ cup cocoa powder, divided
1 cup butter, divided
½ cup cold brewed coffee, divided
¾ cup water
1-¾ cups powdered sugar, divided
3 eggs
1 teaspoon vanilla
3 tablespoons butter, melted
1 tablespoon heavy cream

1. Preheat oven to 350°F. In medium bowl, combine 1-½ cups flour, sugar, and 2 tablespoons cocoa powder. Cut in ½ cup butter until particles are fine. Sprinkle 3 tablespoons coffee over the mixture, tossing until a dough forms. Form into a ball, wrap in plastic wrap, and chill for at least 1 hour.

2. When ready to bake, divide dough into 12 portions. On ungreased cookie sheets, press each portion into a 3" round; form a slight rim. Set aside. In heavy saucepan, combine water, ¼ cup coffee, and ½ cup butter in a large saucepan. Bring to a rolling boil that cannot be stirred down. Add 1 cup flour, ¼ cup powdered sugar, and 2 tablespoons cocoa all at once and beat together. Cook and stir over medium heat until the mixture forms a ball and cleans the sides of the pan. Remove from heat and stir in eggs, one at a time, beating until incorporated. Stir in vanilla.

3. Divide mixture among the twelve crusts on cookie sheets. Bake for 20 to 30 minutes or until pastries are crisp and light golden brown. Let cool on baking sheets for 3 minutes, then remove to wire racks to cool for 30 minutes. In small bowl, combine 1-½ cups powdered sugar, 3 tablespoons melted butter, cream, and 1 tablespoon cold coffee and mix until smooth. Drizzle over rounds and serve.

Orange Nut Swirl Loaf

¼ cup butter, softened
½ cup brown sugar
1 teaspoon cinnamon
½ cup quick-cooking oatmeal
2-½ cups flour
1 cup sugar
2 teaspoons baking powder
1 teaspoon baking soda
1 teaspoons grated orange peel
½ cup frozen orange juice concentrate, thawed
¾ cup milk
3 tablespoons butter, melted
1 egg
½ cup chopped pecans

1. Preheat oven to 350°F. Grease a 9" × 5" loaf pan with unsalted butter and set aside. In small bowl, combine ¼ cup butter, brown sugar, and cinnamon and mix well. Stir in oatmeal and set aside.

2. In large bowl, combine flour, sugar, baking powder, baking soda, orange peel, orange juice concentrate, milk, 3 tablespoons melted butter, and egg and beat for 1 minute on medium speed until combined. Stir in pecans. Pour half of batter into prepared pan and sprinkle with half of oatmeal mixture. Add remaining batter and sprinkle with remaining oatmeal mixture. Using a knife, cut through batter a few times to swirl. Bake for 55 to 65 minutes or until bread is firm and golden brown. Turn out onto wire rack and cool completely.

Storing Quick Breads
Many quick breads, those that use baking powder or baking soda instead of yeast, taste and slice better if allowed to stand overnight. The flavor has a chance to develop, and the crumb, or texture of the bread, has time to set so it slices better. Make sure the bread is completely cooled before you wrap it in plastic wrap or place it in a plastic bag.

YIELDS 1 LOAF (12 SLICES)

CALORIES	341.20
FAT	11.27 GRAMS
SATURATED FAT	4.88 GRAMS
TRANS FAT	0.18 GRAMS*
CARBOHYDRATES	55.71 GRAMS
CHOLESTEROL	36.18 MG

Orange juice concentrate adds lots of flavor to this sweet quick bread recipe. It's perfect for breakfast or brunch.

Kringla

SERVES 24

CALORIES	355.48
FAT	18.18 GRAMS
SATURATED FAT	9.13 GRAMS
TRANS FAT	0.26 GRAMS*
CARBOHYDRATES	44.17 GRAMS
CHOLESTEROL	71.23 MG

This classic coffeecake is for very special occasions. You can buy almond paste in most grocery stores or online.

2 (0.25-ounce) packages active dry yeast
½ cup warm water
4-½ cups flour, divided
1-¼ cups sugar, divided
½ teaspoon salt
1-¼ cups butter, divided
¼ cup coconut oil
½ cup milk
3 egg yolks
1 (8-ounce) can almond paste
2 eggs
1 cup sliced almonds
1 teaspoon vanilla
2 cups powdered sugar
2 to 3 tablespoons heavy cream

1. In small bowl, combine yeast and warm water and set aside. Meanwhile, in large bowl combine 4-¼ cups flour, ¼ cup sugar, and salt and mix well. Cut in ¾ cup butter and coconut oil until particles are the size of cornmeal. Add milk and egg yolks to yeast mixture and stir. Stir into flour mixture until a soft dough forms. Cover and refrigerate overnight.

2. When ready to bake, combine almond paste, 1 cup sugar, ¼ cup butter, ¼ cup flour, and 2 eggs and beat until smooth. Divide dough into 4 parts and roll each part into a rectangle ¼" thick, about 12" × 8". Spread each with almond paste mixture and sprinkle with almonds. Roll up, starting at 12" side. Place two coffeecakes, seam-side down, on a cookie sheet. Cut slits across top of coffeecakes at 2" intervals, being sure not to cut through to bottom layer of dough. Cover and let rise for 1 hour.

3. Preheat oven to 325°F. Bake for 35 to 45 minutes or until coffeecakes are golden brown. Remove to wire racks to cool for about 30 minutes. Meanwhile, melt ¼ cup butter in saucepan. Stir in vanilla, powdered sugar, and enough heavy cream to form a frosting. Spread over warm coffeecakes.

Apricot Sally Lunn

¾ cup apricot nectar, divided
½ cup finely chopped dried apricots
¼ cup milk
½ cup butter
½ cup sugar, divided
1 (0.25-ounce) package active dry yeast
¼ cup warm water
3 eggs
4 to 4-½ cups flour
½ teaspoon salt

SERVES 16

CALORIES	239.56
FAT	7.13 GRAMS
SATURATED FAT	4.02 GRAMS
TRANS FAT	0.15 GRAMS*
CARBOHYDRATES	38.66 GRAMS
CHOLESTEROL	55.10 MG

Be sure that the apricots are chopped very finely for best results. The flavor and aroma of this bread are wonderful.

1. In small saucepan, combine ½ cup apricot nectar and chopped dried apricots. Bring to a simmer over medium high heat. Lower heat and simmer for 5 minutes. Remove from heat and stir in milk, butter, and ⅓ cup sugar; let cool for 30 minutes or until warm. Meanwhile, in large bowl combine yeast and ¼ cup warm water; mix and let stand for 10 minutes.

2. Add eggs to apricot mixture, 1 at a time, beating after each addition. Add yeast mixture. Stir in 2 cups flour and salt and beat for 1 minute. Gradually add remaining flour until soft dough forms, beating after each addition. Cover dough and let rise until doubled, about 1-½ to 2 hours.

3. Grease a 12-cup Bundt pan with unsalted butter and set aside. Punch down dough and shape into a 12" cylinder. Place in prepared pan, sealing ends together; press down. Cover and let rise until doubled, about 45 minutes. Preheat oven to 350°F. Bake for 30 to 40 minutes or until golden brown and set. Invert onto cooling rack. In small saucepan, combine ¼ cup apricot nectar and remaining sugar and heat until sugar melts. Brush over warm loaf until all sugar mixture is used. Cool completely.

The Story of Sally Lunn

The history of the Sally Lunn bread is murky. Sally Lunn may have been the daughter of a French pastry cook. Or the word could be derived from the French word solimeme, *which means a type of brioche. In any case, this bread is baked in a fancy-shaped tube pan, is rich with egg and butter, and is perfect served with tea.*

Chocolate-Chip Crumb Coffeecake

SERVES 24

CALORIES	285.75
FAT	13.37 GRAMS
SATURATED FAT	6.52 GRAMS
TRANS FAT	0.20 GRAMS*
CARBOHYDRATES	40.66 GRAMS
CHOLESTEROL	21.15 MG

Coffeecake is always better with chocolate! And this cake, with a nut-encrusted crumb topping, is perfect for brunch or a fancy tea.

3 cups flour
1 cup sugar
1-½ cups brown sugar, divided
1 cup butter
2 teaspoons cinnamon
½ teaspoon nutmeg
1 teaspoon baking soda
½ teaspoon baking powder
2 cups buttermilk
1 cup chopped pecans
1 cup semisweet chocolate chips
3 tablespoons powdered sugar

1. Preheat oven to 350°F. Grease a 13" × 9" pan with unsalted butter and set aside. In large bowl, combine flour, sugar, and 1 cup brown sugar and mix well. Cut in butter until the particles are the size of peas. Place 1 cup of this mixture into a small bowl and set aside.

2. Add cinnamon, nutmeg, baking soda, and baking powder to remaining crumb mixture and blend well. Add buttermilk and mix just until combined. Pour into prepared pan. To reserved 1 cup of crumb mixture add ½ cup brown sugar, pecans, and chocolate chips. Sprinkle over batter in pan.

3. Bake for 50 to 60 minutes or until coffeecake is golden brown and pulls away from sides of pan. Place on wire rack and let cool for 30 minutes. Place powdered sugar in sieve and sprinkle over cake; let cool completely.

Substituting for Buttermilk
If you're out of buttermilk, it's easy to make a substitute. Just put about a tablespoon of vinegar or lemon juice in a measuring cup. Then add sweet or fresh milk until it reaches the desired amount. Let the mixture stand at room temperature for 5 to 10 minutes, then use as directed in the recipe.

Chapter 6

Salads and Soups

Pumpkin Wild Rice Chowder

You can substitute half-and-half for the heavy cream if you'd like. This hearty chowder is thick and full of flavor.

1 (16-ounce) package baby carrots
2 potatoes, peeled and cubed
1 cup wild rice, rinsed
2 tablespoons olive oil
1 pound beef sirloin tips
1 onion, chopped
4 cloves garlic, minced
1 (15-ounce) can solid pack pumpkin
2 cups Beef Broth (page 119)
4 cups water
1 tablespoon curry powder
1 teaspoon salt
¼ teaspoon white pepper
½ cup heavy cream

1. Place carrots, potatoes, and wild rice in bottom of 4- or 5-quart slow cooker. In large skillet, heat olive oil over medium high heat. Add beef; sauté for 2 to 3 minutes just until meat begins to turn brown; remove with slotted spoon and add to slow cooker. Add onion and garlic to skillet; cook and stir for 3 minutes, then add to slow cooker.

2. Add pumpkin and Beef Broth to skillet. Cook and stir until mixture blends and comes to a simmer. Pour into crock pot; add water, curry powder, salt, and pepper and stir. Cover and cook on low for 8 to 9 hours, until beef and wild rice are tender. Stir in heavy cream and cook for 20 minutes longer; serve.

Sirloin Tips

If you can't find sirloin tips (a beef sirloin steak that has been cut into cubes) you can cut it yourself. Trim the steak of excess fat and cut into 1" cubes, following the grain of the meat. Other cuts of beef will work as well; bottom round steak, sirloin tri-tip, chuck steak, or shoulder steak work well when cooked in the slow cooker.

Red Gazpacho

1 clove garlic
5 ripe tomatoes
3 cucumbers
1 green bell pepper
½ cup minced onion
3 cups tomato juice

¼ cup extra-virgin olive oil
3 tablespoons lemon juice
1 teaspoon salt
⅛ teaspoon pepper
2 tablespoons chopped parsley

1. Cut the garlic in half and rub the serving bowl with garlic; discard garlic. Chop the tomatoes and place half into food processor or blender. Peel cucumber, remove seeds with a spoon, and chop; place half in food processor. Process the tomatoes and cucumbers until smooth; pour into bowl.

2. Chop the green bell pepper and add to serving bowl along with remaining chopped tomatoes, cucumber, and onion. Slowly stir in remaining ingredients. Cover and chill for 2 to 3 hours before serving.

This fabulous and super-easy soup takes only minutes to make using a food processor. You could add just about any cooked seafood if you'd like.

Wilted Spinach Fruit Salad

4 slices bacon
1 onion, chopped
2 apples, chopped
¼ cup sugar

¼ cup apple-cider vinegar
2 (10-ounce) bags baby spinach
½ cup raisins
½ cup toasted chopped walnuts

1. In large skillet, cook bacon until crisp. Remove and drain on paper towels. To drippings remaining in skillet, add onion; cook and stir until crisp-tender, about 4 minutes. Add apples; cook and stir for 2 minutes longer. Stir in sugar and vinegar (watch out—it will boil furiously).

2. While bacon is cooking, combine spinach, raisins, and walnuts in serving bowl. When sugar dissolves in the hot apple and onion mixture, pour mixture over spinach and toss to coat (spinach will wilt). Serve immediately.

Apples and raisins are perfect partners with spinach and bacon in this special salad. Serve it as the main dish for a light lunch or supper.

Four-Bean Salad

SERVES 8

CALORIES	326.23
FAT	14.97 GRAMS
SATURATED FAT	2.11 GRAMS
TRANS FAT	0.0 GRAMS
CARBOHYDRATES	40.17 GRAMS
CHOLESTEROL	0.0 MG

This salad can be served as a vegetarian main course by serving it over mixed salad greens. You could add some chopped toasted walnuts, too, for flavor and crunch.

2 cups frozen green beans
2 cups frozen wax beans
1 (15-ounce) can chickpeas, rinsed
1 (15-ounce) can kidney beans, rinsed
½ cup olive oil
¼ cup lemon juice
¼ cup sugar
½ teaspoon celery seed
¼ teaspoon salt
⅛ teaspoon white pepper

1. Prepare green beans and wax beans as packages direct. Drain well and place in serving bowl along with drained chickpeas and kidney beans.

2. In small bowl, combine olive oil, lemon juice, sugar, celery seed, salt, and pepper and mix well with wire whisk. Drizzle over vegetables and stir to coat. Cover and refrigerate at least 4 hours, stirring occasionally, before serving.

French Salad Dressing

**YIELDS 2 CUPS
(SERVING SIZE
2 TABLESPOONS)**

CALORIES	102.03
FAT	6.82 GRAMS
SATURATED FAT	0.94 GRAMS
TRANS FAT	0.0 GRAMS
CARBOHYDRATES	10.26 GRAMS
CHOLESTEROL	0.0 MG

This dressing keeps well in the fridge for about a week. It's rich, thick, and delicious, especially on baby spinach.

½ cup apple-cider vinegar
½ cup sugar
¼ cup chopped onion
¾ cup ketchup
¼ cup chili sauce
1 teaspoon yellow mustard
½ teaspoon salt
½ teaspoon salt
⅛ teaspoon white pepper
½ cup extra-virgin olive oil

1. In small saucepan, combine vinegar and sugar and bring to a simmer. Reduce heat and simmer for 5 minutes, stirring occasionally, until sugar dissolves completely. Set aside to cool for 30 minutes.

2. In food processor or blender, combine onion and ketchup. Process or blend until mixture is smooth. Add cooled vinegar mixture along with chili sauce, mustard, and seasonings. While mixture is processing, slowly add the olive oil until mixture is thick and blended. Store covered in refrigerator up to 1 week.

Cheese Vegetable Soup

2 tablespoons butter
2 tablespoons olive oil
1 onion, chopped
3 carrots, sliced
2 stalks celery, sliced
3 tablespoons flour
1 teaspoon paprika
½ teaspoon salt
⅛ teaspoon pepper
3 cups Vegetable Broth (page 119)
1 (14-ounce) can diced tomatoes, drained
3 cups milk
1-½ cups cubed Havarti cheese

1. In large pot combine butter and olive oil over medium heat. When butter melts, add onion; cook and stir for 3 minutes. Add carrots; cook and stir 3 minutes longer. Stir in celery and cook for 1 minute. Add flour, paprika, salt, and pepper. Cook and stir for 3 minutes.

2. Add Vegetable Broth and tomatoes, bring to a simmer, and cook for 5 to 10 minutes until vegetables are tender. Slowly stir in milk and heat until the soup steams; do not boil. Place ¼ cup cheese in the bottom of each serving bowl and pour soup over.

SERVES 6

CALORIES	349.74
FAT	21.80 GRAMS
SATURATED FAT	10.67 GRAMS
TRANS FAT	0.10 GRAMS*
CARBOHYDRATES	24.26 GRAMS
CHOLESTEROL	50.33 MG

A hot vegetable soup is poured over cheese placed in soup bowls so the cheese slowly melts as you eat it. Yum!

Cauliflower Radish Salad

SERVES 6

CALORIES	182.49
FAT	14.51 GRAMS
SATURATED FAT	4.44 GRAMS
TRANS FAT	0.08 GRAMS*
CARBOHYDRATES	10.87 GRAMS
CHOLESTEROL	11.37 MG

Radishes and cauliflower provide nice crunch in this delicious salad. Because the vegetables marinate in the dressing, they are very flavorful, too.

1 head cauliflower
12 radishes
½ cup chopped green onion
½ cup sour cream
1 tablespoon Dijon mustard
¼ cup olive oil
¼ cup grated Parmesan cheese
½ teaspoon dried tarragon leaves
2 cups frisée
2 cups baby spinach leaves
2 cups watercress leaves

1. Remove leaves from cauliflower and separate into florets. Thinly slice each floret. Scrub radishes and trim; slice very thin. Combine with green onion in medium bowl. In small bowl, combine sour cream, mustard, oil, cheese, and tarragon and mix well. Pour over cauliflower mixture and toss. Cover and chill in refrigerator for 4 to 8 hours.

2. When ready to eat, add frisée, spinach, and watercress to salad and toss gently. Serve immediately.

Frisée

Frisée *is the French word for "curly." This curly, peppery lettuce can be found in most large grocery stores, and at farmers' markets and gourmet stores. The long, very slender leaves are a nice contrast to softer spinach and lettuces in salads. Trim the stems and rinse in cold water just before using.*

Orzo Vegetable Cheese Salad

1 (12-ounce) package orzo pasta
2 cups frozen baby peas
½ cup yogurt
½ cup buttermilk
½ cup Homemade Mayonnaise (page 31)
¼ cup grated Parmesan cheese
¼ cup crumbled feta cheese
2 cups grape tomatoes
1 red bell pepper, chopped
1 cup chopped celery
¼ cup chopped green onion
1 cup diced Colby cheese

1. In large pot of boiling water, cook pasta according to package directions until tender. Place peas in colander; drain pasta over peas to thaw them. Meanwhile, in large bowl combine yogurt, buttermilk, Mayonnaise, Parmesan cheese, and feta cheese and mix well.

2. Stir in drained pasta and peas along with remaining ingredients and stir gently to coat. Cover and chill in refrigerator for at least 4 hours before serving.

SERVES 8

CALORIES	404.32
FAT	20.23 GRAMS
SATURATED FAT	6.51 GRAMS
TRANS FAT	0.14 GRAMS*
CARBOHYDRATES	42.70 GRAMS
CHOLESTEROL	41.70 MG

Three kinds of cheese make this side-dish salad rich and delicious. You can add some chopped cooked chicken or shrimp to make it a main-dish salad.

Creamy Date and Nut Salad

SERVES 8

CALORIES	325.58
FAT	15.16 GRAMS
SATURATED FAT	4.30 GRAMS
TRANS FAT	0.08 GRAMS*
CARBOHYDRATES	42.69 GRAMS
CHOLESTEROL	17.58 MG

This old-fashioned salad is delicious served at a holiday dinner along with a ham and Garlic and Onion Smashed Potatoes (page 235).

1 (3-ounce) package lemon gelatin
1 cup boiling water
1 (8-ounce) can pineapple tidbits
1 (8-ounce) package low-fat cream cheese
1 (8-ounce) carton lemon yogurt
½ cup finely chopped dates
1 cup chopped walnuts
½ cup dried sweetened cranberries

1. In small bowl, combine gelatin and boiling water; stir until gelatin dissolves completely. Drain pineapple, reserving juice. Add enough cold water to juice to make ¾ cup, if necessary. Add juice to gelatin mixture, stir well, and refrigerate for 20 minutes.

2. In large bowl, beat cream cheese until light and fluffy. Add yogurt gradually, beating until combined and smooth. Gradually beat in cooled gelatin mixture. Fold in drained pineapple, dates, walnuts, and cranberries and stir to combine. Pour into eight 6-ounce serving cups. Cover and chill until firm.

Pitted or Chopped Dates?
When a recipe calls for chopped dates, always buy the whole pitted variety and chop them yourself. Chopped packaged dates are coated in sugar, which will add too much sugar to your recipe. The pre-chopped dates are also usually too dry. Chop dates by snipping them with a kitchen shears, or chopping with a sharp knife.

Wild Rice Cauliflower Chowder

2 tablespoons olive oil
1 onion, chopped
4 cloves garlic, minced
½ teaspoon salt
⅛ teaspoon white pepper
½ teaspoon dried tarragon leaves
1 head cauliflower
1 cup wild rice
4 cups Chicken Broth (page 120) or Vegetable Broth (page 119)
4 cups water
2 cups frozen corn
1 cup frozen sliced carrots
½ cup light cream
3 tablespoons cornstarch
2 cups shredded Gruyère cheese

SERVES 8	
CALORIES	391.71
FAT	18.85 GRAMS
SATURATED FAT	7.94 GRAMS
TRANS FAT	0.29 GRAMS*
CARBOHYDRATES	37.70 GRAMS
CHOLESTEROL	55.06 MG

This creamy soup is delicious served with a drizzle of Basil Pesto (page 23). It's warming and hearty.

1. In large stockpot, combine olive oil, onion, and garlic over medium heat; cook and stir until crisp-tender, about 4 minutes; sprinkle with salt, pepper, and tarragon. Meanwhile, clean cauliflower and break into florets. Add cauliflower and rice to stockpot. Add chicken broth and water.

2. Bring to a boil, then reduce heat and cover; simmer for 30 minutes or until cauliflower is tender and wild rice is tender but still slightly chewy. Add frozen vegetables and simmer for 5 minutes longer. In small bowl, combine cream and cornstarch and blend well. Stir into stockpot and simmer for 5 to 10 minutes longer or until soup is thickened. Stir in cheese and serve.

Melon Pineapple Salad

SERVES 12

CALORIES	108.29
FAT	0.39 GRAMS
SATURATED FAT	0.14 GRAMS
TRANS FAT	0.0 GRAMS
CARBOHYDRATES	27.06 GRAMS
CHOLESTEROL	0.41 MG

This fresh salad can be made with almost any fruit that's in season. Use a different flavor of yogurt if you'd like.

1 cantaloupe
1 honeydew melon
1 ripe pineapple
¼ cup honey

½ cup lemon yogurt
¼ cup pineapple-orange juice
2 tablespoons chopped mint

1. Cut melons in half, remove seeds, and cut into balls with a melon baller, or cut into cubes. Remove leaves from pineapple and cut off skin. Remove center core and slice. Combine fruits in large serving bowl.

2. In small bowl, combine remaining ingredients and mix well. Pour over fruits and toss to coat. Cover and chill for at least 4 hours before serving.

Puffy Dumplings

SERVES 8

CALORIES	184.78
FAT	13.20 GRAMS
SATURATED FAT	7.88 GRAMS
TRANS FAT	0.30 GRAMS*
CARBOHYDRATES	12.79 GRAMS
CHOLESTEROL	84.60 MG

You can add these little dumplings, based on cream puff dough, to any broth or soup recipe. Be sure to simmer the dumplings covered for best results.

½ cup water
½ cup milk
½ cup butter

1 cup flour
¼ teaspoon salt
2 eggs

1. In medium saucepan, combine water, milk, and butter and bring to a full boil over high heat. Add flour and salt all at once. Cook and stir until mixture forms a ball and cleans sides of pan. Remove from heat and add eggs, one at a time, beating well after each addition.

2. Have soup at a simmer over medium heat. Drop dough into the pot, working quickly, using a teaspoon for each dumpling. Cover pot and simmer for 10 minutes without lifting lid. Uncover pot and check if dumplings are cooked through. If not, cover and simmer another 2 to 4 minutes.

Spinach Beet Borscht

4 slices bacon
1 onion, chopped
3 cloves garlic, minced
2 (15-ounce) cans sliced beets
1 (6-ounce) can tomato paste
4 cups Chicken Broth (page 120)
½ teaspoon dill seed
½ teaspoon salt
⅛ teaspoon pepper
1 tablespoon apple-cider vinegar
2 cups baby spinach leaves, chopped
½ cup sour cream
¼ cup chopped parsley

1. In large stockpot, cook bacon until crisp; remove bacon to paper towel to drain; crumble and set aside. In drippings remaining in pot, cook onion and garlic until tender, about 5 minutes. Drain beets and add to pot along with tomato paste, Chicken Broth, dill seed, salt, and pepper.

2. Bring to a boil, then reduce heat and simmer for 15 minutes. Using an immersion blender or potato masher, mash some of the beets, leaving some whole. Stir in apple-cider vinegar and bring just to a simmer again. Divide spinach leaves among six soup bowls and pour soup over leaves. Garnish with sour cream, bacon, and parsley.

SERVES 6

CALORIES	306.49
FAT	17.03 GRAMS
SATURATED FAT	6.40 GRAMS
TRANS FAT	0.05 GRAMS*
CARBOHYDRATES	21.65 GRAMS
CHOLESTEROL	54.38 MG

A hot bacon and beet soup is poured over spinach leaves to wilt the leaves and make them tender. A sour cream garnish finishes the soup to perfection.

Curried Chicken Rice Salad

SERVES 8

CALORIES	369.56
FAT	20.13 GRAMS
SATURATED FAT	3.12 GRAMS
TRANS FAT	0.01 GRAMS*
CARBOHYDRATES	32.42 GRAMS
CHOLESTEROL	52.88 GRAMS

This delicious main-dish salad recipe is full of color and flavor. Serve it for lunch on the porch, along with lemonade and some muffins.

1 cup Chicken Broth (page 120)
1 cup water
1 tablespoon curry powder, divided
3 boneless, skinless chicken breasts
1 cup brown basmati rice
½ cup golden raisins
1 cup chopped celery
⅓ cup chopped green onion

½ cup chopped walnuts
1 (8-ounce) can pineapple tidbits
½ cup Homemade Mayonnaise (page 31)
¼ cup low-fat sour cream
½ cup mango chutney
2 tablespoons lemon juice

1. In large saucepan, combine Chicken Broth, water, and 1 teaspoon curry powder. Bring to a boil over high heat. Add chicken breasts, lower heat, cover, and simmer for 7 to 11 minutes or until chicken is just cooked through. Remove chicken from broth and set aside. Add rice to skillet and bring to a simmer. Cover and simmer for 15 to 20 minutes or until rice is tender and liquid is absorbed.

2. Cut chicken into bite-size pieces and combine in large bowl with rice, raisins, celery, green onion, and walnuts. Drain pineapple, reserving juice. Add pineapple to chicken mixture.

3. In small bowl, combine ¼ cup reserved pineapple liquid, remaining 2 teaspoons curry powder, Mayonnaise, sour cream, chutney, and lemon juice and mix well. Pour over chicken mixture and stir. Cover and chill for 4 hours before serving.

Light Mayonnaise
Most, if not all, brands of light mayonnaise contain artificial trans fats, even if less than 0.5 grams per serving. Making your own mayonnaise (see Homemade Mayonnaise, page 31) is the only way to make sure that the mayo you use in cooking and sandwiches is trans fat–free.

Thousand Island Salad Dressing

¾ cup Homemade Mayonnaise (page 31)
¼ cup chili sauce
3 tablespoons ketchup
1 tablespoon Worcestershire sauce
1 tablespoon sugar
3 tablespoons pickle relish
2 tablespoons apple-cider vinegar

1. Combine all ingredients in small bowl and stir with wire whisk to blend. Taste and adjust seasonings if necessary, adding more sugar if the dressing is too tart, or adding more vinegar or chili sauce if it's too sweet.

Homemade Salad Dressings

Homemade salad dressings are easy and fun to make. Kept in the fridge, well-covered, they will keep for about one week. You can adjust the ingredients to suit your tastes and health needs, too. Use low-sodium products and omit the salt if you're watching your sodium intake; or substitute low-fat ingredients if desired.

YIELDS 1 CUP (SERVING SIZE 2 TABLESPOONS)

CALORIES	187.97
FAT	17.56 GRAMS
SATURATED FAT	2.54 GRAMS
TRANS FAT	0.0 GRAMS
CARBOHYDRATES	8.12 GRAMS
CHOLESTEROL	26.33 MG

Serve this dressing over iceberg lettuce wedges and sprinkle it with some chopped cooked egg and crumbled crisp bacon for a retro salad.

Old-Fashioned Chicken Soup

SERVES 8

CALORIES	368.89
FAT	16.32 GRAMS
SATURATED FAT	4.03 GRAMS
TRANS FAT	0.01 GRAMS*
CARBOHYDRATES	15.28 GRAMS
CHOLESTEROL	110.25 MG

You can use Puffy Dumplings (page 110) instead of the egg noodles; be sure to add the nutrition numbers for Puffy Dumplings if you choose to use them instead.

2 tablespoons olive oil

4 bone-in, skin-on chicken breasts

2 tablespoons flour

1 teaspoon salt, divided

¼ teaspoon pepper, divided

1 onion, chopped

4 cloves garlic, minced

2 stalks celery, chopped

4 carrots, peeled and sliced

1 bay leaf

1 teaspoon dried thyme leaves

4 cups Chicken Broth (page 120)

4 cups water

2 cups egg noodles

1. In large stockpot, heat olive oil over medium heat. Sprinkle chicken breasts with flour, ½ teaspoon salt, and ⅛ teaspoon pepper, and place, skin-side down, in the hot oil. Cook until browned, about 4 to 6 minutes, then remove and set aside. To drippings remaining in skillet, add onion and garlic; cook and stir until crisp-tender, about 4 minutes.

2. Return chicken to pot along with celery, carrots, ½ teaspoon salt, bay leaf, ⅛ teaspoon pepper, thyme, Chicken Broth, and 4 cups water. Bring to a simmer, then reduce heat, cover, and simmer until chicken is cooked, about 35 minutes. Remove chicken from pot; remove and discard skin and bones. Tear chicken into bite-size pieces and return to soup.

3. Bring soup to a simmer over medium heat. Either drop egg noodles into the soup or drop Puffy Dumpling batter into soup by teaspoonfuls; cover and simmer for 10 to 15 minutes or until egg noodles or Dumplings are cooked through. Remove bay leaf and serve soup immediately.

Ranch Salad Dressing

1 tablespoon olive oil
2 cloves garlic, minced
1 shallot, finely minced
¼ cup sour cream
¾ cup Homemade Mayonnaise (page 31)
2 tablespoons milk
1 teaspoon white-wine vinegar
1 teaspoon Worcestershire sauce
½ teaspoon dried thyme leaves
½ teaspoon dried dill weed
1 tablespoon chopped fresh parsley

1. In small saucepan, heat olive oil over medium heat. Add garlic and shallot; cook and stir until tender, about 3 to 5 minutes. Remove from heat and place in medium bowl; set aside to cool for 15 minutes.

2. Add remaining ingredients to vegetables in bowl; stir with wire whisk until smooth. Store covered in the refrigerator up to 4 days.

Shallots

Shallots are a member of the onion family. They look like large cloves of garlic, and are usually a light purple color. An average shallot, peeled and chopped, yields about 2 tablespoons. Shallots have a mild onion flavor and grow like garlic, which is why they are shaped the same as garlic cloves.

YIELDS 1 CUP (SERVING SIZE 2 TABLESPOONS)

CALORIES	193.68
FAT	20.76 GRAMS
SATURATED FAT	3.75 GRAMS
TRANS FAT	0.02 GRAMS*
CARBOHYDRATES	1.57 GRAMS
CHOLESTEROL	29.80 MG

This creamy dressing is full of flavor. It's delicious in Cobb Salad Sandwiches (page 132), or simply drizzled over a mixed green salad.

Cranberry Peach Salad

SERVES 10

CALORIES	232.85
FAT	3.84 GRAMS
SATURATED FAT	0.36 GRAMS
TRANS FAT	0.0 GRAMS
CARBOHYDRATES	47.92 GRAMS
CHOLESTEROL	0.0 MG

Old-fashioned molded salads are great for entertaining because they must be made ahead of time. And leftovers are delicious for breakfast!

2 (3-ounce) packages peach-flavored gelatin
2 cups boiling water
¼ cup orange juice
1 (8-ounce) can crushed pineapple, drained
1 (16-ounce) can whole berry cranberry sauce
1 (15-ounce) can peach slices, drained and chopped
½ cup chopped walnuts

1. In large bowl, combine gelatin and boiling water; stir until gelatin is completely dissolved. Add remaining ingredients and mix well. Pour into 2-quart mold or glass baking dish and chill until firm. Cut into squares to serve.

Gelatin Salads

There are a few tricks to making gelatin salads. First, be sure to completely dissolve the gelatin in the boiling liquid in the first step. Spoon up a small amount and make sure you can't see any grains of sugar or gelatin. And never use fresh or frozen pineapple, kiwi, or guava in gelatin salads; they will keep it from setting.

Vegetable Dumpling Soup

2 tablespoons olive oil

1 onion, chopped

4 cloves garlic, minced

3 carrots, sliced

4 cups Vegetable Broth (page 119)

4 cups water

2 cups frozen corn

1 recipe Puffy Dumplings (page 110)

1 cup frozen green beans

1 yellow summer squash, sliced

1 teaspoon dried Italian seasoning

½ cup grated Parmesan cheese

1. In large stock pot, heat olive oil over medium heat. Add onion, garlic, and carrot; cook and stir for 5 minutes. Add Vegetable Broth, water, and corn, and bring to a boil. Reduce heat, partially cover pot, and simmer for 15 minutes.

2. Prepare dough for Dumplings. Add green beans, summer squash, and Italian seasoning to soup and simmer for 5 minutes longer. Drop Dumplings by teaspoonfuls into simmering soup. Cover and simmer for 10 to 15 minutes or until Dumplings are puffed and cooked through. Sprinkle with cheese and serve.

SERVES 8

CALORIES	335.77
FAT	20.59 GRAMS
SATURATED FAT	9.76 GRAMS
TRANS FAT	0.34 GRAMS*
CARBOHYDRATES	31.57 GRAMS
CHOLESTEROL	90.10 MG

Dumplings add great texture to this rich vegetable soup. All you need to add is a fruit salad, and dinner is complete.

Carrot and Tomato Salad

SERVES 8

CALORIES	169.79
FAT	9.50 GRAMS
SATURATED FAT	1.34 GRAMS
TRANS FAT	0.0 GRAMS
CARBOHYDRATES	21.44 GRAMS
CHOLESTEROL	0.0 MG

This colorful salad is perfect with a grilled steak for a summer dinner. Serve it with some grilled cheese bread for the finishing touch.

1 (16-ounce) package baby carrots
1 pint grape tomatoes
1 green bell pepper, chopped
½ cup sugar
¼ cup apple-cider vinegar
⅓ cup olive oil
1 teaspoon Worcestershire sauce
2 tablespoons Dijon mustard
8 cups mixed lettuces

1. In medium saucepan, place carrots; cover with cold water. Bring to a boil over high heat; reduce heat to medium and simmer for 4 to 7 minutes until carrots are tender when pierced with fork. Immediately drain and cover with cold water. Drain again and combine with tomatoes and bell pepper in serving bowl.

2. In small bowl, combine sugar, vinegar, olive oil, Worcestershire sauce, and mustard and mix well until blended. Pour over carrot mixture; cover and refrigerate for 1 hour. When ready to eat, toss with lettuces and serve.

Cooked Versus Uncooked Carrots

Cooking carrots helps break down the cell structure and fiber in the vegetable and makes the nutrients—especially beta carotene, a precursor to vitamin A—more available to your body. The cooked vegetable is also sweeter than it is when raw, because sugars are readily available to interact with taste buds on your tongue.

Vegetable Broth

2 tablespoons olive oil
2 onions, chopped
3 carrots, chopped
2 tomatoes, sliced
3 stalks celery, sliced

4 cloves garlic
1 teaspoon salt
¼ teaspoon white pepper
7 cups water

1. In large heavy skillet, heat olive oil over medium high heat. Add onions and carrots; cook and stir until vegetables begin to brown. Remove to 4- to 5-quart slow cooker. Add 1 cup water to skillet. Bring to a boil; boil for 1 minute, stirring to loosen any vegetables left in bottom of pan.

2. Pour mixture into slow cooker and add remaining ingredients. Cover and cook on low for 8 to 10 hours.

3. Remove solids. Discard vegetables and let broth cool for 30 minutes. Strain broth into freezer containers and seal. Freeze for up to 3 months.

YIELDS 8 CUPS

CALORIES	54.79
FAT	3.50 GRAMS
SATURATED FAT	0.49 GRAMS
TRANS FAT	0.0 GRAMS
CARBOHYDRATES	5.79 GRAMS
CHOLESTEROL	0.0 MG

These are the best vegetables to use when making broth. You could also add bell peppers and a turnip, but don't use potatoes; they make the broth cloudy.

Beef Broth

2 pounds beef shank
2 pounds beef soup bones
1 onion, sliced
1 cup water
1 onion, quartered
4 cloves garlic, sliced
2 tomatoes, chopped

3 carrots, sliced
2 slices fresh ginger root
1 bay leaf
1 teaspoon salt
¼ teaspoon pepper
10 cups water

1. Heat skillet over medium high heat. Add beef shank; brown on one side until beef can be easily moved; add to 5- to 6-quart slow cooker. Repeat with beef soup bones. Add onion to skillet; cook and stir to loosen pan drippings. Pour 1 cup water into skillet and boil for 1 minute; pour into slow cooker. Add remaining ingredients. Cover and cook on low for 8 hours.

2. Remove solids; remove meat from bones and freeze for another use. Discard vegetables and let broth cool for 30 minutes. Strain broth into freezer containers and seal. Freeze for up to 3 months.

YIELDS 12 CUPS

CALORIES	118.83
FAT	3.02 GRAMS
SATURATED FAT	0.99 GRAMS
TRANS FAT	0.02 GRAMS*
CARBOHYDRATES	5.13 GRAMS
CHOLESTEROL	29.48 MG

Your own beef broth adds fabulous richness to any soup, including Pumpkin Wild Rice Chowder (page 102).

Chicken Broth

YIELDS 8 CUPS

CALORIES	136.31
FAT	8.44 GRAMS
SATURATED FAT	2.27 GRAMS
TRANS FAT	0.01 GRAMS*
CARBOHYDRATES	2.42 GRAMS
CHOLESTEROL	39.53 MG

Browning the chicken pieces before adding them to the slow cooker makes the broth richer and more flavorful.

2 tablespoons olive oil
1 tablespoon butter
3 pounds cut-up chicken pieces
2 onions, sliced
2 carrots, sliced
8 cups water
1 teaspoon salt
½ teaspoon dried thyme leaves
2 tablespoons lemon juice

1. In large skillet, heat olive oil and butter over medium heat. Add chicken pieces, skin-side down. Cook for 5 to 8 minutes or until chicken can be moved; place chicken in 4- to 5-quart slow cooker.

2. Add onions to drippings remaining in skillet; cook and stir until brown bits are loosened; pour into slow cooker. Add carrots, water, salt, and thyme leaves. Cover and cook on low for 8 to 9 hours.

3. Remove solids; remove meat from chicken bones and freeze for another use. Discard vegetables and let broth cool for 30 minutes. Strain broth and stir in lemon juice, then ladle into freezer containers. Label and freeze for up to 3 months.

Freezing Broth

You can freeze cooled broth in large containers, in 1-cup portions, or in ice cube trays. If you'd like, you can refrigerate the broth overnight and remove the fat that will solidify on the surface, then freeze it. Add directly to soup recipes, or let the broth stand overnight in the refrigerator to thaw before using.

Chapter 7

Sandwiches

Vegetarian Picadillo Filling

1 tablespoon olive oil
1 onion, chopped
3 cloves garlic, minced
1 red bell pepper, chopped
1 (15-ounce) can black-eyed peas, drained
1 (8-ounce) can tomato sauce
1 teaspoon Tabasco sauce
½ teaspoon salt
½ cup raisins
¼ cup sliced green olives
¼ cup sliced almonds
Pita Bread, optional

1. In large skillet, heat olive oil over medium heat. Add onion and garlic; cook and stir for 3 minutes. Add bell pepper; cook and stir for 3 minutes longer. Add black-eyed peas, tomato sauce, Tabasco, and salt and bring to a simmer.

2. Simmer mixture for 10 to 15 minutes, stirring occasionally, until thickened. Add raisins, olives, and almonds and simmer for 5 minutes longer. Serve in Pita Breads.

SERVES 6

CALORIES	194.09
FAT	5.37 GRAMS
SATURATED FAT	0.67 GRAMS
TRANS FAT	0.0 GRAMS
CARBOHYDRATES	31.79 GRAMS
CHOLESTEROL	0.0 MG

You can keep this filling in the fridge and let your kids heat up a portion at a time in the microwave oven (about 30 seconds on high) to make their own sandwiches using Pita Bread (page 41).

Baked Ham and Peach Sandwiches

¼ cup butter, softened
3 tablespoons peach preserves
3 tablespoons honey mustard
8 ounces shaved ham slices
8 (1-ounce) slices Havarti cheese
8 Glazed Honey Rolls (page 51), cut in half

1. Preheat oven to 350°F. In small bowl, combine butter, preserves, and honey mustard; mix well. Make sandwiches with the spread, ham, and cheese on the Glazed Honey Rolls.

2. Wrap sandwiches in foil and place on cookie sheet. Bake for 8 to 12 minutes or until sandwiches are hot and cheese is melted. Serve immediately.

SERVES 6–8

CALORIES	394.65
FAT	21.64 GRAMS
SATURATED FAT	12.66 GRAMS
TRANS FAT	0.43 GRAMS*
CARBOHYDRATES	34.09 GRAMS
CHOLESTEROL	80.24 MG

Tangy and sweet fruits like peaches and apricot blend well with salty, tender ham. These sandwiches are special enough to serve for tea!

Ham and Fig Panini

1 loaf Italian Loaves (page 46)
2 tablespoons butter, softened
3 tablespoons apricot preserves
6 (1-ounce) slices ham
6 (1-ounce) slices Gruyère cheese
3 fresh figs, thinly sliced

1. Cut loaf in half lengthwise and cut into 6 sections. In small bowl, combine butter and apricot preserves and mix well. Spread mixture on cut sides of all bread pieces.

2. Layer ham, cheese, and fig slices on half of bread pieces; cover with remaining bread pieces. Prepare and preheat panini grill or indoor grill. Spray grill with nonstick cooking spray. Cook two sandwiches at a time on the grill, pressing down to flatten sandwiches. Cut in half and serve immediately.

Fresh Figs

Did you know that the fig is actually a flower folded in on itself? Figs are a nutritious "fruit," high in antioxidants, iron, fiber, and calcium. They ripen fully on the tree, so are usually available fresh only in late summer and fall. You can substitute dried figs for fresh figs in most recipes; just slice them thin and use.

SERVES 6

CALORIES	468.98
FAT	18.17 GRAMS
SATURATED FAT	9.42 GRAMS
TRANS FAT	0.23 GRAMS*
CARBOHYDRATES	53.79 GRAMS
CHOLESTEROL	76.85 MG

If you can't find fresh figs, thin apple slices can be substituted. This rich sandwich is exotic and delicious.

Chicken Cheese Pitas

SERVES 6

CALORIES	254.78
FAT	11.78 GRAMS
SATURATED FAT	5.57 GRAMS
TRANS FAT	0.19 GRAMS*
CARBOHYDRATES	14.14 GRAMS
CHOLESTEROL	59.01 MG

You can substitute any cheese you'd like in this simple recipe—any vegetable, too, for that matter. It's quick and delicious for an easy lunch.

1 tablespoon olive oil
3 boneless, skinless chicken breasts
1 green bell pepper, chopped
2 cloves garlic, minced
½ teaspoon salt
⅛ teaspoon cayenne pepper
1 cup diced Muenster cheese
¼ cup grated Parmesan cheese
2 tablespoons honey Dijon mustard
3 Pita Breads (page 41), cut in half
6 slices butter lettuce

1. Place olive oil in skillet and heat over medium heat. Cut chicken into cubes and add to skillet. Cook and stir until almost cooked, about 4 minutes. Add bell pepper and garlic; cook and stir for 2 to 4 minutes longer until chicken is cooked. Sprinkle with salt and cayenne pepper and stir.

2. Remove from heat and sprinkle with both cheeses. Cover and let stand for 5 to 8 minutes. Meanwhile, spread mustard inside the cut Pita Bread halves. Add lettuce, then fill with chicken mixture and serve.

Spinach Pesto Turkey Sandwiches

SERVES 4

CALORIES	503.80
FAT	31.88 GRAMS
SATURATED FAT	9.38 GRAMS
TRANS FAT	0.16 GRAMS*
CARBOHYDRATES	30.34 GRAMS
CHOLESTEROL	84.76 MG

Sometimes simple things are the best. Be sure the tomatoes are red and ripe, and the spinach leaves are tiny and fresh for the perfect sandwich.

¼ cup Basil Pesto (page 23)
1 cup baby spinach leaves, divided
1 tablespoon lemon juice
2 tablespoons Homemade Mayonnaise (page 31)
4 (3" × 3") slices Focaccia (page 57)
4 (1-ounce) slices cooked turkey breast
4 slices ripe tomato
4 (1-ounce) slices Swiss cheese

1. In food processor, combine Pesto, ¼ cup spinach, lemon juice, and Mayonnaise. Process until blended.

2. Cut Focaccia slices in half and place cut-side up on work surface. Spread each with some of the Pesto mixture. Make sandwiches with the bread, turkey breast, tomato, and cheese. Serve immediately.

Apple Bagel Sandwiches

2 tablespoons butter
4 apples, thinly sliced
2 tablespoons brown sugar
4 Cinnamon Glazed Bagels (page 48), cut in half
¼ cup pineapple preserves
1-½ cups shredded Havarti cheese

1. In medium skillet, melt butter over medium heat. Add apples; cook and stir for 2 minutes or until apples start to soften. Sprinkle with sugar; cook and stir for 2 minutes longer.

2. Preheat broiler. Place bagels, cut-side up, on broiler pan. Spread each with pineapple preserves and top with cooked apples. Sprinkle with cheese and place under broiler for 3 to 6 minutes or until cheese melts and begins to brown. Serve immediately.

Tart Apples

Tart and crisp apples are best for sandwiches. Granny Smith apples turn brown much more slowly than most other types, so are a good choice. Other tart apples slow to brown include Cortlands, Jonagold, and Pippin. Slice the apples just before you use them for best results. You can peel them or not, as you desire.

SERVES 8

CALORIES	390.16
FAT	11.97 GRAMS
SATURATED FAT	6.37 GRAMS
TRANS FAT	0.26 GRAMS*
CARBOHYDRATES	62.08 GRAMS
CHOLESTEROL	29.31 MG

These wonderfully flavored open-faced sandwiches are perfect for lunch or even breakfast on the run.

Chicken Veggie Mini Subs

SERVES 4

CALORIES	476.89
FAT	25.04 GRAMS
SATURATED FAT	11.72 GRAMS
TRANS FAT	0.39 GRAMS*
CARBOHYDRATES	23.45 GRAMS
CHOLESTEROL	115.87 MG

These big sandwiches will feed your hungry teenagers easily. For more delicate appetites, cut each in half.

4 boneless, skinless chicken breasts
2 tablespoons olive oil
½ teaspoon salt
⅛ teaspoon pepper
½ teaspoon paprika
1 green bell pepper, sliced
1 cup sliced yellow summer squash
4 Almost Sourdough Rolls (page 47), cut in half
2 tablespoons butter, softened
1 cup shredded Cheddar cheese

1. Prepare and preheat indoor dual-contact grill. Sprinkle chicken breasts with oil, salt, pepper, and paprika. Place on grill and cook for 7 to 9 minutes or until chicken is thoroughly cooked. Set chicken aside and cover with foil.

2. Place bell pepper and summer squash slices on grill; cover, and cook for 2 to 3 minutes or until browned. Remove from grill. Spread butter on cut sides of rolls and place, cut-side down, on grill just to brown, about 2 to 3 minutes.

3. Thinly slice chicken and combine with cooked vegetables; pile on bottom half of the grilled rolls and sprinkle with cheese. Cover with top half of rolls and press down slightly; serve immediately.

Veggie Pitas

1 cucumber
¼ cup chopped green onion
½ cup plain yogurt
¼ cup sour cream
½ teaspoon salt
⅛ teaspoon cayenne pepper
2 carrots, shredded
1 tablespoon fresh oregano leaves
1 cup grape tomatoes, sliced
4 Pita Breads (page 41)
8 leaves red lettuce

SERVES 4

CALORIES	133.81
FAT	3.61 GRAMS
SATURATED FAT	1.64 GRAMS
TRANS FAT	0.04 GRAMS*
CARBOHYDRATES	21.31 GRAMS
CHOLESTEROL	5.44 MG

This low-calorie, low-fat sandwich is delicious, fresh, and crunchy. Try using other vegetables, too, including bell peppers, summer squash, and mushrooms.

1. Peel cucumber and cut in half. Remove seeds with spoon. Coarsely chop cucumber. Combine with remaining ingredients except Pita Breads and lettuce in medium bowl. Cover and chill for 2 to 3 hours before serving.

2. When ready to serve, heat Pita Breads in toaster oven until warm and pliable. Cut in half and line with lettuce; fill with cucumber mixture. Serve immediately.

Storing Sandwich Spreads

Any sandwich spread made with mayonnaise, yogurt, or sour cream can be stored, covered, in the refrigerator up to 4 days. Make a couple of these spreads and keep them on hand so your family can make sandwiches or use them as a dip whenever they get hungry.

Peanut Butter Apple Wraps

SERVES 4–6

CALORIES	279.17
FAT	13.26 GRAMS
SATURATED FAT	2.34 GRAMS
TRANS FAT	0.0 GRAMS
CARBOHYDRATES	35.33 GRAMS
CHOLESTEROL	0.0 MG

This sandwich is kind of like the Girl Scout snack "Ants on a Log" wrapped up in a tortilla. Your kids will love it!

½ cup natural crunchy peanut butter
1 apple, chopped
½ cup raisins
1 cup chopped celery
4 whole-wheat tortillas

1. In small bowl, combine peanut butter, apple, raisins, and celery. Arrange tortillas on work surface. Spread with peanut butter mixture and roll up. Cut into thirds and serve.

Apple and Almond Sandwich Spread

**YIELDS 2 CUPS
(SERVING SIZE ¼ CUP)**

CALORIES	86.84
FAT	5.11 GRAMS
SATURATED FAT	1.27 GRAMS
TRANS FAT	0.02 GRAMS*
CARBOHYDRATES	9.59 GRAMS
CHOLESTEROL	3.55 MG

Toast some English Muffins (page 60) and spread this recipe on them. Top with sliced chicken, turkey, or some smoked salmon for an excellent sandwich.

2 Granny Smith apples
2 tablespoons lemon juice
¼ cup vanilla yogurt
¼ cup sour cream
2 tablespoons applesauce
¼ cup ground almonds
⅓ cup sliced almonds, toasted
½ teaspoon cinnamon
¼ teaspoon salt

1. Peel apples and cut into quarters; sprinkle with half of lemon juice. Chop finely and combine with remaining ingredients in small bowl. Cover and chill for 2 to 3 hours before serving.

Purchasing Yogurt
Read labels even when you're purchasing whole foods like yogurt. Some yogurts are made with stabilizers and emulsifiers and other artificial ingredients. If you can't find a natural flavored yogurt, you can make your own. Add ½ teaspoon vanilla to 1 cup of plain yogurt, or stir in some fresh fruit or coconut.

Gourmet Grilled-Cheese Sandwich Spread

½ cup Homemade Mayonnaise (page 31)
1 (3-ounce) package cream cheese, softened
2 tablespoons butter, softened
1 cup shredded Cheddar cheese
1 cup shredded Swiss cheese
¼ cup shredded Parmesan cheese
½ cup finely chopped sun-dried tomatoes in oil

1. In medium bowl, combine Mayonnaise, cream cheese, and butter and beat until smooth and combined. Stir in Cheddar, Swiss, Parmesan, and sun-dried tomatoes until mixed. Cover and chill in refrigerator for 1 to 2 hours before using.

2. To make sandwiches, place bread on work surface. Spread each with 3 tablespoons of the cheese spread. Top with remaining bread slices, then spread outsides of each sandwich with some softened butter.

3. Preheat griddle or skillet over medium heat. Grill sandwiches, covered, for 3 to 5 minutes on first side or until first side is golden brown. Turn sandwiches and press down slightly. Grill on second side for 3 to 5 minutes or until bread is toasted and cheese is melted.

YIELDS 3 CUPS (SERVING SIZE 3 TABLESPOONS)

CALORIES	152.12
FAT	14.27 GRAMS
SATURATED FAT	5.95 GRAMS
TRANS FAT	0.20 GRAMS*
CARBOHYDRATES	1.55 GRAMS
CHOLESTEROL	33.43 MG

You can keep the cheese spread stored in the refrigerator for up to 4 days. It's delicious cold or hot, spread on any bread and topped with meats and lettuces.

Grilled Fruit and Cheese Sandwiches

SERVES 16

CALORIES	430.40
FAT	17.76 GRAMS
SATURATED FAT	10.61 GRAMS
TRANS FAT	0.33 GRAMS*
CARBOHYDRATES	55.92 GRAMS
CHOLESTEROL	63.95 MG

Fruit is an unusual pairing with cheese for a sandwich, but it is delicious. This spread can also be refrigerated for up to 4 days.

2 firm pears, peeled and cored
1 tablespoon lemon juice
1 (8-ounce) can pineapple rings
1 (8-ounce) package cream cheese, softened
2 tablespoons heavy cream
1 cup grated Havarti cheese
1 cup grated Gouda cheese
32 slices Oatmeal Bread (page 43)
6 tablespoons butter, softened

1. Slice pears into ½" thick slices; sprinkle with lemon juice. Drain pineapple rings and discard juice; place on paper towels to drain further. Prepare and preheat indoor dual-contact grill. Place pear slices on grill; close and grill for 2 to 3 minutes or just until pears develop grill marks. Remove from grill and add pineapple rings to grill. Close grill and cook for 3 to 5 minutes or until pineapple develops grill marks.

2. Let fruit cool for 10 minutes, then coarsely chop. In medium bowl, beat cream cheese with cream until light and fluffy. Stir in Havarti and Gouda and mix well. Stir in fruit; cover, and refrigerate for at least 2 hours before serving.

3. To make sandwiches, place about ¼ cup fruit spread in between bread slices. Butter outsides of sandwiches. Grill until bread is toasted and cheese melts, about 3 to 5 minutes on each side.

About Pears

Pears have a slightly gritty texture because they contain stone cells, or cells with a thick wall. If the pears are ripened off the tree, they will contain fewer stone cells. If pears are cooked in a recipe, you can use fruit that isn't quite ripe. The best pears for cooking include the green Anjou and the reddish-brown Bosc.

Garden Quesadillas

2 tablespoons olive oil, divided
1 onion, chopped
1 red bell pepper, chopped
½ cup chopped mushrooms
1 cup Fresh and Spicy Salsa (page 38)
8 whole-wheat tortillas
1 cup baby spinach leaves
1 cup shredded pepper jack cheese

1. In medium skillet, heat 1 tablespoon olive oil over medium heat. Add onion; cook and stir until crisp-tender, about 4 minutes. Add bell pepper and mushrooms; cook and stir for 2 to 4 minutes longer until tender. Drain and combine in medium bowl with Salsa.

2. Arrange tortillas on work surface. Top half of the tortillas with some of the baby spinach leaves and spoon onion mixture on top. Top with cheese, then remaining tortillas and press down gently.

3. Heat griddle or skillet over medium heat. Brush with remaining olive oil, then grill quesadillas, turning once and pressing down occasionally with spatula, until cheese melts and tortillas are toasted. Cut into quarters and serve immediately.

Freezing Sandwiches

Many sandwiches can be frozen. If they don't use mayonnaise, the end result will be better. Wrap sandwiches well in plastic wrap, label, and freeze for up to 3 months. You can let them thaw in a lunchbox until it's time for lunch, or wrap them in foil and bake in a 350°F oven for 15 to 25 minutes until warm, depending on the size of the sandwich.

SERVES 4–6

CALORIES	297.10
FAT	16.04 GRAMS
SATURATED FAT	5.85 GRAMS
TRANS FAT	0.16 GRAMS*
CARBOHYDRATES	29.07 GRAMS
CHOLESTEROL	19.58 MG

Quesadillas are simply made from two tortillas with a filling, toasted on a griddle until crisp.

Cobb Salad Sandwiches

SERVES 4–6

CALORIES	485.51
FAT	28.98 GRAMS
SATURATED FAT	8.18 GRAMS
TRANS FAT	0.05 GRAMS*
CARBOHYDRATES	31.97 GRAMS
CHOLESTEROL	131.33 MG

Cobb salad transformed into sandwiches! You could also serve the sandwich filling in Pita Breads (page 41), or Almost Sourdough Rolls (page 47).

4 slices bacon
1 tablespoon olive oil
3 boneless, skinless chicken breasts, chopped
2 hard-cooked eggs
1 cup grape tomatoes
½ cup Ranch Salad Dressing (page 115)
⅓ cup crumbled feta cheese
1 avocado, peeled and sliced
4 slices romaine lettuce
8 slices White Bread (page 44), toasted

1. In heavy skillet, cook bacon until crisp. Drain bacon on paper towels, crumble, and set aside. Drain drippings from skillet and add olive oil. Add chicken; cook and stir over medium heat for 4 to 7 minutes or until chicken is thoroughly cooked. Combine in medium bowl with crumbled bacon.

2. Chop the hard-cooked eggs and cut the grape tomatoes in half. Add to bowl with chicken. Add Ranch Salad Dressing and feta cheese and mix gently. Cover and store in refrigerator up to 3 days.

3. When ready to eat, prepare avocado and lettuce. Make a sandwich with these ingredients and the chicken mixture on toasted White Bread. Cut in half to serve.

Hard-Cooked Eggs
To hard-cook eggs, start with large eggs that are a couple of days old. Place the eggs in a pan with water to cover them by 1 inch. Bring to a full rolling boil, cover, remove from heat, and let stand for 15 minutes. Immediately place pan under cold running water until eggs feel cold. Crack against pan sides under water and peel.

Hummus Tomato Sandwiches

1 tablespoon olive oil
1 onion, chopped
½ cup sun-dried tomatoes in oil
1 cup grape tomatoes, cut in half
1 cup diced Havarti cheese
4 Pita Breads (page 41)
¾ cup Creamy and Crunchy Hummus (page 32)
8 leaves butter lettuce

1. In medium saucepan, combine olive oil and onion over medium heat. Cook and stir until onion is soft, about 7 to 8 minutes. Meanwhile, slice the sun-dried tomatoes very thin. When onions begin to brown around the edges, add grape tomatoes and sun-dried tomatoes to saucepan; cook and stir for 2 minutes longer. Sprinkle with cheese, cover, and remove from heat.

2. Cut Pita Breads in half and spread the insides of each half with some Hummus. Line with butter lettuce and spoon the warm tomato and cheese mixture into the center; serve immediately.

SERVES 8

CALORIES	229.33
FAT	11.87 GRAMS
SATURATED FAT	3.59 GRAMS
TRANS FAT	0.12 GRAMS*
CARBOHYDRATES	23.77 GRAMS
CHOLESTEROL	13.31 MG

A warm caramelized onion and tomato mixture topped with melted cheese is spooned into hummus-lined pita breads in this spectacular sandwich.

Open-Faced Breakfast Waffle Sandwiches

SERVES 6–8

CALORIES	335.34
FAT	20.99 GRAMS
SATURATED FAT	11.35 GRAMS
TRANS FAT	0.35 GRAMS*
CARBOHYDRATES	20.79 GRAMS
CHOLESTEROL	220.55 MG

Wow—these sandwiches put fast-food breakfasts to shame. They're perfect for breakfast on the run.

4 slices bacon
5 eggs, beaten
1 tablespoon honey mustard
¼ cup heavy cream
½ teaspoon salt
⅛ teaspoon white pepper
3 Fluffy Waffles (page 68)
1 cup shredded Colby cheese
2 pears, peeled and thinly sliced
1 cup shredded Havarti cheese

1. In small saucepan, cook bacon until crisp. Drain on paper towels, crumble, and set aside. In small bowl, combine eggs, mustard, cream, salt, and pepper and beat until smooth.

2. Divide waffles into fourths along the lines from the waffle maker and place on cookie sheet. Spoon 2 tablespoons of the egg mixture onto each fourth, filling up the little squares. Sprinkle with bacon and Colby cheese. Bake for 13 to 18 minutes or until egg mixture is puffed and set.

3. Remove from oven and top with pear slices. Sprinkle with Havarti cheese. Return to oven and bake for 5 to 10 minutes longer or until cheese is melted. Serve immediately.

About Waffles
Most waffle irons are divided into four sections. To use the waffles as sandwich bread, each "slice" should be one-fourth of the whole waffle. Be sure that the waffles don't have any holes or thin spots so the filling stays intact. You can make grilled sandwiches with waffles; just don't press down on them when they're grilling to keep the shape intact.

Pizza English Muffins

4 English Muffins (page 60), split in half
½ cup grated carrots
¼ cup tomato paste
2 tablespoons ricotta cheese
½ teaspoon dried Italian seasoning
½ cup sliced pepperoni
1 (4-ounce) jar sliced mushrooms, well drained
1-¼ cups shredded mozzarella cheese
¼ cup grated Parmesan cheese

1. Preheat oven to 375°F. Split English Muffins with a fork and toast in toaster oven until light golden brown. Remove and set aside.

2. In small bowl, combine carrots, tomato paste, ricotta, and Italian seasoning and mix well. Divide among the English Muffins. Top with pepperoni and sliced mushrooms. Sprinkle with mozzarella cheese, then Parmesan cheese. Arrange on cookie sheet.

3. Bake pizzas for 8 to 13 minutes, or until cheese melts and begins to brown. Let cool for 5 minutes, then serve.

SERVES 4–6

CALORIES	296.37
FAT	15.31 GRAMS
SATURATED FAT	7.73 GRAMS
TRANS FAT	0.26 GRAMS*
CARBOHYDRATES	23.44 GRAMS
CHOLESTEROL	44.98 MG

Think of a pizza as an open-faced sandwich! You can top these simple little treats with anything you'd like. Add Roasted Vegetables (page 226) for more nutrition.

Tex-Mex Club Sandwiches

SERVES 4–6

CALORIES	508.50
FAT	29.74 GRAMS
SATURATED FAT	10.98 GRAMS
TRANS FAT	0.27 GRAMS*
CARBOHYDRATES	40.62 GRAMS
CHOLESTEROL	84.32 MG

A classic club sandwich is updated with some Tex-Mex ingredients, including Manchego cheese and chipotle peppers.

4 slices bacon
2 tablespoons chipotle peppers in adobo sauce
¼ cup Homemade Mayonnaise (page 31)
1 tablespoon grated Cotija cheese
¼ cup Fresh and Spicy Salsa (page 38)
2 tablespoons butter
8 slices Oatmeal Bread (page 43)
8 (1-ounce) slices Roasted Turkey Tenderloin (page 144)
4 (1-ounce) slices Manchego cheese
8 thin slices tomato
1 avocado, peeled and sliced

1. In small skillet, cook bacon until crisp. Drain on paper towels, crumble, and set aside. Remove peppers from adobo sauce and mince finely. Stir into Homemade Mayonnaise along with the adobo sauce, Cotija cheese, Salsa, and bacon.

2. Spread butter on one side of Oatmeal Bread slices and toast under broiler or in toaster oven. Make sandwiches with Mayonnaise mixture, turkey slices, Manchego cheese, tomato, and avocado. Cut sandwiches into four quarters each and serve.

Chipotle Peppers in Adobo

Chipotle peppers in adobo are smoked jalapeño peppers packed in a spicy red sauce. It's really two condiments in one; you can remove the peppers and slice or chop them to add to recipes, and you can add the adobo sauce to mayonnaise or sour cream for an appetizer dip or sandwich spread.

Egg and Mushroom Luncheon Rolls

1 tablespoon butter
1 cup chopped mushrooms
2 cloves garlic, minced
½ teaspoon salt
3 hard-cooked eggs, chopped
1 cup shredded Muenster cheese
⅓ cup chili sauce
2 tablespoons minced fresh parsley
8 Yeast Knot Rolls (page 50)

1. In small saucepan, heat butter over medium heat. Add mushrooms and garlic; cook until mushrooms give up their liquid. Sprinkle with salt and continue cooking, stirring frequently, until the liquid has almost completely evaporated. Set aside to cool for 30 minutes.

2. Preheat oven to 350°F. In medium bowl, combine cooled mushroom mixture, eggs, cheese, chili sauce, and parsley. Cut Rolls in half and scoop out some of the centers (reserve for bread crumbs). Fill with mushroom mixture and reassemble. Wrap sandwiches in foil, place on baking sheet, and bake for 20 to 25 minutes or until heated.

SERVES 8

CALORIES	243.38
FAT	11.76 GRAMS
SATURATED FAT	6.59 GRAMS
TRANS FAT	0.26 GRAMS*
CARBOHYDRATES	24.69 GRAMS
CHOLESTEROL	117.06 MG

These delicate little rolls are perfect for lunch on the porch. To hard-cook eggs, see the tip on page 132.

Monte Cristo Sandwiches

SERVES 6–8

CALORIES	372.80
FAT	19.32 GRAMS
SATURATED FAT	10.06 GRAMS
TRANS FAT	0.19 GRAMS*
CARBOHYDRATES	27.29 GRAMS
CHOLESTEROL	79.22 MG

Bacon adds a salty crispness to these grilled sandwiches. Serve them with more raspberry jam for dipping.

4 slices bacon
2 boneless, skinless chicken breasts
¼ cup raspberry jam
8 slices White Bread (page 44)
8 thin slices Gouda cheese
4 (1-ounce) slices ham
¼ cup butter, softened

1. In medium skillet, cook bacon until crisp. Remove from pan and drain on paper towels; crumble and set aside. Pour drippings from skillet and discard; do not wipe skillet. Add chicken; cook over medium heat, turning once, until browned and cooked, about 8 minutes. Remove chicken from pan and let stand.

2. Spread jam on one side of each slice of bread. Layer half of slices with cheese, then ham. Thinly slice chicken breasts and place over ham. Cover with remaining cheese slices, sprinkle with bacon, and make sandwiches with remaining bread slices.

3. Spread outsides of sandwiches with softened butter. Prepare and preheat griddle, indoor dual-contact grill, or panini maker. Grill sandwiches on medium for 4 to 6 minutes for dual-contact grill or panini maker, or 6 to 8 minutes, turning once, for griddle, until bread is golden brown and cheese is melted. Cut in half and serve immediately.

Sliced Ham
You have several choices when buying sliced ham for sandwiches. You can purchase the super-thin slices packaged in plastic bags, boiled ham in ⅛" slices, or deli ham that you can have sliced to order. Just be sure that the amount of ham you use weighs about 1 ounce per serving to keep the nutrition information constant.

Pizza Burgers by the Yard

1 loaf Italian Loaves (page 46)
2 tablespoons butter, softened
3 tablespoons Dijon mustard
1 tablespoon olive oil
2 onions, chopped
4 cloves garlic, minced
1 (8-ounce) package sliced mushrooms
1 (12-ounce) package frozen meatless crumbles, thawed
1 (6-ounce) can tomato paste
½ teaspoon dried basil leaves
½ teaspoon dried oregano leaves
¼ teaspoon cayenne pepper
3 tomatoes, sliced
3 cups shredded CoJack cheese

SERVES 12	
CALORIES	353.55
FAT	17.09 GRAMS
SATURATED FAT	8.38 GRAMS
TRANS FAT	0.29 GRAMS*
CARBOHYDRATES	32.23 GRAMS
CHOLESTEROL	42.03 MG

This is the sandwich to make when you're serving a crowd! Top it with anything that strikes your fancy.

1. Preheat oven to broil. Cut Italian Loaf in half lengthwise and place, cut-side up, on cookie sheet. In small bowl, combine butter and mustard and mix well. Spread over each piece of bread. Broil for 1 to 2 minutes or until bread is almost crisp.

2. In medium saucepan, combine olive oil, onion, garlic, and mushrooms over medium heat. Cook and stir until tender, about 6 minutes. Continue cooking until liquid evaporates, about 4 minutes longer. Stir in crumbles, tomato paste, basil, oregano, and pepper and mix well.

3. Spread crumbles mixture on each half of loaf. Broil about 6" from heat source for 7 to 9 minutes or until hot. Remove from oven and arrange tomato slices on top. Sprinkle with cheese. Return to oven and broil for 3 to 5 minutes longer until cheese melts and begins to bubble. Cut into slices to serve.

Meatball Pitas

SERVES 8

CALORIES	359.23
FAT	18.01 GRAMS
SATURATED FAT	7.16 GRAMS
TRANS FAT	0.18 GRAMS*
CARBOHYDRATES	21.88 GRAMS
CHOLESTEROL	92.30 MG

You can make the filling ahead of time, then chill it in the fridge. Tell anybody who's hungry to take out about 1/3 cup of the filling, heat in the microwave, then fill a pita bread and eat!

1 tablespoon olive oil
1 green bell pepper, chopped
4 cloves garlic, minced
1 (14-ounce) can diced tomatoes, undrained
1 (8-ounce) can tomato sauce
½ teaspoon dried oregano
½ teaspoon salt
⅛ teaspoon cayenne pepper
15 Classic Meatballs (page 175)
½ cup grated Parmesan cheese
4 leaves romaine lettuce, shredded
4 Pita Breads (page 41)
1 cup grated mozzarella cheese

1. In large skillet, heat olive oil over medium heat. Add bell pepper and garlic; cook and stir for 4 minutes until tender. Add tomatoes, tomato sauce, oregano, salt, and cayenne pepper. Bring to a boil, then reduce heat to low and simmer for 20 to 25 minutes or until sauce thickens.

2. Cut meatballs in half and stir into sauce along with Parmesan cheese; simmer for 5 minutes longer. Remove from heat. Make sandwiches with lettuce, Pita Breads, meatball filling, and mozzarella cheese.

Spaghetti Sauce

If you can find a spaghetti or pasta sauce that says "No Trans Fat," you can substitute it for the sauce in almost any pasta or sandwich recipe. You can also make your own sauce and freeze it in 1-cup portions; to thaw, let stand in refrigerator overnight, or put the sauce in a saucepan over very low heat and cook slowly until it bubbles.

Chapter 8

Chicken and Turkey Entrees

Chicken Wheat-Berry Casserole

SERVES 8

CALORIES	239.05
FAT	4.21 GRAMS
SATURATED FAT	1.01 GRAMS
TRANS FAT	0.09 GRAMS*
CARBOHYDRATES	30.81 GRAMS
CHOLESTEROL	70.59 MG

Wheat berries are the whole kernel of wheat and are nutritious and full of fiber. Plus they taste great!

1 cup wheat berries
1-½ pounds boneless skinless chicken thighs
3 carrots, sliced
2 cups frozen corn
1 onion, chopped
3 cloves garlic, minced
2 cups Chicken Broth (page 120)
1 teaspoon cumin
1 teaspoon salt
¼ teaspoon pepper
1 tablespoon cornstarch
¼ cup water

1. Rinse wheat berries and drain well. Cut chicken into 1-½" pieces and combine with remaining ingredients, except for cornstarch and ¼ cup water, in a 4- to 5-quart slow cooker. Cover and cook on low for 8 to 9 hours or until wheat berries are tender and chicken is cooked.

2. In small bowl, combine cornstarch and water and blend well. Add to casserole in slow cooker, cover, and cook on high for 20 to 30 minutes until thickened, then stir again and serve.

Buying Grains in Bulk
One of the best places to buy grains and legumes in bulk is at a food co-op. These stores usually have a high turnover rate and their bulk products are quite fresh. These stores are also great places to find more unusual grains like the wheat berries used in this stew, along with grains like amaranth and quinoa.

Parmesan Turkey Cutlets

⅓ cup Homemade Mayonnaise (page 31)

1 teaspoon paprika

½ teaspoon salt

⅛ teaspoon cayenne pepper

4 (5-ounce) turkey cutlets

⅓ cup grated Parmesan cheese

¼ cup dry bread crumbs

2 tablespoons butter

1 tablespoon olive oil

1. In small bowl, combine Mayonnaise with paprika, salt, and pepper and mix well. Spread mixture on both sides of turkey cutlets. On shallow plate, combine cheese and bread crumbs; mix well. Drop coated cutlets into cheese mixture, pressing to coat both sides.

2. In heavy skillet, combine butter and olive oil; heat over medium heat until butter starts to sizzle. Add cutlets. Cook on first side for 5 minutes, then carefully turn and cook for 3 to 5 minutes longer until coating is brown and cutlets are thoroughly cooked. Serve immediately.

SERVES 4

CALORIES	407.87
FAT	25.20 GRAMS
SATURATED FAT	6.58 GRAMS
TRANS FAT	0.13 GRAMS*
CARBOHYDRATES	5.44 GRAMS
CHOLESTEROL	120.58 MG

Turkey cutlets are an excellent cut, with little fat and no waste. You can flavor them any way you'd like.

Roasted Turkey Tenderloin

SERVES 4–6

CALORIES	273.57
FAT	5.43 GRAMS
SATURATED FAT	2.90 GRAMS
TRANS FAT	0.10 GRAMS*
CARBOHYDRATES	6.48 GRAMS
CHOLESTEROL	135.66 MG

This recipe is a great substitute for traditional stuffed turkey on Thanksgiving, or you can use it to make sandwiches, like Tex-Mex Club Sandwiches (page 136).

4 (8-ounce) turkey tenderloins, cut in half crosswise
2 tablespoons butter, melted
½ cup dried bread crumbs
2 teaspoons chopped fresh thyme leaves
1 tablespoon chopped fresh parsley
1 teaspoon seasoned salt
⅛ teaspoon white pepper

1. Preheat oven to 325°F. Fold the thin end of each tenderloin under on itself. In small bowl, combine butter, bread crumbs, and remaining ingredients. Place turkey tenderloin halves on a cookie sheet with sides. Sprinkle with bread crumb mixture, patting to adhere.

2. Roast tenderloins for 35 to 45 minutes until internal temperature reaches 165°F. Remove from oven, cover with foil, and let stand for 10 minutes before carving.

Turkey Tenderloins
Like chicken tenderloins (also known as chicken tenders), this is the muscle that lies underneath the turkey breast. Each tenderloin weighs about 8 ounces. You can find them plain, or pre-marinated with a variety of seasonings. They have very little fat and cook quickly; be careful not to overcook them. They can also be stuffed, as in Turkey Tenderloins with Rice Stuffing (page 152).

Pecan Chicken with Pesto

6 boneless, skinless chicken breast halves
¼ cup flour
1 teaspoon salt
⅛ teaspoon white pepper
¾ cup Basil Pesto (page 23), divided
¾ cup finely chopped pecans
¼ cup dried bread crumbs
½ teaspoon dried basil leaves
3 tablespoons butter
1 tablespoon olive oil
½ cup grated Parmesan cheese

SERVES 6	
CALORIES	516.38
FAT	36.37 GRAMS
SATURATED FAT	7.68 GRAMS
TRANS FAT	0.10 GRAMS*
CARBOHYDRATES	11.18 GRAMS
CHOLESTEROL	89.60 MG

Chicken, pesto, and pecans—what's not to like? You can use this coating and cooking method with pounded pork tenderloin, too.

1. Place each chicken breast between two pieces of wax paper and pound gently with meat mallet or rolling pin until about ¼" thick. On shallow plate, combine flour, salt, and pepper. On another plate, place ½ cup of the Basil Pesto. On a third plate, combine pecans, bread crumbs, and basil leaves.

2. One at a time, dip pounded chicken breasts into flour mixture and shake off excess. Dip into pesto, then into pecan mixture, pressing to coat. Set coated chicken on wire rack as you work.

3. In large saucepan, heat butter and olive oil over medium heat. Cook chicken, three at a time, for 2 to 4 minutes on each side, turning once, until chicken is thoroughly cooked and pecans are toasted. In small bowl, combine remaining Pesto with Parmesan cheese. Serve Pesto mixture with chicken.

Scampi Roasted Chicken

SERVES 4

CALORIES	457.30
FAT	19.68 GRAMS
SATURATED FAT	6.45 GRAMS
TRANS FAT	0.07 GRAMS*
CARBOHYDRATES	0.33 GRAMS
CHOLESTEROL	209.48 MG

Scampi flavors include garlic, butter, and lemon. What better seasonings to infuse tender and juicy roasted chicken?

1 (3-pound) roasting chicken
¼ cup butter, divided
1 teaspoon salt, divided
⅛ teaspoon white pepper
4 cloves garlic, minced, divided
¼ cup lemon juice, divided
1 whole lemon
4 whole cloves garlic

1. Preheat oven to 350°F. Rinse chicken, remove giblets, and pat dry. Loosen skin from flesh. In small bowl, combine 1 tablespoon butter, ½ teaspoon salt, pepper, 1 clove minced garlic, and 1 tablespoon lemon juice. Rub in between skin and flesh. Smooth skin back over flesh.

2. Rub chicken skin with remaining 3 tablespoons butter. On work surface, combine ½ teaspoon salt with 3 cloves minced garlic and work into a paste. Rub over chicken. Drizzle chicken with 3 tablespoons lemon juice. Cut lemon in half and place inside chicken cavity. Smash whole cloves garlic and place inside chicken cavity.

3. Roast chicken for 80 to 95 minutes or until juices run clear and meat thermometer inserted into breast registers 165°F. Let chicken stand for 10 minutes, then carve.

Flavoring as Stuffing
When you stuff a chicken or turkey with ingredients just used for flavoring, don't remove them or serve them to your guests. Lemons, garlic, onions, carrots, celery, and other ingredients, when not made into a stuffing, are only used to flavor the chicken from the inside out. Just carve the bird, discarding the vegetables later.

Simple Baked Chicken

6 bone-in, skin-on chicken breasts
1 teaspoon seasoned salt
⅛ teaspoon pepper
2 tablespoons lemon juice
1 teaspoon paprika
2 tablespoons olive oil

1. Place chicken, skin-side up, in 9" × 13" glass baking dish. In small bowl, combine salt, pepper, lemon juice, paprika, and olive oil. Drizzle over chicken and turn to coat. Cover and refrigerate for at least 8 hours before baking.

2. When ready to bake, preheat oven to 350°F. Place chicken, uncovered, in oven and roast for 40 to 50 minutes or until a meat thermometer registers 165 degrees F., juices run clear and chicken is thoroughly cooked.

3. You can serve this as is, or cool and remove meat to use in other recipes. Save the bones and skin for making Chicken Broth (page 120).

SERVES 6

CALORIES	273.53
FAT	9.56 GRAMS
SATURATED FAT	2.05 GRAMS
TRANS FAT	0.0 GRAMS
CARBOHYDRATES	0.0 GRAMS
CHOLESTEROL	120.42 MG

Use this recipe whenever another recipe calls for cooked chicken; also use in Cobb Salad Sandwiches (page 132) and Moroccan Chicken Pie (page 154)

Chicken and Mushrooms

6 bone-in, skin-on chicken breasts
3 tablespoons flour
1 teaspoon salt
⅛ teaspoon pepper
1 teaspoon paprika
2 tablespoons butter
2 tablespoons olive oil
1 cup sliced button mushrooms
½ cup sliced cremini mushrooms
3 cloves garlic, sliced
⅔ cup cream
¼ cup grated Parmesan cheese

1. Preheat oven to 350°F. Sprinkle chicken with flour, salt, pepper, and paprika. In large ovenproof skillet, melt butter and olive oil over medium heat. Add chicken, skin-side down; cook until browned, about 5 to 6 minutes. Remove chicken from pan and place in 13" × 9" glass baking pan.

2. To drippings remaining in skillet, add mushrooms and garlic. Cook and stir for 2 to 3 minutes to deglaze pan. Pour cream into pan and bring to a simmer. Pour mixture over chicken in pan and sprinkle with cheese.

3. Bake for 30 to 40 minutes or until chicken is thoroughly cooked and mushrooms are very tender. Serve immediately.

SERVES 6

CALORIES	472.45
FAT	27.13 GRAMS
SATURATED FAT	10.33 GRAMS
TRANS FAT	0.29 GRAMS*
CARBOHYDRATES	6.29 GRAMS
CHOLESTEROL	158.18 MG

Serve this easy and simple chicken dish with hot cooked rice. Wilted Spinach Fruit Salad (page 103) would be a nice accompaniment.

Healthy Chicken Fingers

SERVES 6–8

CALORIES	243.79
FAT	10.22 GRAMS
SATURATED FAT	4.60 GRAMS
TRANS FAT	0.19 GRAMS*
CARBOHYDRATES	8.59 GRAMS
CHOLESTEROL	84.90 MG

Children love chicken fingers; they are easy to eat and flavorful. You can vary this coating any way you like; use your favorite herbs and spices.

1 cup buttermilk
1 cup Ranch Salad Dressing (page 115)
2 pounds chicken tenders
1 cup dried bread crumbs
¼ cup cornmeal
1 teaspoon salt
¼ teaspoon pepper
½ teaspoon dried oregano leaves
½ teaspoon dried basil leaves
⅓ cup butter

1. In glass baking dish, combine buttermilk and Salad Dressing and mix well. Place chicken tenders in dish and turn to coat. Cover and refrigerate for at least 8 hours.

2. When ready to eat, on shallow plate combine bread crumbs, cornmeal, salt, pepper, oregano, and basil and mix well. Remove tenders from marinade (discard marinade) and drop into bread crumb mixture, turning to coat. Set aside on wire rack to sit for 30 minutes.

3. Preheat oven to 400°F. Place butter in heavy-duty 15" × 10" jelly roll pan and place in oven to melt. Remove from oven and arrange coated tenders in hot butter. Bake for 12 minutes, then carefully turn and bake for 10 to 15 minutes longer or until tenders are golden brown and cooked through. Remove from pan and let stand on wire rack for 10 minutes, then serve.

Dipping Sauces

These chicken fingers, or any baked or fried coated chicken, can be dipped in Ranch Salad Dressing (page 115) mixed with softened cream cheese. Or combine Basil Pesto (page 23) or Fresh and Spicy Salsa (page 38) with Homemade Mayonnaise (page 31). Mustard or ketchup combined with sour cream is also an excellent dipper.

Chicken with Three-Fruit Stuffing

6 (5-ounce) boneless skinless chicken breasts
¼ cup dried currants
¼ cup dried cranberries, chopped
¼ cup peeled, chopped apple
3 tablespoons soft bread crumbs
1 teaspoon salt, divided
½ teaspoon dried thyme leaves
3 tablespoons butter, melted
½ cup dried bread crumbs
⅛ teaspoon white pepper
1 egg, beaten
2 tablespoons milk

1. Preheat oven to 350°F. Spray a roasting pan with nonstick cooking spray and set aside. Cut a pocket in the side of each chicken breast, being careful not to cut through to the other side. In medium bowl, combine currants, cranberries, apple, soft bread crumbs, ½ teaspoon salt, and thyme leaves and toss to mix. Drizzle melted butter over mixture and toss to coat.

2. Stuff mixture into pockets cut into chicken breasts. On shallow plate, combine dried bread crumbs and pepper and mix well. In shallow bowl, combine egg with milk and beat well. Dip stuffed chicken breasts into egg mixture, then into bread crumb mixture to coat.

3. Arrange chicken in prepared pan. Bake for 35 to 45 minutes or until chicken is thoroughly cooked. Serve immediately.

About Chicken Breasts
A whole chicken breast consists of two halves joined by cartilage. When a recipe calls for a chicken breast, technically it means half of a whole breast. You can buy them already split, or split them yourself to save a bit of money. If you buy bone-in breasts, you can remove the meat from the bone; save the bones to make Chicken Broth (page 120).

SERVES 6

CALORIES	398.50
FAT	12.53 GRAMS
SATURATED FAT	5.55 GRAMS
TRANS FAT	0.16 GRAMS*
CARBOHYDRATES	21.72 GRAMS
CHOLESTEROL	171.32 MG

This stuffing is reminiscent of Thanksgiving turkey stuffing but has more fruit. Serve with Brown Rice Stir-Fry (page 227) and sautéed broccoli.

Crispy Chicken Patties

SERVES 4

CALORIES	318.75
FAT	13.76 GRAMS
SATURATED FAT	4.11 GRAMS
TRANS FAT	0.09 GRAMS*
CARBOHYDRATES	16.49 GRAMS
CHOLESTEROL	128.22 MG

Serve these patties on a bun with mustard and relish, or serve them on top of mashed potatoes, with creamed peas for a retro meal.

2 tablespoons olive oil, divided
¼ cup finely chopped onion
¼ cup finely chopped red bell pepper
2 tablespoons finely chopped mushrooms
1 slice White Bread (page 44)
1 egg, beaten
½ teaspoon salt
⅛ teaspoon cayenne pepper
¼ teaspoon poultry seasoning
1 pound ground chicken breast
½ cup dried bread crumbs
2 tablespoons butter

1. In large skillet, heat 1 tablespoon olive oil over medium heat. Add onion, bell pepper, and mushrooms; cook and stir until tender, about 4 minutes. Continue cooking, stirring frequently, until liquid evaporates. Remove from heat.

2. Make soft bread crumbs from the slice of Bread. In medium bowl, combine bread crumbs, egg, salt, cayenne pepper, poultry seasoning, and onion mixture; stir to combine. Add ground chicken and mix gently but thoroughly. Form into four patties. Dip patties in dried bread crumbs to coat.

3. Wipe out skillet. Add another tablespoon of olive oil and the butter; melt together over medium heat. Add chicken patties; cook for 5 minutes on first side. Carefully turn; cook for 3 to 6 minutes on second side until juices run clear and chicken is thoroughly cooked.

Ground Chicken

You can usually purchase ground chicken at the supermarket; you may have to ask the butcher to grind some for you. You can also grind it yourself. Just take boneless, skinless chicken breasts and cut into pieces. Place in food processor and pulse until the chicken is ground, but still has texture. Use the same day the chicken is ground.

Crisp and Healthy Fried Chicken

6 boneless, skinless chicken breasts
1-½ cups buttermilk
8 cloves garlic, minced
½ cup flour
2 tablespoons cornstarch
1 teaspoon seasoned salt
½ teaspoon garlic powder
1 tablespoon paprika
2 eggs
¼ cup milk
¾ cup dried bread crumbs
2 cups corn or canola oil

SERVES 6

CALORIES	372.56
FAT	13.64 GRAMS
SATURATED FAT	2.54 GRAMS
TRANS FAT	0.06 GRAMS
CARBOHYDRATES	21.36 GRAMS
CHOLESTEROL	154.02 MG

Yes, you can enjoy fried chicken, with very little trans fat. To cook boneless, skinless chicken thighs, just add 10 minutes to the total frying time.

1. Place chicken breasts in glass baking dish and add buttermilk and garlic. Cover and refrigerate for at least 8 hours.

2. When ready to cook, place flour, cornstarch, salt, garlic powder, and paprika on a shallow plate. In shallow bowl, beat eggs with milk. Place bread crumbs on another shallow plate. Remove chicken from marinade (discard marinade) and drain briefly. Dip chicken into flour mixture, then egg mixture, then bread crumbs. Place on wire rack to stand for 30 minutes until coating becomes sticky.

3. Heat oil in heavy deep saucepan over medium heat until temperature reaches 375°F. Carefully add chicken; fry until browned, about 10 minutes. Turn the chicken, cover, and fry for 5 to 10 minutes longer or until chicken is thoroughly cooked.

Fried Bone-In Chicken

You can also fry bone-in chicken with the skin on. Marinate as directed in the recipe above, coat as directed, brown, then fry covered for 25 to 30 minutes or until juices run clear and chicken is cooked. The dark meat (legs and thighs) will take longer to cook than the breasts, so put them in the oil 10 minutes before you add the breasts.

Turkey Tenderloins with Rice Stuffing

SERVES 8

CALORIES	397.19
FAT	15.60 GRAMS
SATURATED FAT	5.40 GRAMS
TRANS FAT	0.12 GRAMS*
CARBOHYDRATES	12.51 GRAMS
CHOLESTEROL	141.76 MG

A flavorful stuffing is delicious in moist turkey tenderloins. Serve it with Wilted Spinach Fruit Salad (page 103) and Orange-Scented Broccoli (page 230).

4 (12-ounce) turkey tenderloins
1 tablespoon olive oil
¼ cup finely chopped onion
¼ cup brown basmati rice
¼ teaspoon salt
¼ teaspoon dried basil leaves
½ cup Chicken Broth (page 120)
¼ cup Basil Pesto (page 23)

1 cup diced Swiss cheese
¾ cup dried bread crumbs
¼ cup flour
½ teaspoon seasoned salt
⅛ teaspoon pepper
1 egg, beaten
1 tablespoon water

1. Preheat oven to 325°F. Cut turkey tenderloins in half crosswise. Cut a pocket into the side of each tenderloin half, being careful not to cut through to the other side; set aside. In small saucepan, combine olive oil and onion over medium heat. Cook and stir until onion is tender, about 5 minutes. Add rice, salt, and basil; cook and stir until rice is translucent, about 2 minutes longer.

2. Add chicken broth to rice mixture. Bring to a boil, then reduce heat, cover, and simmer for 15 to 20 minutes or until rice is almost tender and liquid is absorbed. Remove from heat and stir in Pesto. Let stand for 10 minutes, then stir in cheese.

3. Stuff tenderloins with rice mixture. On shallow plate, combine bread crumbs, flour, seasoned salt, and pepper and mix well. In shallow bowl, combine egg and water and mix well. Dip tenderloins into egg mixture, then into bread crumb mixture to coat.

4. Arrange stuffed tenderloins on a cookie sheet. Bake for 20 minutes, then carefully turn tenderloins over with a spatula and bake for 20 to 25 minutes longer, until juices run clear and turkey is thoroughly cooked. Serve immediately.

Baked Fried Chicken

6 boneless, skinless chicken breast halves
2 cups buttermilk
¾ cup flour
2 tablespoons nonfat dry milk
1 teaspoon salt
¼ teaspoon pepper
10 tablespoons butter, divided

SERVES 6

CALORIES	298.16
FAT	10.64 GRAMS
SATURATED FAT	6.02 GRAMS
TRANS FAT	0.23 GRAMS*
CARBOHYDRATES	13.16 GRAMS
CHOLESTEROL	105.71 MG

The crisp coating on this chicken is flavorful and tender, too. And the chicken stays moist. It's perfect served with Garlic and Onion Smashed Potatoes (page 235).

1. Place chicken breasts in large baking dish and pour buttermilk over. Cover and refrigerate for at least 8 hours. In medium bowl, combine flour, dry milk powder, salt, and pepper and mix well. Cut in 4 tablespoons butter until particles are fine. Cover and refrigerate.

2. When ready to cook, preheat oven to 400°F. Spray a heavy-duty 15" × 10" jelly roll pan with nonstick cooking spray and set aside. Remove chicken from buttermilk and discard buttermilk. Drain chicken, then drop into flour mixture, pressing to coat. Let chicken dry on wire rack for 30 minutes.

3. Cut 6 tablespoons butter into pieces and place in prepared pan. Place in oven for 4 to 5 minutes or until butter melts. Remove from oven and carefully place chicken in hot butter. Bake for 10 minutes, then turn chicken and bake for 10 to 15 minutes longer or until juices run clear and internal temperature reaches 165°F.

Chicken Parts

You can make this recipe with boneless, skinless chicken thighs. Just increase the baking time by 10 to 15 minutes or until chicken registers 170°F on a thermometer. It can also be made with bone-in chicken breasts, or cut-up chicken parts. Again, increase the baking time by 10 to 15 minutes and always use your thermometer to check the temperature.

Moroccan Chicken Pie

SERVES 8

CALORIES	429.22
FAT	19.38 GRAMS
SATURATED FAT	5.14 GRAMS
TRANS FAT	0.11 GRAMS*
CARBOHYDRATES	37.41 GRAMS
CHOLESTEROL	66.48 MG

Take a trip to Morocco with this exotic pie. Serve it like a casserole, scooping out some filling and crisp pastry for each diner.

2 tablespoons olive oil, *divided*
3 cloves garlic, *minced*
1 teaspoon grated fresh ginger root
½ teaspoon turmeric
1 teaspoon cumin
1 cup basmati rice
2 cups Chicken Broth (page 120)
1 teaspoon salt
⅛ teaspoon cayenne pepper
3 servings Simple Baked Chicken (page 147)
1 onion, *chopped*
1 (14-ounce) can diced tomatoes, *drained*
1 (15-ounce) can chickpeas, *drained*
½ cup slivered almonds
4 (15" × 18") sheets frozen filo pastry, *thawed*
3 tablespoons butter, *melted*

1. Preheat oven to 375°F. In large saucepan, combine 1 tablespoon olive oil and garlic over medium heat. Cook and stir for 1 minute. Then stir in ginger root, turmeric, and cumin; cook and stir for 1 minute longer. Add rice; cook and stir for 2 minutes. Add Chicken Broth and bring to a boil. Reduce heat, cover, and simmer for 20 to 25 minutes or until rice is tender. Stir in salt and pepper, cover, and remove from heat.

2. Remove meat from Chicken and dice. Stir into rice mixture. In large skillet, heat 1 tablespoon olive oil over medium heat. Add onion; cook and stir for 5 minutes until tender. Add tomatoes, chickpeas, and almonds; simmer for 5 minutes or until slightly thickened.

3. In 10-inch deep-dish pie pan, layer half of rice mixture, then half of tomato mixture. Repeat layers. Layer filo pastry, brushing with butter between layers. Place on top of pie pan, folding to fit. Brush with remaining butter. Bake for 25 to 30 minutes or until pastry is browned and crisp. Let stand for 10 minutes, then serve.

Stir-Fried Chicken Tahiti

1 (15-ounce) can pineapple tidbits
2 tablespoons soy sauce
2 tablespoons cornstarch
½ cup frozen orange juice concentrate, thawed
1 tablespoon minced fresh ginger root
⅛ teaspoon cayenne pepper
4 boneless, skinless chicken breasts
2 tablespoons olive oil
1 onion, chopped
2 cups sugar snap peas
½ cup chopped toasted macadamia nuts

SERVES 4–6

CALORIES	332.75
FAT	14.29 GRAMS
SATURATED FAT	2.23 GRAMS
TRANS FAT	0.0 GRAMS
CARBOHYDRATES	30.97 GRAMS
CHOLESTEROL	45.63 MG

This fresh stir-fry has wonderful tropical flavors. You could also top it with a bit of toasted coconut.

1. Drain pineapple tidbits, reserving ½ cup juice. In medium bowl, combine reserved juice, soy sauce, cornstarch, juice concentrate, ginger root, and pepper; set aside. Cut chicken into 1" pieces and add to cornstarch mixture; stir and let marinate in refrigerator for 30 minutes.

2. When ready to cook, heat oil in wok or heavy skillet over medium-high heat. Remove chicken from marinade with slotted spoon; add to oil. Reserve marinade. Stir-fry for 4 to 5 minutes or until chicken is almost cooked. Remove chicken from wok and set aside. Add onion to wok; stir-fry for 2 minutes. Add sugar snap peas; stir-fry for 3 minutes. Then add pineapple and chicken to wok.

3. Stir marinade and add to wok. Stir-fry for 3 to 5 minutes or until sauce thickens and bubbles. Serve over hot cooked rice; top each serving with macadamia nuts.

Macadamia Nuts
Macadamia trees are actually evergreens, grown in any climate where coffee also grows. The nut is encased in a very hard shell that is difficult to crack; in fact, a bench vise is one of the best tools to use. Macadamia nuts have a very high fat content, which means they go rancid easily. Store the nuts in the refrigerator for up to 3 months.

Cilantro Chicken Tacos

SERVES 6

CALORIES	368.14
FAT	19.64 GRAMS
SATURATED FAT	6.33 GRAMS
TRANS FAT	0.03 GRAMS
CARBOHYDRATES	24.33 GRAMS
CHOLESTEROL	56.79 MG

Manufactured taco shells can have as much as 2.5 grams of artificial trans fat per shell! You'll still have a bit of trans fat in these tacos, but the amount is very small.

6 (6") flour or whole-wheat tortillas
2 cups corn or canola oil
1 tablespoon olive oil
1 onion, chopped
3 boneless, skinless chicken breasts
1 green bell pepper, chopped
1 jalapeño pepper, minced
1 cup Fresh and Spicy Salsa (page 38)
⅓ cup chopped fresh cilantro
½ cup sour cream
1 cup chopped plum tomatoes
1 cup shredded lettuce
1 cup shredded jalapeño Monterey jack cheese

1. Pour corn or canola oil into a large deep saucepan and place over medium high heat. Heat until oil temperature reaches 375°F. One at a time, fold tortillas in half and slip into the oil. Hold the taco shape with tongs as the tortilla fries, turning once during frying. Fry for 2 to 4 minutes on each side until the tortilla browns and puffs. Carefully remove from the oil, draining excess oil over the pot, and place on paper towels to drain. Repeat with remaining tortillas.

2. In large skillet, heat olive oil over medium heat. Add onion; cook and stir for 3 minutes. Meanwhile, cut chicken into 1" pieces. Add to skillet; cook and stir for 4 minutes longer. Add bell pepper and jalapeño; cook and stir for 1 minute longer.

3. Stir Salsa and cilantro into chicken mixture; remove from heat. Make tacos with the cooled shells, chicken mixture, sour cream, plum tomatoes, lettuce, and shredded cheese.

Chicken and Tomato Pizza

1 Homemade Pizza Crust (page 49), partially baked
1 tablespoon olive oil
1 onion, chopped
3 cloves garlic, minced
3 boneless, skinless chicken breasts
1 teaspoon salt
⅛ teaspoon cayenne pepper
½ cup Ranch Salad Dressing (page 115)
½ cup crumbled feta cheese
1-½ cup chopped plum tomatoes
1-½ cups shredded mozzarella cheese
¼ cup grated Romano cheese

SERVES 8

CALORIES	418.24
FAT	23.47 GRAMS
SATURATED FAT	9.07 GRAMS
TRANS FAT	0.26 GRAMS*
CARBOHYDRATES	28.02 GRAMS
CHOLESTEROL	75.36 MG

Make this excellent pizza that has wonderful flavor and texture. It's perfect for a cozy movie night at home.

1. Preheat oven to 400°F. Place partially baked Crust on cookie sheet and set aside. In large saucepan, heat olive oil over medium heat. Add onion and garlic; cook and stir until tender, about 5 minutes. Meanwhile, cut chicken into 1" pieces and sprinkle with salt and pepper. Add chicken to skillet; cook and stir until chicken is thoroughly cooked, about 5 to 7 minutes. Remove from heat.

2. Drain chicken mixture thoroughly and add Salad Dressing and feta cheese. Spoon onto Crust. Sprinkle with tomatoes, mozzarella cheese, and Romano cheese. Bake for 20 to 30 minutes or until Pizza Crust is golden brown, sauce is bubbling, and cheese is melted and beginning to brown.

Grilling Pizzas
You can grill most pizzas! Prepare and preheat the grill, and arrange the coals for indirect grilling: an open space without coals in the center, with coals piled to the edges. Place the pizza on the rack above the open space, cover, and grill for 6 to 10 minutes, checking frequently to make sure the pizza isn't burning.

Chicken Spinach Pie

SERVES 10

CALORIES	452.27
FAT	27.84 GRAMS
SATURATED FAT	16.08 GRAMS
TRANS FAT	0.45 GRAMS*
CARBOHYDRATES	27.49 GRAMS
CHOLESTEROL	169.74 MG

This rich and delicious pie serves a crowd! It's delicious paired with a simple fruit salad and perhaps some cooked carrots.

1 Recipe Traditional Pie Crust (page 260)
1 tablespoon olive oil
1 onion, chopped
3 boneless, skinless chicken breasts
½ teaspoon salt
⅛ teaspoon white pepper
1 (9-ounce) package frozen chopped spinach, thawed
5 eggs, reserving 1 yolk
½ cup part-skim ricotta cheese
1-½ cups shredded part-skim mozzarella cheese
½ cup shredded Romano cheese

1. Preheat oven to 375°F. Line a 9" pie pan with one Crust, letting excess drape over sides. In large skillet, combine olive oil and onion over medium heat. Cook and stir until onion is crisp-tender, about 4 minutes.

2. Cut chicken into 1" pieces and sprinkle with salt and pepper. Add to skillet with onion; cook and stir until chicken is almost cooked, about 5 minutes. Drain spinach and add to skillet; cook and stir until liquid evaporates. Remove from heat.

3. In large bowl, place 5 eggs (minus 1 yolk). Beat well, then add ricotta cheese and beat until blended. Stir in chicken mixture, then fold in mozzarella and Romano cheeses. Pour into Pie Crust. Top with second Crust, folding excess up to form a rim. Pinch edges and flute.

4. Cut a decorative pattern into the top crust with a knife. Brush with egg yolk. Bake pie for 50 to 60 minutes or until the pie is browned and filling is set. Remove from oven and let cool for 15 minutes before slicing.

Curried Chicken with Rice Pilaf

6 boneless, skin-on chicken
   breasts
1 tablespoon olive oil
1 onion, chopped
3 cloves garlic, minced
1 tablespoon curry powder
1 red bell pepper, chopped
1-½ cups brown basmati rice

1-½ cups Chicken Broth (page 120)
1 cup water
1 (3-ounce) package light cream
   cheese, softened
½ cup shredded Gouda cheese
½ cup light cream
1 cup frozen peas

SERVES 6

CALORIES	647.54
FAT	25.97 GRAMS
SATURATED FAT	9.95GRAMS
TRANS FAT	0.17 GRAMS*
CARBOHYDRATES	46.01 GRAMS
CHOLESTEROL	160.77 MG

Stuffing a curry-flavored cheese mixture under the skin of chicken breasts is a wonderful way to flavor the flesh. Serve this elegant dish with a spinach salad.

1. Preheat oven to 400°F. Loosen skin from chicken, but leave attached at the edges. In large saucepan, heat olive oil over medium heat. Add onion and garlic; cook and stir until crisp-tender, about 4 minutes. Add curry powder; cook and stir for 1 minute longer. Remove ½ cup of this mixture and place in small bowl.

2. Add bell pepper and rice to saucepan; cook and stir for 1 minute. Add Chicken Broth and water, bring to a simmer, cover, and cook for 15 minutes or until rice is almost cooked.

3. Add cream cheese to onion mixture in small bowl and mix well. Stir in Gouda cheese. Stuff this mixture between the skin and flesh of the chicken breasts. Stir cream and peas into rice mixture and place in 2-quart baking dish. Top with stuffed chicken. Bake for 30 to 40 minutes or until chicken is thoroughly cooked and rice is tender. Serve immediately.

Boning Chicken Breasts

To bone chicken breasts, first cut them in half if you have a whole breast, which is about 6" wide. Then, with a sharp knife, carefully work the knife between the bone and the flesh. Keep cutting until the meat comes away from the bone. You can remove the long thin muscle under the breast (the tenderloin) and reserve for another use, like Healthy Chicken Fingers (page 148).

Crisp Cornmeal Chicken

SERVES 6

CALORIES	237.54
FAT	4.21 GRAMS
SATURATED FAT	0.79 GRAMS
TRANS FAT	0.04 GRAMS
CARBOHYDRATES	18.13 GRAMS
CHOLESTEROL	68.85 MG

This crisp and spicy chicken is first fried for crispness, then baked to keep the chicken moist.

6 boneless, skinless chicken breasts
1 cup buttermilk
¼ cup chipotle peppers in adobo sauce
¾ cup yellow cornmeal
¼ cup flour
1 teaspoon salt
¼ teaspoon cayenne pepper
1 tablespoon chili powder
1 tablespoon ground red chile powder
½ cup corn oil

1. Place chicken breasts in glass baking dish. In small bowl, combine buttermilk and peppers with adobo sauce and mix well. Pour over chicken; cover and refrigerate for at least 8 hours.

2. When ready to cook, on shallow plate combine cornmeal, flour, salt, cayenne pepper, chili powder, and ground red chile powder and mix well. Remove chicken from buttermilk (discard buttermilk mixture) and drain. Drop into cornmeal mixture and turn to coat, pressing coating onto chicken. Let stand on wire racks for 30 minutes. Preheat oven to 350°F.

3. In large skillet, pour corn oil. Heat over medium heat until oil shimmers. Fry three chicken breasts at a time, turning once, until browned, about 3 to 5 minutes total. Place fried chicken in roasting pan. Repeat with remaining breasts. Bake chicken for 18 to 25 minutes or until thoroughly cooked.

Chapter 9

Beef and Pork Entrees

Slow-Cooker Sausage and Cabbage

SERVES 6

CALORIES	395.57
FAT	28.19 GRAMS
SATURATED FAT	9.62 GRAMS
TRANS FAT	0.02 GRAMS*
CARBOHYDRATES	20.99 GRAMS
CHOLESTEROL	69.93 MG

This hearty recipe is satisfying on a cold winter night. Serve it with dark crusty bread, toasted and spread with butter.

1-½ pounds bratwurst	¼ cup sugar
1 onion, chopped	¼ cup red wine vinegar
4 cloves garlic, minced	½ teaspoon salt
2 cups chopped red cabbage	⅛ teaspoon pepper
2 cups chopped green cabbage	¼ cup English mustard

1. In large skillet, cook bratwurst over medium heat until it begins to brown. Remove from heat. Add onion and garlic; cook and stir until onion is crisp-tender, about 4 minutes.

2. In 4- or 5-quart slow cooker, combine onion, garlic, cabbages, sugar, wine vinegar, salt, and pepper and mix. Top with bratwurst and spread bratwurst with mustard. Cover and cook on low for 7 to 8 hours or until cabbage is tender and sausage is thoroughly cooked.

Bulgogi

SERVES 6

CALORIES	407.35
FAT	28.94 GRAMS
SATURATED FAT	9.99 GRAMS
TRANS FAT	0.15 GRAMS*
CARBOHYDRATES	5.38 GRAMS
CHOLESTEROL	101.81 MG

Serve this tender and flavorful beef over hot cooked rice. You could add other vegetables as well; asparagus and mushrooms would be nice choices.

3 tablespoons soy sauce	2 tablespoons sesame seeds
2 tablespoons brown sugar	3 tablespoons olive oil, divided
½ cup pineapple juice	1-½ pounds beef sirloin tip
3 cloves garlic, minced	2 red bell peppers, sliced
¼ teaspoon cayenne pepper	3 green onions, chopped

1. In medium bowl, combine soy sauce, brown sugar, pineapple juice, garlic, cayenne pepper, sesame seeds, and 1 tablespoon olive oil. Slice beef into thin strips across the grain. Add to bowl with marinade; cover, and refrigerate for at least 2 hours, up to 8 hours.

2. When ready to eat, remove meat from marinade; discard marinade. Heat 2 tablespoons olive oil in wok or heavy skillet over medium high heat. When oil ripples, add beef and bell peppers. Stir-fry for 4 to 6 minutes or until beef is desired doneness and bell peppers are crisp-tender. Sprinkle with green onions and serve.

Ham and Potato Casserole

2 tablespoons olive oil	⅛ teaspoon white pepper
1 tablespoon butter	1-½ cups milk
1 onion, chopped	1 cup shredded Havarti cheese
1 green bell pepper, chopped	1-½ cups cubed cooked ham
3 tablespoons flour	6 potatoes, thinly sliced
1 teaspoon salt	¼ cup grated Parmesan cheese

SERVES 8

CALORIES	269.08
FAT	11.85 GRAMS
SATURATED FAT	5.36 GRAMS
TRANS FAT	0.31 GRAMS*
CARBOHYDRATES	30.44 GRAMS
CHOLESTEROL	30.52 MG

This old-fashioned recipe is pure comfort food. Make it when you have leftover ham after holiday dinners.

1. Preheat oven to 350°F. In large saucepan, melt olive oil and butter over medium heat. Add onion; cook and stir for 3 minutes. Then add green bell pepper; cook and stir for 2 minutes longer. Remove vegetables from pan with slotted spoon and set aside.

2. Add flour to fat remaining in pan; cook and stir for 3 minutes. Add salt, pepper, and milk; bring to a simmer, stirring constantly with a wire whisk. Cook for 4 to 5 minutes or until sauce thickens. Remove from heat and stir in reserved vegetables, Havarti cheese, and ham.

3. Place ¼ cup sauce in the bottom of a 13" × 9" glass baking dish. Layer with one-third of the potatoes and top with one-third of the remaining sauce. Repeat layers, ending with sauce. Sprinkle with Parmesan cheese. Cover with foil and bake for 1 hour, then remove foil and bake 30 to 35 minutes longer or until potatoes are tender, casserole is bubbling, and top is beginning to brown. Cool for 10 minutes, then serve.

White Sauce

White sauces are the base for many recipes, including scalloped potatoes and gumbo. There are a few secrets to making the best white sauce. Be sure to cook the flour for at least 2 minutes so the starch granules swell and the "raw" taste goes away. And when adding the liquid, stir constantly with a wire whisk to prevent lumps.

Garden Chili

SERVES 8

CALORIES	364.78
FAT	16.61 GRAMS
SATURATED FAT	5.61 GRAMS
TRANS FAT	0.0 GRAMS
CARBOHYDRATES	36.60 GRAMS
CHOLESTEROL	32.32 MG

Chili can be made with almost any vegetable. Have some summer squash or zucchini from your garden? Throw it in!

1 pound hot Italian sausage
2 tablespoons extra-virgin olive oil
2 onions, chopped
4 cloves garlic, minced
1 jalapeño pepper, minced
1 green bell pepper, chopped
1 (6-ounce) can tomato paste
1 (28-ounce) can stewed tomatoes, chopped
2 cups water
2 (15-ounce) cans kidney beans, drained
2 tablespoons cornstarch
1 cup Beef Broth (page 119)

1. In large pot, brown sausage, stirring to break up. Remove sausage from pot with slotted spoon and set aside. Drain drippings from pan. Add olive oil to pan and cook onions, garlic, and jalapeño in drippings until crisp-tender, about 5 minutes. Add green bell pepper, tomato paste, tomatoes, water, beans, and reserved sausage. Bring to a boil, reduce heat, and simmer for 30 minutes.

2. In small bowl, combine cornstarch and Beef Broth and mix well. Stir this mixture into the chili. Bring back to a simmer and simmer for 10 to 15 minutes or until thickened. Serve with sour cream, tortilla chips, and salsa.

Beef Barley Stew

1-½ pounds beef stew meat
3 tablespoons flour
1 teaspoon paprika
1 teaspoon salt
⅛ teaspoon pepper
2 tablespoons olive oil
1 onion, chopped
3 cloves garlic, minced
1 teaspoon dried thyme leaves

1 (4-ounce) jar sliced
    mushrooms, undrained
4 carrots, sliced
3 cups Beef Broth (page 119)
4 cups water
¾ cup pearl barley
1 (14-ounce) can diced
    tomatoes, undrained
3 tablespoons tomato paste

SERVES 6–8	
CALORIES	358.32
FAT	11.51 GRAMS
SATURATED FAT	3.19 GRAMS
TRANS FAT	0.08 GRAMS*
CARBOHYDRATES	30.39 GRAMS
CHOLESTEROL	98.61 MG

This rich stew is perfect for a cold winter's day. Serve it with Triple-Cheese Muffins (page 71) for a warming and easy meal.

1. Cut beef stew meat into 1-½" pieces. Sprinkle with flour, paprika, salt, and pepper and toss to coat. In large stockpot, heat olive oil over medium heat. Add cubes of beef; brown on all sides, stirring occasionally, about 10 minutes total. Remove beef from pot. Add onion and garlic; cook and stir until crisp-tender, about 4 minutes.

2. Add thyme, mushrooms with their liquid, carrots, and Beef Broth to pot; stir to loosen drippings from bottom of pan. Return beef to pot along with water. Bring to a boil, then reduce heat, cover pot, and simmer for 1 hour. Add barley, cover, and simmer for 25 minutes longer. Stir in undrained tomatoes and tomato paste; simmer for 20 to 30 minutes until beef, vegetables, and barley are tender, then serve.

Tomato Paste

Tomato paste is most often sold in 6-ounce cans. If a recipe doesn't call for a whole can, freeze the rest! Portion it into 2-tablespoon mounds and freeze. Then place the mounds in a food-storage bag and freeze up to 3 months. You can also find tomato paste in a tube; just store it in the fridge and measure out the amount you need.

Beef and Hummus Pizza

SERVES 8

CALORIES	409.52
FAT	18.79 GRAMS
SATURATED FAT	8.16 GRAMS
TRANS FAT	0.20 GRAMS*
CARBOHYDRATES	34.65 GRAMS
CHOLESTEROL	63.49 MG

This unusual pizza is delicious and good for you, too!

1 pound extra-lean ground beef
1 onion, chopped
1 (8-ounce) package sliced mushrooms
1 Homemade Pizza Crust (page 49), partially baked

1 cup Creamy and Crunchy Hummus (page 32)
1-¼ cups shredded Monterey jack cheese
¼ cup grated Parmesan cheese
2 tablespoons chopped fresh parsley

1. Preheat oven to 400°F. In heavy skillet, combine ground beef, onion, and mushrooms. Stir until ground beef is browned and vegetables are tender.

2. Place Pizza Crust on a cookie sheet and spread with Hummus. Top with ¼ cup cheese. Drain ground beef mixture thoroughly and sprinkle over pizza. Top with remaining Monterey jack and Parmesan cheeses.

3. Bake for 25 minutes, or until crust is golden brown and cheese is melted and brown. Sprinkle with parsley, let stand for 5 minutes, then slice to serve.

Kung Pao Pork

SERVES 4

CALORIES	483.34
FAT	33.94 GRAMS
SATURATED FAT	6.98 GRAMS
TRANS FAT	0.08 GRAMS
CARBOHYDRATES	14.60 GRAMS
CHOLESTEROL	72.11 MG

You can control the spiciness of this recipe by preparing the jalapeños. Discard the seeds and it will be milder; use the seeds for a hotter dish.

1 pound boneless pork chops
3 tablespoons soy sauce
1 teaspoon sesame oil
3 tablespoons canola oil, divided
2 tablespoons white-wine vinegar
2 tablespoons cornstarch
1 tablespoon sugar

1 teaspoon chile paste
2 jalapeño peppers, minced
1 red bell pepper, sliced
1 yellow bell pepper, sliced
1 cup Chicken Broth (page 120)
½ cup chopped peanuts

1. Cut pork into 2" × ⅛" slices. In bowl, combine soy sauce, sesame oil, 1 tablespoon canola oil, vinegar, cornstarch, sugar, chile paste, and jalapeños. Add pork and stir. Cover and refrigerate for 1 hour. Drain pork, reserving marinade. Heat a wok or skillet over medium high heat. Add 2 tablespoons canola oil, then add pork; stir-fry until browned. Add peppers; stir-fry for 3 minutes.

2. Add Chicken Broth to marinade, stir, and add to wok. Stir-fry for 2 to 3 minutes longer or until sauce boils and thickens. Sprinkle with peanuts and serve with hot cooked rice.

Pork Chops with Spicy Fruit Salsa

2 Granny Smith apples, peeled and chopped
2 oranges, peeled and chopped
1 jalapeño pepper, minced
3 tablespoons orange marmalade
1 tablespoon sugar
2 tablespoons lemon juice
1 teaspoon salt, divided
¼ teaspoon cayenne pepper
¼ cup brown sugar
1 tablespoon olive oil
1 teaspoon ground ginger
1 tablespoon cornstarch
6 boneless pork rib chops

1. For salsa, prepare apples and oranges and place in medium bowl. Add jalapeño, marmalade, 1 tablespoon sugar, lemon juice, ½ teaspoon salt, and cayenne pepper and mix gently. Cover and refrigerate for at least one hour. Drain salsa, reserving liquid.

2. In saucepan, combine ⅓ cup liquid from the salsa, ¼ cup brown sugar, olive oil, ginger, ½ teaspoon salt, and cornstarch and bring to a boil. Boil for 1 minute. Remove from heat and brush half of sauce over pork chops.

3. Prepare and preheat grill. Place pork chops 6" from medium coals. Grill for 10 to 12 minutes, turning once and brushing frequently with sauce, until pork registers 160°F on a meat thermometer. Remove pork from grill and let stand for 5 minutes (discard remaining sauce). Serve pork with drained salsa.

About Pork Chops

Pork chops are usually cut from the back of the pig, which is the most tender meat. Blade chops are closest to the shoulder. Rib chops come next; they are very tender and flavorful. Loin chops aren't quite as tender because they don't contain as much fat. And the sirloin chop is drier with not as much flavor. Boneless chops usually come from the loin.

SERVES 6

CALORIES	322.21
FAT	13.15 GRAMS
SATURATED FAT	4.36 GRAMS
TRANS FAT	0.0 GRAMS
CARBOHYDRATES	30.94 GRAMS
CHOLESTEROL	58.24 MG

This fruit salsa can be served with almost any grilled meat; it's delicious with chicken and fish fillets, or even shrimp.

Stuffed Mini Meatloaves

SERVES 4

CALORIES	559.84
FAT	29.95 GRAMS
SATURATED FAT	15.06 GRAMS
TRANS FAT	0.45 GRAMS*
CARBOHYDRATES	23.51 GRAMS
CHOLESTEROL	205.08 MG

You can flavor the filling in these mini meatloaves any way you'd like. Use Cheddar cheese and omit the onion. Add curry powder and omit the Gouda cheese. You decide!

1 tablespoon olive oil
¼ cup finely chopped onion
4 cloves garlic, minced
⅓ cup brown basmati rice
⅔ cup Beef Broth (page 119)
1 (3-ounce) package low-fat cream cheese, softened
½ cup light sour cream, divided
1 cup shredded Gouda cheese, divided
1 egg
¼ cup dried Italian bread crumbs
½ teaspoon salt
⅛ teaspoon pepper
1 pound extra-lean ground beef
2 tablespoons heavy cream

1. Preheat oven to 375°F. In small saucepan, heat olive oil over medium heat. Add onion and garlic; cook and stir for 4 minutes. Add rice; cook and stir for 1 minute longer. Add Beef Broth; bring to a boil, then cover, reduce heat, and simmer for 20 to 25 minutes or until rice is cooked. Remove from heat and place in medium bowl.

2. Stir in cream cheese and ¼ cup sour cream, along with half of the Gouda cheese; set aside. In large bowl, combine egg, bread crumbs, salt, and pepper and mix well. Add beef; mix gently until combined.

3. Place a sheet of foil on work surface. Divide beef into four balls; gently pat each ball into a 5" × 6" rectangle. Divide rice mixture among ground beef rectangles. Gently roll each, starting with 6" side. Place in 13" × 9" glass baking dish.

4. Bake for 15 minutes. Meanwhile, in small bowl combine ¼ cup sour cream with heavy cream and mix well. Remove meatloaves from oven and top with sour cream mixture; sprinkle with remaining ½ cup Gouda cheese. Return to oven and bake for 10 to 15 minutes longer or until beef is thoroughly cooked. Serve immediately.

Garlic and Onion Pot Roast

8 cloves garlic, divided
1 teaspoon salt
3 tablespoons Dijon mustard
2 tablespoons horseradish
⅛ teaspoon cayenne pepper
1 (2-pound) bottom round beef roast
2 onions, chopped
1 (16-ounce) bag baby carrots
2 parsnips, peeled and cubed
½ cup Beef Broth (page 119)

SERVES 6	
CALORIES	346.23
FAT	13.20 GRAMS
SATURATED FAT	4.87 GRAMS
TRANS FAT	0.40 GRAMS*
CARBOHYDRATES	18.55 GRAMS
CHOLESTEROL	79.71 MG

Serve this fabulous old-fashioned dinner with a fruit salad and some crusty rolls.

1. Finely mince 4 cloves of garlic and place on work surface. Sprinkle with salt. With side of knife, work garlic and salt together into a paste. Place in small bowl and mix with mustard, horseradish, and cayenne pepper.

2. Rub this mixture over the roast. Place a skillet over medium high heat. Sear roast on both sides until browned, about 5 minutes total.

3. Place remaining garlic, onions, carrots, and parsnips in a 4- or 5-quart slow cooker. Top with beef. Pour Beef Broth over. Cover and cook on low for 8 to 9 hours, or until vegetables and beef are very tender.

Beef and the Slow Cooker
Your slow cooker is the ideal appliance in which to cook a pot roast. The moist heat and low temperature make the most tender roast ever. The meat used for pot roast is too tough to cook quickly. The slow cooking melts the fat and spreads it through the meat, while dissolving tougher fibers.

Country-Style Pork Kiev

2 slices Oatmeal Bread (page 43)
2 tablespoons grated Parmesan
   cheese
½ teaspoon dried basil leaves
½ teaspoon dried oregano leaves

½ teaspoon garlic salt
½ cup butter
2 (12-ounce) pork tenderloins
¼ cup dry white wine
2 tablespoons chopped parsley

SERVES 6

CALORIES	392.10
FAT	21.85 GRAMS
SATURATED FAT	11.72 GRAMS
TRANS FAT	0.41 GRAMS*
CARBOHYDRATES	8.66 GRAMS
CHOLESTEROL	147.36 MG

Coating pork tenderloins with seasoned bread crumbs and baking it and serving with a butter sauce makes a wonderful elegant dish, perfect to serve to company.

1. Preheat oven to 425°F. Make bread crumbs from Oatmeal Bread; mix in small bowl with Parmesan cheese, basil, oregano, and salt. Melt butter in small saucepan. Mix 4 tablespoons melted butter with the bread crumbs.

2. Place pork on a shallow roasting pan. Press crumb mixture onto the top and sides of the pork tenderloins. Bake for 35 to 45 minutes or until pork registers 165°F on a meat thermometer and coating is brown and crisp.

3. In small saucepan, combine remaining butter with wine and parsley. Bring to a boil over medium high heat and pour over tenderloins. Slice to serve.

Orange Pork Tenderloin

1 tablespoon olive oil
1 orange, sliced
1 pound pork tenderloin
½ teaspoon salt
⅛ teaspoon white pepper

½ teaspoon dried thyme leaves
1 orange, peeled and diced
½ cup orange juice
1 teaspoon orange zest

SERVES 4

CALORIES	261.83
FAT	9.06 GRAMS
SATURATED FAT	2.37 GRAMS
TRANS FAT	0.0 GRAMS
CARBOHYDRATES	11.27 GRAMS
CHOLESTEROL	89.53 MG

Fresh oranges scent a tender pork tenderloin in this wonderful and super-easy recipe.

1. Preheat oven to 425°F. Coat a small roasting pan with olive oil, then arrange orange slices in bottom. Place pork tenderloin on oranges; sprinkle with salt, pepper, and thyme leaves.

2. In small bowl, combine diced orange, orange juice, and orange zest. Spoon this mixture over the pork tenderloin. Roast for 25 minutes, then baste tenderloin. Continue roasting for 15 to 25 minutes longer or until internal temperature reads at least 155°F. Let stand for 10 minutes, then serve.

Grilled Steaks with Romesco Sauce

3 tomatoes
4 to 6 tablespoons olive oil, divided
8 cloves garlic, peeled
1 teaspoon salt
⅛ teaspoon pepper
⅛ teaspoon cayenne pepper
½ cup slivered almonds
¼ cup chopped walnuts
1 slice Oatmeal Bread (page 43), toasted
2 tablespoons diced pimentos
½ teaspoon paprika
1 tablespoon balsamic vinegar
6 (6-ounce) rib-eye steaks
1 teaspoon grill seasoning

SERVES 6

CALORIES	458.83
FAT	26.24 GRAMS
SATURATED FAT	4.83 GRAMS
TRANS FAT	0.22 GRAMS*
CARBOHYDRATES	9.97 GRAMS
CHOLESTEROL	78.17 MG

Romesco sauce is made with roasted tomatoes, garlic, and toasted almonds. It's traditionally served with fish or pork, but is delicious with grilled steak.

1. Make the sauce at least two hours before cooking the meat. Preheat oven to 400°F. Cut tomatoes in half and place, cut-side up, on a roasting pan. Drizzle with 1 tablespoon olive oil. Roast for 30 minutes, then add garlic to pan. Roast for 15 to 20 minutes longer or until tomatoes start to brown.

2. Place tomatoes and garlic in food processor with salt, peppers, almonds, walnuts, Oatmeal Bread, pimentos, paprika, and balsamic vinegar. Process until mixture is blended, then stream in enough olive oil to form a thick sauce; cover and refrigerate.

3. When ready to eat, remove sauce from refrigerator. Prepare and preheat grill. Sprinkle steaks with grill seasoning; grill 6" from medium coals for 15 to 20 minutes, turning once. Remove steaks to serving platter, cover with foil, and let stand for 10 minutes. Then serve with Romesco Sauce.

Standing Time

Beef needs standing time after it's cooked and before it's sliced or served. This allows the juice to redistribute from the surface, where it is drawn by heat, to the center of the meat. If you slice beef the second it's cooked, the juices will run out and you'll be left with flavorless, tough meat.

Pepperoni Pizza

SERVES 8

CALORIES	376.65
FAT	19.13 GRAMS
SATURATED FAT	9.93 GRAMS
TRANS FAT	0.29 GRAMS*
CARBOHYDRATES	36.09 GRAMS
CHOLESTEROL	49.07 MG

The secret to this pizza is the combination of pizza sauce and mustard. It's so much better than take-out!

1 tablespoon olive oil
1 onion, chopped
3 cloves garlic, minced
1 cup sliced mushrooms
1 (6-ounce) can tomato paste
1 (14-ounce) can diced tomatoes, undrained
2 tablespoons Dijon mustard
1 teaspoon Italian seasoning
1 Homemade Pizza Crust (page 49)
½ cup Three-Cheese Pasta Sauce (page 220)
1 (3-ounce) package sliced pepperoni
1 cup grated mozzarella cheese
1 cup grated Cheddar cheese

1. Preheat oven to 400°F. In large saucepan, heat olive oil over medium heat. Add onion, garlic, and mushrooms; cook and stir until tender, about 5 minutes. Add tomato paste and diced tomatoes. Simmer for 8 to 10 minutes or until sauce thickens. Stir in mustard and Italian seasoning.

2. Spread sauce over Pizza Crust and drizzle with Three-Cheese Pasta Sauce. Arrange pepperoni on pizza and sprinkle with mozzarella and Cheddar cheeses. Bake for 20 to 30 minutes or until crust is golden brown and cheese melts and begins to brown.

Asian Stuffed Peppers

1 pound ground pork
1 onion, chopped
½ cup chopped carrot
2 teaspoons grated fresh ginger root
½ cup long-grain rice
1-⅓ cups Beef Broth (page 119), divided
3 tablespoons soy sauce
3 tablespoons hoisin sauce
⅛ teaspoon cayenne pepper
½ teaspoon chile paste
6 red bell peppers

SERVES 6

CALORIES	303.44
FAT	12.22 GRAMS
SATURATED FAT	4.43 GRAMS
TRANS FAT	0.0 GRAMS
CARBOHYDRATES	27.89 GRAMS
CHOLESTEROL	55.83 MG

These well-flavored peppers are delicious served with a cool fruit salad and some steamed broccoli or asparagus.

1. Preheat oven to 375°F. In large saucepan, combine pork and onion; cook and stir until pork crumbles and turns brown. Add carrot and ginger; cook and stir for 3 minutes longer. Remove from saucepan with slotted spoon and set aside. Drain off drippings and discard; do not wipe saucepan.

2. Add rice to saucepan; cook and stir for 1 minute. Add 1 cup Beef Broth and soy sauce. Bring to a boil, reduce heat, cover, and simmer for 15 minutes or until rice is almost cooked. Remove from heat and stir in hoisin sauce, pepper, chile paste, and pork mixture.

3. Cut tops off bell peppers and remove ribs and seeds. Stuff with rice mixture. Arrange in a glass baking dish. Pour ⅓ cup Beef Broth around peppers. Cover and bake for 30 minutes, then uncover and bake for 10 to 15 minutes longer or until peppers are tender. Serve immediately.

Chile Paste

Chile paste is a combination of jalapeño and other chiles and garlic. It is very potent and adds a lot of flavor to recipes. Use it sparingly, and be sure that it is mixed very well with other ingredients. You don't want to have a lump of chile paste waiting for an unsuspecting diner!

Lemon Pork Scallops

SERVES 4

CALORIES	358.90
FAT	20.28 GRAMS
SATURATED FAT	7.22 GRAMS
TRANS FAT	0.15 GRAMS*
CARBOHYDRATES	6.94 GRAMS
CHOLESTEROL	122.06 MG

This recipe would be delicious served with a rice pilaf and some roasted asparagus for a springtime meal.

1 pound pork tenderloin
¼ cup flour
½ teaspoon salt
⅛ teaspoon white pepper
½ teaspoon dried thyme leaves
2 tablespoon butter, divided
2 tablespoons olive oil
1 shallot, minced
3 tablespoons lemon juice
½ cup Chicken Broth (page 120)
½ teaspoon grated lemon zest

1. Cut pork tenderloin into ¼" slices crosswise. Place on work surface and cover with wax paper or parchment paper. Pound pork pieces until ⅛" thick. On shallow plate, combine flour, salt, pepper, and thyme. Coat pork in flour mixture.

2. In large saucepan, combine 1 tablespoon butter and olive oil over medium heat. When mixture is hot, add pork scallops. Cook for 2 to 3 minutes on each side, turning once, until pork is almost cooked. Remove to plate. Add shallot to saucepan; cook and stir for 2 minutes. Then add lemon juice, Chicken Broth, and lemon zest; bring to a boil. Boil for 3 minutes until sauce is reduced. Return pork to saucepan and cook over medium heat for 1 to 2 minutes until pork is thoroughly cooked. Swirl in 1 tablespoon butter and serve pork with sauce.

Classic Meatballs

2 slices bacon
1 onion, chopped
2 tablespoons olive oil
3 slices Oatmeal Bread (page 43)
2 eggs
1 teaspoon salt
¼ teaspoon pepper
½ cup grated Parmesan cheese
1-½ pounds extra-lean ground beef
½ pound ground pork sausage

1. Preheat oven to 375°F. In food processor, combine bacon pieces and half of the onion; process until finely chopped. Place in large saucepan with olive oil and remaining chopped onion. Cook and stir for 5 to 8 minutes or until onion is tender. Remove from heat and pour into a large bowl.

2. Using your hands, make small bread crumbs from the Oatmeal Bread. Add to onion mixture along with eggs, salt, pepper, and cheese; mix well. Stir in beef and pork sausage and mix with your hands until combined. Form into 30 meatballs and place on a broiler pan.

3. Bake meatballs for 25 to 30 minutes or until meatballs are thoroughly cooked. Use immediately in pasta sauce or in other recipes, or cool and freeze.

Freezing Meatballs
Meatballs freeze beautifully. For best results, first flash-freeze them. Arrange them in a single layer on a cookie sheet, making sure they are not touching each other. Freeze until hard. Then pack the meatballs into a hard-sided container, label, and freeze up to 3 months. To thaw, let stand in the refrigerator overnight, or add directly to simmering sauce.

YIELDS 30 MEATBALLS (3 PER SERVING)

CALORIES	317.25
FAT	17.20 GRAMS
SATURATED FAT	6.26 GRAMS
TRANS FAT	0.27 GRAMS*
CARBOHYDRATES	9.60 GRAMS
CHOLESTEROL	126.67 MG

Two kinds of meat and Parmesan cheese make these meatballs tender and flavorful. Use them in Meatball Pizza (page 177), or Meatball Pitas (page 140).

Wild Rice Meatball Casserole

SERVES 6

CALORIES	500.66
FAT	22.15 GRAMS
SATURATED FAT	8.53 GRAMS
TRANS FAT	0.27 GRAMS*
CARBOHYDRATES	35.98 GRAMS
CHOLESTEROL	143.85 MG

Wild rice is a delicious accompaniment to tender meatballs. Serve this one-dish meal with a green salad and some apple slices.

3 slices bacon
1 onion, chopped
1 cup wild rice
1 cup Beef Broth (page 119)
1 cup water
½ cup light sour cream
1 cup sliced carrots
⅛ teaspoon pepper
½ teaspoon dried thyme leaves
18 Classic Meatballs (page 175), baked

1. Preheat oven to 375°F. In large saucepan, cook bacon until crisp. Remove bacon, drain on paper towels, crumble, and refrigerate. Cook onion in bacon drippings until crisp-tender, about 4 minutes. Add wild rice; cook and stir for 1 minute. Stir in Beef Broth and water. Bring to a boil, cover, and simmer for 25 minutes.

2. Remove from heat and stir in sour cream, carrots, pepper, and thyme. Then add Meatballs, stir gently. Pour mixture into 2-quart baking dish. Bake, covered, for 30 minutes, then uncover and sprinkle with bacon. Bake for 10 to 15 minutes longer or until rice is tender and casserole is hot. Serve immediately.

Meatball Pizza

1 Homemade Pizza Crust (page 49), partially baked
1 tablespoon olive oil
1 onion, chopped
½ cup grated carrot
1 (14-ounce) can diced tomatoes, undrained
1 (6-ounce) can tomato paste
½ cup Beef Broth (page 119)
2 tablespoons yellow mustard
1 teaspoon dried Italian seasoning
15 Classic Meatballs (page 175), baked
1 cup grated part-skim mozzarella cheese
1 cup grated Cheddar cheese

SERVES 8

CALORIES	498.85
FAT	23.71 GRAMS
SATURATED FAT	10.94 GRAMS
TRANS FAT	0.41 GRAMS*
CARBOHYDRATES	40.39 GRAMS
CHOLESTEROL	111.10 MG

Make your own pizza and control what goes into your body! You can add any cooked vegetable to this easy pizza.

1. Preheat oven to 400°F. Place Pizza Crust on cookie sheet and set aside. In large skillet, heat olive oil over medium heat. Add onion and carrot; cook and stir until onion is tender and carrot softens, about 5 to 6 minutes. Stir in tomatoes, tomato paste, Beef Broth, mustard, and Italian seasoning and stir well. Simmer for 15 minutes.

2. Cut Meatballs in half. Spread tomato sauce over Pizza Crust and arrange Meatballs on top. Sprinkle with cheeses. Bake for 20 to 25 minutes or until pizza crust is crisp and golden brown and cheeses are melted and start to brown. Let stand for 5 minutes, then serve.

Yellow Versus Dijon Mustard

Yellow, or American-style, mustard has the mildest flavor, while Dijon mustard is one of the strongest. Yellow mustard is made of white mustard seeds with vinegar, salt, and spices. Dijon mustard is made of brown mustard seeds, and includes white wine, wine vinegar, salt, and spices.

Pepperoni-Stuffed French Toast

SERVES 8–10

CALORIES	326.59
FAT	16.12 GRAMS
SATURATED FAT	6.99 GRAMS
TRANS FAT	0.17 GRAMS*
CARBOHYDRATES	31.96 GRAMS
CHOLESTEROL	107.48 MG

French Toast doesn't have to be sweet! This savory dish is a good choice for a cold winter's night.

1 loaf Italian Loaves (page 46)
1 (3-ounce) package low-fat cream cheese, softened
½ cup part-skim ricotta cheese
2 tablespoons heavy cream
3 ounces pepperoni, chopped
¼ cup finely sliced green onion
¾ cup milk
4 eggs
1 teaspoon salt
⅛ teaspoon cayenne pepper
¼ cup grated Parmesan cheese
3 tablespoons butter
1 tablespoon olive oil
1-½ cups Fresh and Spicy Salsa (page 38)

1. Slice bread into 1" slices. Cut a pocket in the side of each slice. In small bowl, combine cream cheese, ricotta cheese, and cream and beat until smooth. Stir in pepperoni and green onion. Stuff bread with this mixture.

2. In shallow bowl, mix milk, eggs, salt, cayenne pepper, and Parmesan cheese until combined. In large skillet, melt butter and olive oil together over medium heat.

3. Dip stuffed bread pieces into egg mixture, turning once to coat. Then cook bread in skillet, turning once, until dark golden brown. Serve immediately with Salsa.

Chapter 10

Seafood and Meatless Entrees

Seafood Pizza

SERVES 6–8

CALORIES	393.41
FAT	18.86 GRAMS
SATURATED FAT	10.79 GRAMS
TRANS FAT	0.26 GRAMS*
CARBOHYDRATES	28.65 GRAMS
CHOLESTEROL	103.23 MG

Gourmet pizza at home! This rich pizza is loaded with seafood. You can substitute cooked fish fillets for some of the shrimp or crab if you'd like.

1 Homemade Pizza Crust (page 49)
1 (8-ounce) package low-fat cream cheese
⅔ cup milk
1 tablespoon cornstarch
½ teaspoon salt
⅛ teaspoon cayenne pepper
½ teaspoon dried dill weed
2 tablespoons butter
4 cloves garlic, minced
1 red bell pepper, chopped
6 ounces raw cleaned shrimp
6 ounces fresh lump crabmeat
1 (6-ounce) can red salmon, drained
1-½ cups shredded baby Swiss cheese
¼ cup grated Parmesan cheese

1. Preheat oven to 400°F. Place Pizza Crust on cookie sheet and set aside. Cut cream cheese into cubes and, in medium microwave-safe bowl, combine with milk. Microwave on 50 percent power for 1 minute; remove and stir. Return to microwave and cook on 50 percent power for 1 to 2 minutes longer, or until cheese is melted. Stir with wire whisk until smooth, then add cornstarch, salt, pepper, and dill weed. Set aside.

2. In large saucepan, melt butter over medium heat. Add garlic and bell pepper; cook and stir until crisp-tender, about 3 minutes. Add shrimp; cook and stir until shrimp turn pink. Remove from heat.

3. Spread cream cheese mixture over Pizza Crust. Top with crabmeat and salmon. Remove shrimp and vegetables from saucepan with slotted spoon and arrange over crust. Sprinkle with cheeses.

4. Bake for 20 to 25 minutes or until cheese melts and begins to brown. Let stand for 5 minutes, then cut into slices to serve.

Seafood Newburg

¼ cup butter, divided
1 shallot, peeled and minced
2 cloves garlic, minced
8 ounces medium raw shrimp
8 ounces fish fillets
2 tablespoons flour
½ teaspoon salt

⅛ teaspoon cayenne pepper
¾ cup whole milk
¼ cup chili sauce
2 teaspoons Worcestershire sauce
2 English Muffins (page 60), split
1 tablespoon minced chives

SERVES 4	
CALORIES	381.95
FAT	18.92 GRAMS
SATURATED FAT	9.74 GRAMS
TRANS FAT	0.33 GRAMS*
CARBOHYDRATES	24.39 GRAMS
CHOLESTEROL	158.94 MG

This indulgent recipe is delicious and perfect to serve company for brunch.

1. In large skillet, melt 2 tablespoons butter over medium heat. Add shallot and garlic; cook and stir until tender, about 4 minutes. Add shrimp to skillet; cook and stir until shrimp turn pink, about 3 to 4 minutes. Remove with slotted spoon and set aside. Add fish fillets to skillet; cook for 4 minutes, then carefully turn and cook for 2 to 3 minutes longer or until fish flakes. Remove from skillet.

2. Add flour, salt, and cayenne pepper to skillet; cook and stir until bubbly. Add whole milk; cook and stir until mixture bubbles and thickens. Remove from heat and stir in chili sauce and Worcestershire sauce. Add reserved seafood.

3. With remaining butter, butter the split English Muffins and toast under broiler or in toaster oven. Return skillet to medium heat; cook and stir until heated through. Place Muffins on serving plates and spoon seafood mixture over; sprinkle with chives and serve immediately.

Fish Fillets
When a recipe calls for "fish fillets" or "white fish fillets" there are several good species to choose. Orange roughy, cod, grouper, mahi-mahi, tilapia, or striped bass fillets will always work well. They cook very quickly, so be sure to remove the fish from the pan or grill just as they begin to flake when you insert a fork into the flesh and twist.

Veggie Omelet

SERVES 4

CALORIES	361.49
FAT	27.26 GRAMS
SATURATED FAT	13.61 GRAMS
TRANS FAT	0.47 GRAMS*
CARBOHYDRATES	9.38 GRAMS
CHOLESTEROL	419.88 MG

This recipe is a great way to use up any leftover vegetables. Or you could just sauté any combination along with the onions.

3 tablespoons butter
1 onion, finely chopped
3 cloves garlic, minced
1 cup Roasted Vegetables (page 226)
7 eggs
⅓ cup whole milk
1 teaspoon salt
⅛ teaspoon pepper
1 cup shredded Havarti cheese

1. In large nonstick skillet, melt butter over medium heat. Add onion and garlic; cook and stir until crisp-tender, about 4 minutes. Add Roasted Vegetables; cook and stir just until hot. Remove vegetables from skillet with slotted spoon and set aside.

2. In medium bowl, combine eggs, milk, salt, and pepper and beat well until foamy. Place same skillet over medium heat and pour in egg mixture. Cook for 3 minutes without stirring, then run a spatula around the edges of the egg mixture, lifting to let uncooked egg flow underneath.

3. Continue cooking egg until bottom is lightly browned and egg is just set, about 5 to 9 minutes longer. Add reserved vegetables to omelet and sprinkle cheese over all. Carefully fold omelet in half, cover, and let cook for 2 minutes to melt cheese. Serve immediately.

Seafood-Stuffed Potatoes

4 baking potatoes
¼ pound small raw shrimp
¼ pound fresh lump crabmeat
¼ cup butter
½ cup finely chopped onion
2 cloves garlic, minced
¼ cup light cream
½ teaspoon salt
⅛ teaspoon cayenne pepper
2 cups shredded Gruyère cheese
1 teaspoon paprika

SERVES 8

CALORIES	270.37
FAT	15.91 GRAMS
SATURATED FAT	9.38 GRAMS
TRANS FAT	0.42 GRAMS*
CARBOHYDRATES	16.41 GRAMS
CHOLESTEROL	76.77 MG

You can serve these elegant potatoes as a main dish, or alongside a grilled steak for a surf and turf dinner.

1. Preheat oven to 400°F. Rinse potatoes, dry, and prick with fork. Place on baking rack and bake for 40 to 45 minutes, until soft when pressed with fingers. Remove potatoes from oven and let cool for 30 minutes.

2. Meanwhile, clean and devein shrimp. Pick over crabmeat to remove any cartilage. In medium saucepan, melt butter. Add onion and garlic; cook and stir until crisp-tender, about 4 minutes. Add shrimp; cook and stir just until shrimp turn pink; remove from heat.

3. When potatoes are cool enough to handle, cut in half lengthwise. Scoop out the flesh, leaving a ¼" thick shell. Place flesh in large mixing bowl. Drain butter from shrimp and vegetables and add to potatoes; mash until smooth. Add cream, salt, and cayenne pepper and beat well.

4. Fold in shrimp, vegetables, crabmeat, and cheese. Pile mixture back into potato shells. Sprinkle with paprika. Bake potatoes for 15 to 20 minutes longer or until hot and potatoes begin to brown. Serve immediately.

Baking Potatoes

The best potatoes for baking are russet potatoes, those oblong, golden-brown globes. Before they are put into the oven, wash them well, dry, and prick with a fork to prevent explosions in the oven. You can rub them with a bit of olive oil or butter for a crisper skin, but it's not necessary.

Onion Quiche

For onion lovers! This vegetarian quiche is a good choice for brunch; serve it with some homemade pastries and lots of fruit salad.

1 tablespoon olive oil
1 onion, chopped
1 onion, sliced
½ cup sour cream
½ cup whole milk
3 eggs, beaten
½ teaspoon salt
⅛ teaspoon cayenne pepper
2 tablespoons grated Romano cheese
1 cup shredded Muenster cheese
½ Recipe Traditional Pie Crust (page 260)

1. Preheat oven to 375°F. In large skillet, heat olive oil over medium heat. Add chopped and sliced onion; cook and stir for 8 to 9 minutes or until onions are translucent. Remove from heat and set aside.

2. In medium bowl, combine sour cream, milk, eggs, salt, and pepper and beat well. Sprinkle Romano cheese in bottom of Pie Crust. Remove onions from skillet with slotted spoon and arrange in an even layer. Sprinkle with Muenster cheese, then top with egg mixture. Bake for 35 to 45 minutes or until filling is set and golden brown in spots. Let stand for 5 minutes, then serve.

Quiche

Quiche is a good choice for breakfast or brunch. It freezes well. Simply cut the completely cooled quiche into slices, wrap well in freezer wrap, label, and freeze for up to 6 months. To defrost, reheat each individual slice on 50 percent power for 2 to 4 minutes, then on 100 percent power for 1 minute, until hot. Let stand for 3 minutes, then serve.

Vegetable Lasagna Rolls

2 potatoes, peeled
2 tablespoons butter
1 onion, diced
2 cloves garlic, minced
8 lasagna noodles
1 cup frozen peas
1 cup shredded carrots

1 (8-ounce) package low-fat cream cheese
½ cup milk
¼ cup Vegetable Broth (page 119)
1 cup shredded Colby cheese
1 (8-ounce) can tomato sauce
½ teaspoon dried Italian seasoning
¼ cup grated Parmesan cheese

1. Preheat oven to 350°F. Bring a large pot of salted water to a boil. Dice potatoes and add to large skillet along with butter. Cook over medium heat until potatoes start to soften, about 5 minutes. Add onion and garlic; cook and stir until onion and potatoes are tender, about 5 to 7 minutes longer.

2. In boiling water, cook lasagna noodles according to package directions until tender. Drain and rinse with cold water; drain again. Add peas and carrots to potato mixture; cook and stir for 3 minutes.

3. In microwave-safe bowl, combine cream cheese, milk, and Vegetable Broth and microwave on high for 2 minutes until cheese is melted; stir with wire whisk. Add Colby cheese and stir. Add ⅓ cup of this mixture to the vegetables in skillet.

4. Arrange noodles on work surface. Spread each with some of the vegetable mixture and roll up, starting with short end. Spoon half of cream-cheese sauce into 13" × 9" glass baking dish and arrange filled noodles, seam-side down, on sauce. Pour remaining sauce over, then top with tomato sauce; sprinkle with seasoning and Parmesan cheese. Bake for 35 to 40 minutes or until casserole is bubbling. Serve immediately.

SERVES 8

CALORIES	351.28
FAT	14.66 GRAMS
SATURATED FAT	8.71 GRAMS
TRANS FAT	0.26 GRAMS*
CARBOHYDRATES	39.42 GRAMS
CHOLESTEROL	40.25 MG

These lovely little rolls are filled with a cheesy vegetable blend. You could substitute any other vegetable in this recipe if you'd like.

Curried Shrimp Stir-Fry

SERVES 4

CALORIES	289.81
FAT	10.32 GRAMS
SATURATED FAT	1.18 GRAMS
TRANS FAT	0.05 GRAMS
CARBOHYDRATES	21.43 GRAMS
CHOLESTEROL	177.21 MG

Curry powder's flavor is developed when it's heated; that's why it's used to coat the shrimp in the first step of this simple and delicious stir-fry recipe.

1 pound medium raw shrimp
2 tablespoons cornstarch, divided
1 tablespoon curry powder, divided
½ teaspoon salt
⅛ teaspoon cayenne pepper
1 onion, sliced
4 cloves garlic, minced
2 cups sugar snap pea pods
1 yellow bell pepper, sliced
½ cup Chicken Broth (page 120)
¼ cup mango chutney
2 tablespoons lemon juice
2 tablespoons canola oil

1. Clean and devein shrimp and place in medium bowl. Sprinkle with 1 tablespoon cornstarch, 1 teaspoon curry powder, salt, and pepper and toss to coat. Set aside. Prepare all the vegetables. In a small bowl, combine Chicken Broth, chutney, lemon juice, 2 teaspoons curry powder, and 1 tablespoon cornstarch and set aside.

2. Heat a large wok or skillet over medium high heat. Add canola oil; add shrimp and stir-fry until shrimp curl and turn pink. Remove to a clean plate. Add onion and garlic; stir-fry for 2 minutes. Then add pea pods and bell pepper; stir-fry for 3 minutes longer. Return shrimp to skillet.

3. Stir chicken broth mixture and add to skillet. Continue stir-frying until sauce bubbles and thickens. Serve immediately over hot cooked rice.

Curry Powder

Curry powder is actually a blend of spices and herbs, not one single spice. It is commonly used in Indian cooking. The blend usually contains cinnamon, coriander, cumin, ginger, turmeric, pepper, cardamom, and cloves. You can make your own blend by combining different spices; have fun experimenting! Use it in Curried Chicken with Rice Pilaf (page 159).

Shrimp Kebabs

2 tablespoons olive oil
2 tablespoons lemon juice
2 tablespoons Dijon mustard
1 shallot, finely minced
1 teaspoon grated fresh ginger root
1 teaspoon salt

⅛ teaspoon cayenne pepper
1 teaspoon dried dill weed
2 pounds large raw shrimp
8 ounces button mushrooms
2 yellow bell peppers, sliced

1. In bowl, combine olive oil, lemon juice, mustard, shallot, ginger root, salt, pepper, and dill weed. Add shrimp, mushrooms, and sliced peppers and toss to coat. Cover and chill for 4 hours in the refrigerator, up to 8 hours.

2. When ready to cook, prepare and preheat grill. Thread shrimp, mushrooms, and peppers onto metal skewers. Grill 6" from medium coals, brushing with remaining marinade, for 5 minutes, turning once, until shrimp curl and turn pink and vegetables are crisp-tender. Discard remaining marinade.

SERVES 6

CALORIES	221.96
FAT	7.46 GRAMS
SATURATED FAT	1.16 GRAMS
TRANS FAT	0.0 GRAMS
CARBOHYDRATES	5.56 GRAMS
CHOLESTEROL	229.69 MG

Wow—this flavorful recipe is perfect for a summer night cookout. Serve it with rice pilaf and some crusty grilled bread.

Pesto Fish en Papillote

4 (6-ounce) white fish fillets
½ teaspoon salt
⅛ teaspoon white pepper
½ cup Basil Pesto (page 23)
1 lemon, thinly sliced

1 cup baby carrots
2 green onions, chopped
1 cup thinly sliced mushrooms
2 tablespoons olive oil

1. Preheat oven to 400°F. Cut four large rectangles of parchment paper; fold in half and cut half a heart shape. Unfold. Place one fish fillet close to the fold on one side of the heart.

2. Sprinkle fish with salt and pepper and spread pesto on each fillet. Top with lemon. Cut baby carrots in half lengthwise and arrange them, along with onions and mushrooms, around fish. Drizzle all with olive oil.

3. Fold heart shapes in half and crimp to close by folding the paper over tightly at the edge. Place on large cookie sheets and bake for 13 to 17 minutes, rotating cookie sheets halfway through baking time. Let your guests unwrap the bundles warning them to be careful of the steam.

SERVES 4

CALORIES	399.96
FAT	27.80 GRAMS
SATURATED FAT	4.60 GRAMS
TRANS FAT	0.0 GRAMS
CARBOHYDRATES	4.90 GRAMS
CHOLESTEROL	110.75 MG

This dish is a good choice for a birthday party because it's another present to unwrap! You could substitute thinly sliced zucchini or small peas for the vegetables.

Salmon with Dill

SERVES 4

CALORIES	323.40
FAT	17.98 GRAMS
SATURATED FAT	3.01 GRAMS
TRANS FAT	0.0 GRAMS
CARBOHYDRATES	1.89 GRAMS
CHOLESTEROL	105.46 MG

Serve these steaks for a Fourth of July barbecue, along with some potato salad and grilled corn on the cob.

1 teaspoon dill seed
½ teaspoon salt
⅛ teaspoon white pepper
4 salmon steaks
¼ cup orange juice
1 tablespoon lemon juice
2 tablespoons olive oil

1. In a mini food processor, coffee grinder, or with a mortar and pestle, grind dill seed with salt and pepper until very fine. Sprinkle on both sides of salmon steaks. Place salmon in a large glass baking dish. In small bowl, combine orange juice, lemon juice, and olive oil; pour over salmon. Cover and refrigerate for 1 hour.

2. When ready to cook, prepare and preheat grill. Remove salmon from marinade. Grill salmon 6" over medium coals until desired doneness (3 to 5 minutes for rare, 5 to 8 minutes for medium, 8 to 10 minutes for well done), turning once. Brush salmon with remaining marinade as it grills (discard unused marinade). Serve immediately.

Dill Seed Versus Weed

Dill seed is just that; the seed of the dill plant. Dill weed is the feathery fronds of the dill plant, which is usually dried and found in the baking aisle of your supermarket. Don't substitute one for the other; the flavor of dill seed is intense and smoky, while dill weed is lighter and more lemony.

Polenta Seafood Casserole

3 tablespoons butter, divided
1 onion, chopped
2 yellow summer squash, sliced
1 zucchini, sliced
1 tablespoon flour
2 tablespoons yellow cornmeal
½ teaspoon salt
⅛ teaspoon white pepper

½ teaspoon dried thyme leaves
1-½ cups Vegetable Broth (page 119)
¾ cup light sour cream
1 cup shredded Havarti cheese
6 ounces fresh lump crabmeat
6 ounces cooked small shrimp
2 slices White Bread (page 44)
⅓ cup grated Romano cheese

SERVES 6

CALORIES	338.49
FAT	18.33 GRAMS
SATURATED FAT	10.97 GRAMS
TRANS FAT	0.39 GRAMS*
CARBOHYDRATES	21.51 GRAMS
CHOLESTEROL	121.98 MG

This elegant casserole layers polenta with sautéed squash, zucchini, and seafood. You can make it ahead of time and keep it in the fridge—add 10 to 15 minutes to the baking time.

1. Preheat oven to 350°F. In large saucepan, melt 2 tablespoons butter over medium heat. Add onion; cook and stir until crisp-tender, about 4 minutes. Add yellow squash; cook and stir until squash begins to soften. Remove squash and onions with slotted spoon and set aside. Add zucchini to saucepan; cook and stir until it begins to soften, about 4 to 5 minutes. Remove with slotted spoon and combine with the onions and squash, leaving liquid in pan.

2. Add flour, cornmeal, salt, pepper, and thyme leaves to saucepan. Cook and stir until mixture bubbles. Gradually stir in Broth; cook and stir until thickened. Then add sour cream and Havarti cheese; remove from heat.

3. Grease a 2-quart casserole with unsalted butter. Place half of the vegetable mixture into the bottom of the casserole. Add the crabmeat, then half of the cornmeal mixture. Layer remaining vegetable mixture, shrimp, and remaining cornmeal mixture on top. Melt remaining 1 tablespoon butter. Make crumbs out of bread and mix with melted butter and Romano cheese; sprinkle over casserole.

4. Bake for 35 to 45 minutes or until casserole bubbles and bread crumb topping is golden brown. Let stand for 5 minutes before serving.

Salmon Rice Loaf

SERVES 4

CALORIES	376.64
FAT	17.95 GRAMS
SATURATED FAT	6.89 GRAMS
TRANS FAT	0.19 GRAMS*
CARBOHYDRATES	23.24 GRAMS
CHOLESTEROL	169.43 MG

This comforting, homey dish is true classic comfort food. Serve with mashed potatoes and peas sautéed in butter.

1 tablespoon butter
½ cup finely chopped onion
¼ cup shredded carrot
½ cup brown rice
1 cup Vegetable Broth (page 119)
2 eggs, beaten
1 (14-ounce) can sockeye salmon, drained
½ cup shredded Havarti cheese
1 tablespoon lemon juice
1 teaspoon dried dill weed
½ teaspoon salt
⅛ teaspoon white pepper

1. Preheat oven to 350°F. Grease a 9" × 5" loaf pan with unsalted butter and set aside. In medium skillet, melt 1 tablespoon butter over medium heat. Add onion; cook and stir for 3 minutes. Add carrot; cook and stir for 2 minutes longer. Add brown rice; cook and stir for 2 minutes. Add Vegetable Broth and bring to a boil. Reduce heat, cover, and simmer for 35 to 40 minutes or until rice is tender.

2. When rice is done, add eggs, drained and flaked salmon, cheese, lemon juice, and seasonings to pan; stir well. Spoon into prepared loaf pan and smooth top. Bake for 40 to 50 minutes or until loaf is set and top is browned. Let cool for 5 minutes, then slice and serve.

Canned Salmon

The skin and bones you'll find in a can of salmon are edible. You can eat them (and get lots of calcium) or discard them; it's your choice! Canned salmon comes in two varieties: pink, which is less expensive, and red sockeye, which is more expensive but very flavorful. You can also now find salmon in a pouch, which has less liquid.

Fried Fish

2 pounds fish fillets
1 cup beer
½ cup water
1 teaspoon Tabasco sauce
1 egg

¾ cup all-purpose flour, divided
¼ cup ground oatmeal
1 teaspoon salt
¼ teaspoon cayenne pepper
3 cups canola oil

1. Rinse fish and pat dry with paper towels. Sprinkle with 2 tablespoons flour. In shallow bowl, combine beer, water, Tabasco sauce, and egg, and beat well. Add remaining flour, oatmeal, salt, and cayenne pepper and mix just until combined.

2. In deep skillet, heat canola oil over medium high heat until it reaches 375°F. One at a time, dip fish into the batter and let excess drip off for a few minutes. Carefully place fish in hot oil. Fry for 8 to 10 minutes, turning once, until coating is deep golden brown. Drain on paper towels and serve.

SERVES 8	
CALORIES	244.16
FAT	8.94 GRAMS
SATURATED FAT	0.90 GRAMS
TRANS FAT	0.05 GRAMS
CARBOHYDRATES	14.18 GRAMS
CHOLESTEROL	75.17 MG

Adding some ground oatmeal to the batter makes the fish crisper and adds a nice nutty flavor.

Crispy Baked Fillets

6 red snapper fillets
2 tablespoons flour
1 teaspoon salt
⅛ teaspoon cayenne pepper
1 egg
¼ cup milk
1 cup crushed Crisp Cheese Crackers (page 67)
1 tablespoon olive oil

1. Preheat oven to 450°F. Pat fish dry and sprinkle with flour, salt, and pepper. In shallow bowl, combine egg and milk and beat until combined. Place crushed Crackers on a plate. Dip fish into egg mixture, then into Crackers to coat.

2. Brush a 15" × 10" jelly roll pan with olive oil and arrange fillets in pan. Bake for 20 minutes or until fish flakes when tested with fork. Serve immediately.

SERVES 6	
CALORIES	363.71
FAT	12.19 GRAMS
SATURATED FAT	4.92 GRAMS
TRANS FAT	0.14 GRAMS*
CARBOHYDRATES	10.27 GRAMS
CHOLESTEROL	132.62 MG

Crisp Cheese Crackers (you'll need about 12) form a flavorful and crunchy coating on these tender and moist fish fillets.

Shrimp Puttanesca

SERVES 4–6

CALORIES	454.20
FAT	9.81 GRAMS
SATURATED FAT	1.47 GRAMS
TRANS FAT	0.0 GRAMS
CARBOHYDRATES	55.35 GRAMS
CHOLESTEROL	115.98 MG

Anchovies add a meaty richness to this spicy sauce. Don't overcook the shrimp; they're done when they curl and turn pink.

3 tablespoons olive oil
1 onion, chopped
6 cloves garlic, minced
½ teaspoon crushed red pepper flakes
2 anchovy fillets, minced
2 (14-ounce) cans diced tomatoes, undrained
1 (6-ounce) can tomato paste
⅛ teaspoon pepper
1 cup white wine
¼ cup capers, rinsed
1 pound medium raw shrimp
12 ounces linguine pasta

1. In large skillet, heat olive oil over medium heat. Add onion and garlic; cook and stir for 4 minutes until almost tender. Add red pepper flakes and anchovy fillets. Reduce heat and simmer until anchovies begin to melt into the sauce, about 5 minutes.

2. Stir in tomatoes, tomato paste, pepper, and wine. Bring to a boil, then reduce heat, partially cover, and simmer for 20 to 25 minutes, stirring occasionally, until sauce thickens. Stir in capers and shrimp and bring back to a simmer.

3. Bring a large pot of salted water to a boil. Add pasta; cook until pasta is al dente, according to package directions. When shrimp are pink, remove sauce from heat. Drain pasta and stir into sauce. Serve immediately.

Seared Scallops on Orange Pilaf

1 pound sea scallops
1 tablespoon olive oil
½ cup orange juice, divided
3 tablespoons butter, divided
1 onion, finely chopped
2 cloves garlic, minced
½ cup chopped mushrooms

¾ cup basmati rice
1 cup water
½ teaspoon salt
⅛ teaspoon white pepper
1 orange, peeled and diced
⅓ cup sliced almonds

SERVES 4

CALORIES	406.22
FAT	14.32 GRAMS
SATURATED FAT	4.59 GRAMS
TRANS FAT	0.23 GRAMS*
CARBOHYDRATES	45.06 GRAMS
CHOLESTEROL	52.65 MG

A rice pilaf scented with orange complements these little scallops. Don't let the scallops marinate for more than 30 minutes, or their texture will change.

1. If there is a small muscle attached to each scallop, pull it off and discard. Place scallops on plate; sprinkle with olive oil and 1 tablespoon orange juice; set aside.

2. Meanwhile, in heavy saucepan melt 1 tablespoon butter. Add onion and garlic; cook and stir until tender, about 5 minutes. Add mushrooms; cook and stir for 2 minutes longer. Add rice; cook and stir for 1 minute. Add water and remaining orange juice; bring to a boil. Reduce heat, cover, and simmer for 20 to 25 minutes.

3. When rice is almost done, melt 2 tablespoons butter in another saucepan over medium high heat. When butter sizzles, sprinkle salt and pepper over scallops and add them to the pan. Cook on first side for 3 minutes, then carefully turn and cook for 2 to 3 minutes on second side until scallops are just opaque. Remove from heat.

4. When rice is done, stir in orange and almonds. Place on serving plate and top with scallops. Serve immediately.

Scallops: Bay or Sea?
There are actually three kinds of scallops: bay, sea, and calico. Bay scallops are small, usually around 40 per pound, tender, and more expensive. Sea scallops are larger, less expensive, usually around 10 per pound. And calico scallops are the smallest and least expensive of all; sometimes they are passed off as bay scallops, so beware!

Seafood Enchiladas

SERVES 6–8

CALORIES	431.92
FAT	22.43 GRAMS
SATURATED FAT	11.29 GRAMS
TRANS FAT	0.42 GRAMS*
CARBOHYDRATES	31.93 GRAMS
CHOLESTEROL	98.36 MG

This elegant recipe is perfect for company. You can make it ahead of time and refrigerate until serving; add 10 to 15 minutes to the baking time.

4 tablespoons butter, divided	½ teaspoon salt
1 tablespoon olive oil	⅛ teaspoon cayenne pepper
2 shallots, finely chopped	1-½ cups milk
3 cloves garlic, minced	1 cup shredded Colby cheese
⅓ pound small shrimp	1 cup shredded Havarti cheese
⅓ pound lump crabmeat	½ cup Fresh and Spicy Salsa (page 38)
⅓ pound orange roughy fish fillets	12 (6") flour tortillas
3 tablespoons flour	¼ cup grated Cotija cheese

1. Preheat oven to 350°F. In large skillet, melt together 2 tablespoons butter and olive oil over medium heat. Add shallots and garlic; cook and stir until tender, about 5 minutes.

2. Meanwhile, clean and devein shrimp and pick over crabmeat to remove cartilage. Add shrimp to pan with shallots; cook and stir until pink, about 3 to 4 minutes. Remove shrimp and vegetables from skillet with slotted spoon and place in large bowl with crabmeat. Add fish fillets to pan; cover and cook for 4 to 7 minutes or until fish flakes when tested with fork; add to shrimp and crabmeat.

3. Add another 2 tablespoons butter to skillet. Add flour, salt, and pepper; cook and stir over medium heat until bubbly, about 3 minutes. Add milk; cook and stir with wire whisk until mixture thickens and bubbles, about 5 minutes. Stir in 1 cup Colby and Havarti cheeses and Salsa; stir until blended.

4. Combine 1 cup of the Salsa mixture with seafood in bowl; mix well so fish fillets break up. Fill flour tortillas with seafood mixture and roll up; place in 13" × 9" glass baking dish. Pour remaining Salsa mixture over and sprinkle with Cotija cheese. Bake for 30 to 40 minutes or until casserole bubbles and cheese melts and begins to brown.

Orange Roughy with Almonds

2 tablespoons butter
4 cloves garlic, minced
½ cup sliced almonds
1 pound orange roughy fillets
2 tablespoons flour
½ teaspoon salt
⅛ teaspoon pepper
½ cup pineapple juice
2 tablespoons lemon juice

1. In heavy skillet, melt butter over medium heat. Add garlic and almonds; cook and stir until garlic is tender and almonds begin to brown, about 4 minutes. Remove almonds and garlic from skillet with slotted spoon and set aside.

2. Sprinkle fillets with flour, salt, and pepper on both sides and add to skillet. Cook over medium heat, turning once, until fillets flake when tested with a fork, about 5 to 7 minutes total. Place fish on serving plate. Add pineapple juice and lemon juice to skillet and increase heat to high. Boil rapidly for 2 to 3 minutes until thickened. Pour over fish and sprinkle with almonds and garlic.

Orange Roughy

Orange roughy sudden became very popular in the 1980s. Because these fish live so deep under the ocean's surface, they weren't harvested until new fishing methods were developed. They live for a very long time—up to 150 years. The fish, which is native to New Zealand, has an orange-pink body and delicate, light-flavored flesh.

SERVES 4

CALORIES	240.62
FAT	12.46 GRAMS
SATURATED FAT	4.12 GRAMS
TRANS FAT	0.15 GRAMS*
CARBOHYDRATES	10.93 GRAMS
CHOLESTEROL	83.25 MG

This elegant recipe is perfect for company. It's low calorie, flavorful, and beautiful to look at, too.

Wild Rice Crab Quiche

SERVES 8

CALORIES	428.28
FAT	27.41 GRAMS
SATURATED FAT	16.47 GRAMS
TRANS FAT	0.49 GRAMS*
CARBOHYDRATES	27.66 GRAMS
CHOLESTEROL	174.40 MG

Quiches are perfect for brunch, and this one, with wild rice and crabmeat, is very special. Serve with a fruit salad and brownies for dessert.

½ cup wild rice
1 cup water
¼ cup butter
1 onion, chopped
2 cloves garlic, minced
½ cup chopped green pepper
2 tablespoons flour
½ cup whole milk
¾ cup light sour cream
4 eggs
⅛ teaspoon pepper
½ teaspoon dried thyme leaves
1 cup shredded Havarti cheese
½ recipe Traditional Pie Crust (page 260)
8 ounces fresh lump crabmeat, drained
¼ cup grated Parmesan cheese

1. In small saucepan, combine wild rice and water. Bring to a boil, cover pan, reduce heat, and simmer for 35 to 40 minutes or until rice is tender. Drain if necessary.

2. Preheat oven to 350°F. In heavy saucepan, melt butter over medium heat. Add onion and garlic; cook and stir until crisp-tender, about 5 minutes. Add green pepper; cook and stir for 1 minute longer. Stir in flour; cook and stir until bubbly. Add milk; cook and stir until thick.

3. Remove from heat and stir in sour cream, eggs, pepper, and thyme. Sprinkle a layer of Havarti cheese in pie crust. Top with crabmeat, then remaining Havarti cheese. Pour egg mixture into pie crust, shaking the pie so the filling settles over the cheese. Sprinkle with Parmesan cheese.

4. Bake for 40 to 45 minutes or until quiche is puffed and golden brown. Let stand for 5 minutes, then cut into wedges and serve.

Olive Pizza

1 tablespoon olive oil
8 cloves garlic
1 onion, chopped
1 red bell pepper, chopped
1 cup part-skim ricotta cheese
½ teaspoon salt
⅛ teaspoon cayenne pepper
1 Homemade Pizza Crust (page 49), prebaked
½ cup sliced green olives
½ cup sliced black olives
1 cup shredded CoJack cheese
¼ cup grated Cotija cheese

SERVES 8	
CALORIES	291.44
FAT	14.63 GRAMS
SATURATED FAT	7.28 GRAMS
TRANS FAT	0.20 GRAMS*
CARBOHYDRATES	28.99 GRAMS
CHOLESTEROL	33.33 MG

You can top this simple pizza with any vegetable. Try adding artichoke hearts, steamed asparagus, green bell peppers, or sliced summer squash.

1. Preheat oven to 375°F. In medium skillet, heat olive oil over medium heat. Add whole cloves garlic; toast garlic for 4 to 6 minutes, stirring frequently, until cloves are golden. Remove from skillet. Add onion to skillet; cook and stir until tender, about 5 minutes; remove. Add red bell pepper; cook and stir for 2 minutes. Place garlic and onion in small bowl; mash together. Stir in ricotta cheese, salt, and pepper.

2. Spread ricotta mixture over pizza crust. Top with red bell pepper, olives, and cheeses. Bake for 20 to 30 minutes or until crust is golden brown and cheese is melted and beginning to brown. Cut into pieces and serve.

About Olives

You can't eat fresh olives right off the tree! They contain a substance called oleuropein, which is very bitter. This carbohydrate is removed by soaking the olives in sodium hydroxide, a very powerful base. Green olives are fermented before being bottled. Black, or ripe, olives are not fermented, so they have a milder taste.

Apple and Onion Strata

Stratas are very inexpensive foods to feed a crowd. Have a brunch party and serve this along with some orange juice, coffee, and a nice fruit salad.

2 tablespoons butter
1 onion, finely chopped
1 apple, peeled and chopped
8 eggs
1-½ cups milk
2 tablespoons yellow mustard
½ teaspoon salt
8 slices White Bread (page 44), cubed
1-½ cups shredded Swiss cheese
¼ cup grated Parmesan cheese

1. In medium saucepan, melt butter over medium heat. Add onion; cook and stir for 5 minutes. Then add apple; cook and stir for 3 to 5 minutes or until onion begins to caramelize and apples are tender.

2. Grease a 13" × 9" glass baking dish with butter. In large bowl, combine eggs, milk, mustard, and salt and beat well. Layer one-third of bread cubes in prepared dish. Sprinkle with half of Swiss cheese, then half of onion mixture. Repeat layers, ending with bread cubes. Pour egg mixture over all, gently pressing the bread cubes into the egg mixture. Sprinkle with Parmesan cheese, cover, and refrigerate for 8 to 24 hours.

3. When ready to eat, preheat oven to 350°F. Bake strata, uncovered, for 55 to 65 minutes or until golden brown and set. Let stand for 5 minutes on wire rack, then serve.

About Stratas

Once you know how to make a strata, you can vary the flavor and ingredients. If you have leftover hamburgers from a cookout, crumble the burger and layer it in the strata. Use cooked chicken or turkey. Add other vegetables, especially leftovers that are crisply cooked. And any kind of bread and cheese will work well. Have fun!

Bread-Crumb Frittata

2 slices Orange Cracked-Wheat Bread (page 56), toasted
2 tablespoons butter
½ cup frozen spinach, thawed and drained
7 eggs
¼ cup milk
½ teaspoon salt
Dash white pepper
¼ cup grated Parmesan cheese
1 tomato, chopped
¼ cup chopped fresh basil

SERVES 4

CALORIES	271.53
FAT	17.62 GRAMS
SATURATED FAT	8.15 GRAMS
TRANS FAT	0.19 GRAMS*
CARBOHYDRATES	12.06 GRAMS
CHOLESTEROL	394.00 MG

Leftover toast from breakfast? Save it to make this wonderful and filling frittata the next day.

1. Place toasted bread in plastic food-storage bag and close bag; pound bread with rolling pin to make crumbs. In a large, ovenproof skillet, melt 2 tablespoons butter over medium heat. Add spinach; cook and stir until water evaporates, about 4 to 7 minutes.

2. Meanwhile, preheat broiler. In large bowl, combine eggs with milk, salt, and pepper and beat well. Pour into skillet with spinach. Cook over medium heat until mixture starts to set, about 4 minutes. Then sprinkle bread crumbs over eggs. Continue cooking, lifting edges of frittata to allow uncooked eggs to flow underneath.

3. When eggs are almost set, sprinkle with cheese and place under broiler. Broil for 3 to 6 minutes, watching carefully, until frittata is puffed and top begins to turn brown. Meanwhile, combine chopped tomato and basil. Remove frittata from oven, cut into quarters, top with tomato mixture, and serve.

Frittata Versus Omelet
A frittata is typically denser than an omelet, and can be served warm or even cold. In Italy frittatas are often served as appetizers or street snacks. A classic omelet should be very fluffy and has to be eaten immediately; it's delicate and ethereal. You can make this frittata the night before, then eat it cold for breakfast the next day.

French Toast

SERVES 6–8

CALORIES	366.23
FAT	17.84 GRAMS
SATURATED FAT	6.34 GRAMS
TRANS FAT	0.12 GRAMS*
CARBOHYDRATES	44.66 GRAMS
CHOLESTEROL	120.33 MG

This French toast is the best! A crisp coating of ground pecans, cinnamon, and powdered sugar means you (almost) don't need maple syrup.

3 eggs
¾ cup milk
¼ cup flour, divided
¼ cup powdered sugar, divided
¼ teaspoon salt
1 tablespoon vanilla extract
½ cup ground pecans
1 teaspoon cinnamon
¼ cup butter
12 slices Raisin Spice Swirl Bread (page 42)

1. In shallow bowl, combine eggs, milk, 2 tablespoons flour, 2 tablespoons powdered sugar, salt, and vanilla and beat well. On plate, combine pecans, 2 tablespoons flour, 2 tablespoons powdered sugar, and cinnamon.

2. In large skillet over medium heat, melt butter. Dip bread slices into the egg mixture, turning to coat, then into the pecan mixture, pressing to coat. Pan fry bread, turning once, until crisp and golden brown, about 4 to 5 minutes per side. Serve immediately.

Chapter 11

Pasta

Curried Pasta and Shrimp

SERVES 4

CALORIES	424.75
FAT	11.39 GRAMS
SATURATED FAT	4.53 GRAMS
TRANS FAT	0.15 GRAMS*
CARBOHYDRATES	48.90 GRAMS
CHOLESTEROL	187.52 MG

This unusual pasta, served without cheese, is an Indian take on a typical Italian dish. Serve it with Roasted Vegetables (page 226).

1 tablespoon olive oil
2 tablespoons butter
1 pound raw large shrimp
12 ounces fettuccine pasta
1 onion, chopped
1 tablespoon curry powder
1 apple, peeled and chopped
½ teaspoon salt
½ cup mango chutney

1. Bring a large pot of salted water to a boil. Meanwhile, in large saucepan combine olive oil and butter over medium heat. When butter foams, add shrimp; cook and stir until shrimp are curled and pink, about 3 to 4 minutes. Remove shrimp from pan.

2. Add pasta to boiling water; cook until al dente according to package directions. Meanwhile, add onion and curry powder to saucepan. Cook and stir until onion is tender, about 5 minutes. Add apples to pan, sprinkle with salt, and return shrimp to pan.

3. When pasta is done, drain, reserving ¼ cup pasta water. Add drained pasta along with pasta water to shrimp mixture. Toss over medium heat for 3 to 4 minutes, then add chutney and toss until combined. Serve immediately.

About Chutney
Chutney is a sweet and tart condiment, often used in Indian cooking. The type you buy in the supermarket is usually canned, and is most often made from mango, ginger, raisins, vinegar, sugar, tamarind, and spices. It is delicious added to mayonnaise and used as a sandwich spread, or can be added to cream cheese for an appetizer spread.

Pasta with Spinach Pesto

½ cup Basil Pesto (page 23)
1 cup frozen chopped spinach, thawed and drained
1 (3-ounce) package cream cheese, softened
½ teaspoon dried basil leaves
Pinch grated nutmeg
1 tablespoon lemon juice
2 tablespoons heavy cream
1 pound fettuccine pasta
½ cup grated Romano cheese

1. In food processor or blender, combine Pesto, spinach, cream cheese, basil, nutmeg, lemon juice, and heavy cream; process or blend until smooth.

2. Bring a large pot of salted water to a boil. Add fettuccine; cook until al dente according to package directions. Drain pasta, reserving about ¼ cup of the pasta cooking water. Return pasta to pot and stir in the pesto mixture along with reserved cooking water. Cook and stir over low heat until sauce is creamy and coats pasta. Sprinkle with Romano cheese and serve.

SERVES 6	
CALORIES	382.69
FAT	24.65 GRAMS
SATURATED FAT	9.28 GRAMS
TRANS FAT	0.15 GRAMS*
CARBOHYDRATES	27.37 GRAMS
CHOLESTEROL	43.04 MG

Romano cheese is made from goat's milk and has a slightly richer, sharper taste than Parmesan cheese.

Fresh Tomato with Angel Hair Pasta

SERVES 4–6

CALORIES	276.78
FAT	17.73 GRAMS
SATURATED FAT	1.96 GRAMS
TRANS FAT	0.0 MG
CARBOHYDRATES	25.29 GRAMS
CHOLESTEROL	24.95 MG

This sauce should only be made in the summer when you can find vine-ripened fresh red tomatoes.

½ cup pine nuts
4 ripe beefsteak tomatoes
¼ cup extra-virgin olive oil
1 tablespoon lemon juice
¼ cup packed fresh basil leaves
½ teaspoon salt
⅛ teaspoon white pepper
1 pound angel hair pasta

1. Bring a large pot of salted water to a boil. Since the pasta cooks so quickly, have the sauce ready before you start cooking the pasta. Place small skillet over medium heat for 3 minutes. Add pine nuts; cook and stir for 3 to 5 minutes or until nuts begin to brown and are fragrant. Remove from heat and pour nuts into serving bowl.

2. Chop tomatoes into ½" pieces and add to pine nuts along with olive oil, lemon juice, basil, salt, and pepper. Add pasta to the boiling water; cook and stir until al dente, according to package directions. Drain and add to tomato mixture in bowl. Toss gently and serve immediately.

Fresh Basil

If you have a garden, by all means grow basil; it's easy to grow and requires very little maintenance. You can usually find fresh basil in the produce aisle of your supermarket. Or grow it on a sunny windowsill. There are lots of kits available at the market or on the Internet. Just be sure to use the basil before the plant starts to flower.

Chicken and Broccoli Pasta

4 boneless, skinless chicken breasts
2 tablespoons flour
½ teaspoon salt
⅛ teaspoon cayenne pepper
2 tablespoons olive oil
3 cloves garlic, minced
1 pound fettuccine pasta
1 (12-ounce) bag prepared broccoli florets
1 (14-ounce) can chopped tomatoes, drained
½ cup Basil Pesto (page 23)
¼ cup heavy cream

1. Bring a large pot of salted water to a boil. Meanwhile, cut chicken breasts into 1-½" pieces. Sprinkle with flour, salt, and cayenne pepper; toss and set aside. In large saucepan, heat olive oil over medium heat until it ripples. Add garlic; cook and stir for 1 minute. Add chicken; cook and stir for 4 to 6 minutes or until chicken is almost cooked.

2. Add pasta to boiling water and cook for 5 minutes. Then add broccoli to the pot; bring back to a boil and cook for 3 to 4 minutes longer until pasta is al dente and broccoli is tender. Drain and add to saucepan with chicken. Stir in tomatoes, Pesto, and cream; cook and stir until thoroughly heated, about 4 minutes. Serve immediately.

Fresh Broccoli

You can often find already prepared vegetables in the produce aisle of your supermarket. If the store has a salad bar, you can buy vegetables there. You can also substitute frozen broccoli florets for fresh; just thaw and drain, don't cook them before using in the recipe. Or buy a fresh bunch; just cut off the florets, leaving each with about a 1-½" stem.

SERVES 8

CALORIES	464.34
FAT	17.87 GRAMS
SATURATED FAT	4.40 GRAMS
TRANS FAT	0.07 GRAMS*
CARBOHYDRATES	50.91 GRAMS
CHOLESTEROL	48.87 MG

This fresh and brightly colored chicken and pasta dish is perfect for a family dinner. Enjoy it with some garlic bread and a spinach salad.

Baked Caramelized Onion Ziti

For onion lovers! The caramelized onions become very sweet when they turn brown, adding great flavor to this layered casserole.

1 pound ziti pasta
1 tablespoon olive oil
2 tablespoons butter
3 onions, chopped
6 cloves garlic, minced
1 shallot, minced
2 teaspoons sugar
½ cup light sour cream
½ cup part-skim ricotta cheese
½ cup cottage cheese

1 tablespoon cornstarch
1 (26-ounce) jar pasta sauce
1 (6-ounce) can tomato paste
1 (15-ounce) can tomato sauce
1 cup water
1 teaspoon dried Italian seasoning
2 cups shredded part-skim
   mozzarella cheese
½ cup grated Parmesan cheese

1. Preheat oven to 350°F. Bring a large pot of salted water to a boil. Add pasta; cook according to package directions. Meanwhile, in large skillet combine olive oil and butter over medium heat. Add onion; cook and stir until onion begins to turn brown, about 8 to 10 minutes. Add garlic and shallot; sprinkle with sugar. Cook and stir until onions are browned, about another 5 minutes. Remove from heat.

2. In medium bowl, combine sour cream, ricotta, cottage cheese, and cornstarch and mix well. Stir in onion mixture; set aside. To skillet used for onions, add pasta sauce, tomato paste, tomato sauce, water, and Italian seasoning; bring to a simmer over medium heat.

3. When pasta is done, drain and rinse with cold water; drain again. Stir pasta into the pasta sauce mixture. Grease a 13" × 9" glass baking dish with unsalted butter. Add half of the pasta mixture, half of the ricotta mixture, then half of the mozzarella cheese. Repeat layers. Sprinkle top with Parmesan cheese.

4. Bake casserole for 30 to 40 minutes or until sauce is bubbling and cheeses melt and begin to brown. Let stand for 5 minutes, then serve.

Wild Rice and Onion Pasta

½ cup wild rice
1 cup water
½ pound linguine pasta
1 tablespoon olive oil
2 tablespoons butter
2 onions, chopped
3 cloves garlic, minced
½ cup grated Parmesan cheese
¼ cup chopped parsley
¼ cup chopped fresh basil

1. In small saucepan, combine wild rice and water. Bring to a boil over high heat, cover, reduce heat, and simmer for 35 to 40 minutes or until wild rice is tender. Meanwhile, bring a large pot of salted water to a boil. Add linguine pasta and cook.

2. In heavy saucepan, combine olive oil and butter over medium heat. Add onions and garlic; cook and stir until onions begin to caramelize, about 10 to 15 minutes.

3. When pasta is done, drain in a colander, reserving about ⅓ cup of the pasta water. Add pasta and reserved water to skillet with onions and reduce heat to low. Add wild rice to skillet; cook and stir for 2 minutes. Sprinkle with cheese, parsley, and basil, stir, and serve immediately.

Wild Rice
Wild rice is actually not a rice, but the seed of a grass plant. It grows wild in northern Minnesota; the highest quality rice is harvested by Native Americans who glide through lakes in canoes. Always use long-grain wild rice. Rice with broken grains will cook up mushy and tasteless.

SERVES 4

CALORIES	319.66
FAT	13.64 GRAMS
SATURATED FAT	6.42 GRAMS
TRANS FAT	0.23 GRAMS*
CARBOHYDRATES	38.89 GRAMS
CHOLESTEROL	45.06 MG

Caramelized onions and garlic add fabulous flavor to tender pasta and chewy wild rice. Fresh parsley and basil are the perfect finishing touch.

Lemon Garlic Pasta

SERVES 4–6

CALORIES	313.39
FAT	11.18 GRAMS
SATURATED FAT	5.50 GRAMS
TRANS FAT	0.23 GRAMS*
CARBOHYDRATES	44.68 GRAMS
CHOLESTEROL	25.77 MG

This creamy pasta tastes like shrimp scampi, minus the shrimp. Serve it with steamed asparagus and a fruit salad for a light spring meal.

1 tablespoon olive oil
2 tablespoons butter
4 cloves garlic, minced
½ cup heavy cream
⅓ cup whole milk

2 teaspoons Dijon mustard
¼ teaspoon salt
12 ounces spaghetti pasta
2 tablespoons lemon juice
1 teaspoon grated lemon zest

1. Bring a large pot of salted water to a boil. Meanwhile, in large saucepan combine olive oil and butter over medium heat. Add garlic; cook and stir until garlic is tender, about 3 minutes. Add cream, milk, mustard, and salt; reduce heat to low and simmer, stirring frequently.

2. Cook spaghetti in large pot according to package directions. When al dente, drain and add to saucepan with cream mixture. Add lemon juice and zest and toss gently over low heat until pasta is coated. Serve immediately.

Vegetable Pine Nut Mostaccioli

SERVES 4

CALORIES	399.58
FAT	20.71 GRAMS
SATURATED FAT	6.68 GRAMS
TRANS FAT	0.16 GRAMS*
CARBOHYDRATES	38.60 GRAMS
CHOLESTEROL	29.74 MG

You could add any cooked meat or fish to this simple dish. About a pound of shrimp, cooked tuna, or chicken breasts would be delicious.

⅓ cup pine nuts
1 tablespoon olive oil
1 yellow summer squash, sliced
1 cup sliced cremini mushrooms
1 red bell pepper, sliced

3 cloves garlic, minced
1 cup frozen baby peas
12 ounces mostaccioli pasta
1 tablespoon butter
½ cup grated Romano cheese

1. Bring a large pot of salted water to a boil. Meanwhile, in large skillet place pine nuts over medium heat. Toast, stirring frequently, until nuts are fragrant and begin to brown, about 2 to 4 minutes. Remove from pan and set aside. Add olive oil to pan, and add squash, mushrooms, bell pepper, and garlic. Cook and stir for 4 to 5 minutes until vegetables are crisp-tender. Add peas; cook and stir for 2 to 3 minutes longer.

2. Cook pasta in water until al dente according to package directions. Drain, reserving ¼ cup pasta water. Add pasta to vegetables in pan along with pasta water and butter. Toss to coat. Sprinkle with pine nuts and cheese and serve.

Pasta and Fennel Carbonara

2 tablespoons olive oil
1 tablespoon butter
2 heads fennel, thinly sliced
4 cloves garlic, minced
½ cup chopped walnuts
16 ounces linguine pasta
3 eggs, beaten
½ cup heavy cream
½ teaspoon salt
⅛ teaspoon pepper
½ cup grated Parmesan cheese

1. Bring a large pot of salted water to a boil. Meanwhile, combine olive oil and butter in large skillet over medium heat. When butter foams, add fennel; cook and stir for 5 minutes. Add garlic; cook and stir until fennel begins to brown around the edges, about 5 to 7 minutes longer. Add walnuts and cook until walnuts are fragrant; remove from heat.

2. Cook pasta as directed on package. While pasta is cooking, combine eggs, cream, salt, and pepper in medium bowl. Drain pasta and return to hot pot. Over low heat, stir in egg mixture, tossing to cook eggs. Add fennel mixture and toss. Sprinkle with Parmesan cheese and serve.

Working with Fennel

Fennel is a large white bulb with a licorice taste that is good raw or cooked. It can be difficult to clean; cut off the green stalk and the root end. Cut into pieces lengthwise and separate the layers; place in a bowl of water and swish to remove the grit, which will fall to the bottom. When clean, slice or dice as recipe directs.

SERVES 6

CALORIES	537.40
FAT	22.45 GRAMS
SATURATED FAT	6.92 GRAMS
TRANS FAT	0.24 GRAMS*
CARBOHYDRATES	64.94 GRAMS
CHOLESTEROL	131.87 MG

Fennel has a wonderfully spicy licorice taste. You can find it in the produce aisle of the supermarket. It's delicious with a creamy egg sauce in this pasta recipe.

Fettuccine with Asparagus

SERVES 4

CALORIES	235.31
FAT	5.75 GRAMS
SATURATED FAT	3.16 GRAMS
TRANS FAT	0.14 GRAMS*
CARBOHYDRATES	32.50 GRAMS
CHOLESTEROL	16.87 MG

Fresh asparagus is cooked until just crisp-tender right along with the pasta in this easy vegetarian main dish recipe.

½ cup part-skim ricotta cheese
2 tablespoons chopped green onions
⅛ teaspoon cayenne pepper
1 pound fresh asparagus
12 ounces fettuccine pasta
⅓ cup grated Parmesan cheese
2 tablespoons chopped fresh basil

1. Bring a large pot of salted water to a boil. Meanwhile, in small bowl combine ricotta cheese, onions, and cayenne pepper and mix well.

2. Prepare asparagus and cut into 1" pieces. Cook pasta in water according to package directions until just al dente, adding asparagus during last 3 minutes of cooking time. Drain pasta and asparagus, reserving ¼ cup pasta cooking water.

3. Return pasta and asparagus to pot and stir in ricotta mixture, reserved cooking water, and half of the Parmesan cheese. Toss until pasta is coated and sauce is smooth. Pour onto serving plate and sprinkle with basil and remaining Parmesan cheese; serve immediately.

Preparing Asparagus

When choosing fresh asparagus, pick firm stalks with tightly closed heads. To prepare, bend the asparagus between your fingers. It will naturally break at the point where the stalk becomes tough. Then immerse in water to rinse, since the asparagus can be sandy. Drain well and chop.

Old-Fashioned Mac and Cheese

4 tablespoons butter, divided
1 onion, finely chopped
3 tablespoons flour
2-½ cups whole milk
½ teaspoon salt
⅛ teaspoon cayenne pepper
⅛ teaspoon ground nutmeg
1 pound penne pasta
1 (3-ounce) package low-fat cream cheese
¾ cup shredded Muenster cheese
1 cup shredded Colby cheese
1 cup shredded part-skim mozzarella cheese
¼ cup dried Italian flavored bread crumbs
¼ cup grated Romano cheese

SERVES 6–8

CALORIES	499.57
FAT	20.12 GRAMS
SATURATED FAT	12.11 GRAMS
TRANS FAT	0.49 GRAMS*
CARBOHYDRATES	54.77 GRAMS
CHOLESTEROL	57.00 MG

Oh, this is rich, delicious, and wonderful—just like Grandma's! Yes, it's high in fat and calories, but when you want comfort food, make this rather than going to a fast-food place.

1. Preheat oven to 375°F. Bring a large pot of salted water to a boil. Meanwhile, in large saucepan melt 3 tablespoons butter over medium heat. Add onion; cook and stir until tender, about 5 minutes. Sprinkle flour over onions; cook and stir until bubbly. Add milk, salt, pepper, and nutmeg and stir with wire whisk. Let simmer until thickened, stirring frequently, about 10 minutes.

2. Add pasta to boiling water; cook according to package directions until almost al dente. Drain, rinse, and drain again.

3. Add cream cheese, Muenster, Colby, and mozzarella to the milk mixture. Remove from heat and stir until cheese melts. Add pasta to mixture and stir. Pour into 3-quart casserole. In small bowl, melt remaining 1 tablespoon butter; toss with bread crumbs and Romano cheese. Sprinkle over casserole.

4. Bake casserole for 30 to 40 minutes or until sauce is bubbling and bread crumb top is golden brown. Let stand for 5 minutes, then serve.

Garlic Broccoli Sauce over Pasta

SERVES 4

CALORIES	323.19
FAT	12.27 GRAMS
SATURATED FAT	3.62 GRAMS
TRANS FAT	0.08 GRAMS*
CARBOHYDRATES	37.43 GRAMS
CHOLESTEROL	12.84 MG

This smooth sauce has lots of flavor and a beautiful green color. It can be served as the main dish in a vegetarian meal, or as a side dish with any grilled meat.

1 bunch broccoli
2 tablespoons olive oil
4 cloves garlic, minced
1 cup Vegetable Broth (page 119)
12 ounces linguine pasta
½ cup plain yogurt
1 tablespoon lemon juice
½ teaspoon salt
⅛ teaspoon cayenne pepper
½ cup grated Parmesan cheese

1. Bring a large pot of salted water to a boil. Meanwhile, cut florets from broccoli. Cut stems into 2" pieces and peel. Chop stems. In large skillet, heat olive oil over medium heat. Add broccoli and garlic; stir-fry until broccoli is bright green, about 4 to 5 minutes. Add Broth, bring to a simmer, cover pan, and cook for 3 to 5 minutes until broccoli is tender.

2. Add pasta to boiling water. In food processor, combine all of the broccoli mixture with yogurt, lemon juice, salt, and pepper and blend until smooth.

3. When pasta is done, drain, reserving ¼ cup pasta water. Return pasta to pot. Add broccoli mixture and enough reserved pasta water to make a sauce; toss together over medium heat for 2 minutes. Serve with Parmesan cheese.

Freezing Pasta Sauces

Most pasta sauces—but not those that are cream-based, like Three-Cheese Pasta Sauce (page 220)—will freeze very well. Pour into a hard-sided container, leaving about 1" of room, or head space, at the top. Seal the container, label, and freeze up to 4 months. To thaw, place frozen block of sauce in a saucepan and heat over very low heat.

Classic Spaghetti and Meatballs

1 tablespoon olive oil
1 tablespoon butter
1 onion, chopped
6 cloves garlic, minced
½ cup shredded carrots
1 (6-ounce) can tomato paste
½ cup dry red wine
2 (14-ounce) cans diced tomatoes, undrained
1 teaspoon salt
⅛ teaspoon pepper
1 teaspoon dried basil leaves
16 ounces spaghetti pasta
18 Classic Meatballs (page 175)
½ cup grated Parmesan cheese, divided

SERVES 6–8

CALORIES	467.54
FAT	18.29 GRAMS
SATURATED FAT	7.00 GRAMS
TRANS FAT	0.15 GRAMS*
CARBOHYDRATES	41.70 GRAMS
CHOLESTEROL	104.32 MG

Shredded carrots are the secret ingredient in this classic recipe; they help thicken the sauce and are a sneaky way to get more veggies into your kids.

1. In large skillet, combine olive oil and butter over medium heat. When butter melts, add onion and garlic. Cook and stir for 5 minutes until onion is tender. Add carrots; cook and stir for 3 to 4 minutes longer.

2. Stir in tomato paste and mix. Let mixture cook for 4 to 5 minutes or until paste just begins to brown in spots. Add wine and undrained tomatoes along with salt, pepper, and basil leaves. Bring to a simmer, cover, and simmer for 30 to 40 minutes until sauce is thickened.

3. Bring a large pot of salted water to a boil. Cook spaghetti according to package directions. Add Meatballs to sauce along with 2 tablespoons Parmesan cheese; simmer while pasta is cooking.

4. When pasta is done, drain well and return to pot. Stir in ½ cup of the sauce and toss to coat. Arrange pasta on serving platter and pour remaining sauce over all. Sprinkle with remaining Parmesan cheese and serve.

Pasta and Wilted Spinach

SERVES 6

CALORIES	342.83
FAT	17.17 GRAMS
SATURATED FAT	6.81 GRAMS
TRANS FAT	0.12 GRAMS*
CARBOHYDRATES	29.74 GRAMS
CHOLESTEROL	135.35 MG

Wilted spinach salad takes on a new twist when served as a hot pasta dish. This super-quick recipe is delicious.

6 slices bacon
1 pound spaghetti pasta
¼ cup heavy cream divided
2 tablespoons white vinegar
4 cups chopped spinach
4 cloves garlic, minced
3 eggs, beaten
½ cup grated Parmesan cheese,
2 tablespoons sugar
1 tablespoon apple-cider vinegar
¼ teaspoon salt
¼ teaspoon pepper

1. Bring a large pot of salted water to a boil. Meanwhile, in large skillet cook bacon until crisp. Remove bacon from skillet and drain on paper towels; crumble and set aside. Remove all but 3 tablespoons bacon drippings from skillet. Add garlic to hot skillet and remove from heat.

2. Add pasta to water and cook according to package directions. Meanwhile, beat eggs, cream, and ¼ cup Parmesan cheese in small bowl. When pasta is done, drain and return to pot. Add egg mixture; toss for 2 minutes and remove from heat.

3. Working quickly, place skillet with bacon drippings over medium high heat. Add sugar, vinegars, salt, and pepper and bring to a boil. Add spinach; toss until spinach starts to wilt.

4. Add all of spinach mixture to the pasta mixture. Toss over low heat for 2 minutes or until mixture is hot and spinach is wilted. Serve immediately with remaining ¼ cup Parmesan cheese.

Dark Greens
You can substitute other dark greens for spinach if you'd like. Bok choy, collard greens, kale, and mustard greens would all work well. If the recipe calls for cooking the dark greens, these other vegetables need to be cooked about 40 to 50 percent longer than spinach because they are sturdier. Be sure to prepare the greens the same way.

Pasta Carbonara with Bread Crumbs

1 tablespoon olive oil
1 tablespoon butter
4 cloves garlic, minced
3 slices White Bread (page 44), crumbled
1 pound spaghetti pasta
4 eggs
⅓ cup heavy cream
⅓ cup grated Parmesan cheese
¼ teaspoon white pepper
2 tablespoons chopped fresh parsley

1. Bring a large pot of salted water to a boil. Meanwhile, in large saucepan heat olive oil and butter over medium heat. Add garlic; cook and stir until garlic is fragrant, about 3 minutes. Add bread crumbs. Cook and stir over medium heat for 6 to 9 minutes until bread crumbs are toasted. Remove bread crumbs from pan and place on plate.

2. Add pasta to boiling water and cook until al dente according to package directions. Meanwhile, in medium bowl combine eggs, cream, cheese, and pepper and mix well.

3. Drain pasta and place in pan used to sauté bread crumbs; place over medium heat. Add egg mixture all at once; toss pasta with tongs for 2 minutes (heat will cook eggs). Add half of the bread crumbs and toss. Place on serving plate and sprinkle with remaining bread crumbs and parsley; serve immediately.

SERVES 6

CALORIES	318.53
FAT	13.15 GRAMS
SATURATED FAT	5.93 GRAMS
TRANS FAT	0.19 GRAMS*
CARBOHYDRATES	35.19 GRAMS
CHOLESTEROL	164.00 MG

The garlicky bread crumbs substitute for the bacon in this super-easy and delicious pasta dish.

Pasta with Cabbage

SERVES 4

CALORIES	310.57
FAT	9.51 GRAMS
SATURATED FAT	2.44 GRAMS
TRANS FAT	0.12 GRAMS*
CARBOHYDRATES	42.85 GRAMS
CHOLESTEROL	7.33 MG

This meatless main dish is simple yet flavorful. Serve it with some carrots steamed with dill and a bit of butter, and Caraway Breadsticks (page 59).

2 tablespoons olive oil
1 onion, chopped
3 cloves garlic, minced
3 cups shredded red cabbage
½ teaspoon dried dill weed
½ teaspoon salt
⅛ teaspoon pepper
12 ounces penne pasta
1 cup frozen baby peas, thawed
⅓ cup grated Parmesan cheese

1. Bring a large pot of salted water to a boil. Meanwhile, in large skillet heat olive oil over medium heat. Add onion and garlic; cook and stir for 3 minutes. Add cabbage and sprinkle with dill, salt, and pepper. Cover, reduce heat to low, and cook for 5 to 8 minutes, stirring occasionally, until cabbage is crisp-tender.

2. Cook pasta until just al dente according to package directions. Drain, reserving ¼ cup cooking water. Add pasta along with cooking water and peas to skillet with cabbage. Cook and stir for 3 to 4 minutes or until cabbage is tender and mixture is hot. Sprinkle with cheese and serve.

Shredding Cabbage
Cabbage can be shredded several ways. A food processor with a shredding disc makes the process simple. But you can also just use a chef's knife. Cut the cabbage in half and cut out the core. Then cut in half again and place cut-side down on a work surface. Cut the cabbage into ¼"slices.

Tex-Mex Fettuccine

½ pound pork sausage
1 onion, chopped
3 cloves garlic, minced
1 jalapeño pepper, minced
1 green bell pepper, chopped
1 (14-ounce) can diced tomatoes, undrained
12 ounces fettuccine pasta
2 tablespoons flour
½ cup light cream
⅓ cup grated Cotija cheese

1. Bring a large pot of salted water to a boil. Meanwhile, cook pork sausage along with onion and garlic over medium heat, stirring until sausage is brown and vegetables are tender. Drain well. Add jalapeño, bell pepper, and tomatoes; bring to a simmer.

2. Cook pasta according to package directions until al dente. When pasta is almost done, combine flour and cream in a small bowl and beat well. Add to tomato mixture; bring to a boil and simmer for 3 minutes.

3. Drain pasta and add to saucepan with sauce. Toss for 2 minutes, then sprinkle with cheese and serve.

Cotija Cheese
Cotija cheese is a hard grating cheese similar to Parmesan and Romano cheeses, but with a stronger flavor. You can find it in Mexican markets and sometimes at the regular grocery store. When the cheese is less aged, it resembles feta cheese. It freezes well, like all hard cheeses; grate some and store it in the freezer to use anytime.

SERVES 4	
CALORIES	433.50
FAT	19.09 GRAMS
SATURATED FAT	7.70 GRAMS
TRANS FAT	0.13 GRAMS*
CARBOHYDRATES	46.27 GRAMS
CHOLESTEROL	54.25 MG

This simple fettuccine dish is spicy, creamy, and flavorful. Serve it with a crisp green salad and a fruit salad for a cooling contrast.

Pesto Pasta with Two Peas

SERVES 6–8

CALORIES	457.09
FAT	21.78 GRAMS
SATURATED FAT	5.23 GRAMS
TRANS FAT	0.10 GRAMS*
CARBOHYDRATES	45.64 GRAMS
CHOLESTEROL	19.11 MG

This simple dish can be made in minutes and is a great supper when the cupboard is almost bare. Keep these ingredients on hand to feed your family fast.

2 tablespoons olive oil
2 shallots, minced
1 cup frozen sugar snap peas
1 cup frozen baby peas
¼ cup Vegetable Broth (page 119)
1 pound rotini pasta
½ cup Basil Pesto (page 23)
⅓ cup chopped walnuts
½ cup grated Romano cheese

1. Bring a large pot of salted water to a boil. In large saucepan, heat olive oil over medium heat. Add shallots; cook and stir until they are beginning to brown, about 4 minutes. Add both kinds of frozen peas and Vegetable Broth; bring to a simmer. Cover pan, reduce heat, and simmer for 3 to 4 minutes.

2. Cook pasta according to package directions until al dente. Drain and add to saucepan with peas. Add Pesto and walnuts and toss over medium heat for 2 to 3 minutes, until pasta is coated and vegetables are hot. Serve with Romano cheese.

Sugar Snap Peas

Sugar snap peas are fully edible, pod and all. They are a good source of fiber and vitamins A, B, and C. They can be eaten raw, but taste better if blanched for a minute in boiling water, then refreshed in ice water. Serve them tossed with pasta, or as a dipper for an appetizer like Red Pepper Almond Dip (page 22).

Two-Bean Lasagna

2 tablespoons olive oil

1 onion, chopped

2 jalapeño peppers, minced

1 green bell pepper, chopped

2 (14-ounce) cans diced
    tomatoes, undrained

1 tablespoon chili powder

1 teaspoon cumin

1 teaspoon salt

1 cup Fresh and Spicy Salsa
    (page 38)

1 (15-ounce) can black beans,
    rinsed and drained

1 (15-ounce) can red kidney beans,
    rinsed and drained

1 cup water

1 cup part-skim ricotta cheese

1 (8-ounce) package low-fat cream
    cheese, softened

2 eggs, beaten

¼ cup grated Parmesan cheese

9 uncooked lasagna noodles

1 cup shredded pepper jack cheese

1 cup shredded mozzarella cheese

⅓ cup grated Romano cheese

SERVES 8–10	
CALORIES	529.37
FAT	21.04 GRAMS
SATURATED FAT	10.74 GRAMS
TRANS FAT	0.34 GRAMS*
CARBOHYDRATES	55.61 GRAMS
CHOLESTEROL	93.59 MG

This hearty lasagna must be made ahead of time, so it's perfect for entertaining.

1. In large saucepan, heat olive oil over medium heat. Add onion; cook and stir for 3 minutes. Add jalapeño and bell pepper; cook and stir for 2 minutes longer. Add tomatoes, chili powder, cumin, and salt and bring to a simmer. Simmer for 10 minutes, stirring frequently. Remove from heat and add Salsa, black beans, kidney beans, and water.

2. In medium bowl, combine ricotta cheese and cream cheese and beat until combined. Add eggs and Parmesan cheese and mix well.

3. In 13" × 9" glass baking dish, place ½ cup of the bean mixture. Add 3 lasagna noodles, then top with one-third of the cheese mixture, then one-third of the remaining bean mixture. Repeat layers, ending with bean mixture. Cover and refrigerate for at least 8 hours.

4. When ready to eat, preheat oven to 350°F. Place covered lasagna in oven. Bake for 1 hour or until lasagna noodles are almost tender when pierced with a fork. Uncover and sprinkle with pepper jack, mozzarella, and Romano cheeses. Bake for 15 to 20 minutes longer or until cheeses are melted and bubbling.

Three-Cheese Pasta Sauce

SERVES 6

CALORIES	266.17
FAT	16.88 GRAMS
SATURATED FAT	10.48 GRAMS
TRANS FAT	0.48 GRAMS*
CARBOHYDRATES	11.77 GRAMS
CHOLESTEROL	52.80 MG

Serve this delicious sauce over any cooked pasta. You can make it ahead of time and refrigerate for up to 3 days. To reheat, just put the sauce in a pan over low heat and stir.

2 tablespoons butter
1 onion, finely chopped
3 tablespoons flour
½ teaspoon salt
⅛ teaspoon white pepper
Pinch nutmeg
2 cups whole milk
½ cup mascarpone cheese
1 cup shredded mozzarella cheese
1 cup grated Parmesan cheese

1. In large saucepan, melt butter over medium heat. Add onion; cook and stir until tender, about 5 minutes. Add flour, salt, pepper, and nutmeg; cook and stir until mixture bubbles, about 3 minutes.

2. Add milk all at once, stirring with wire whisk. Cook over medium heat, stirring constantly, until sauce thickens and bubbles, about 5 to 7 minutes. Remove from heat and stir in all three cheeses. Stir until melted. Serve immediately over cooked pasta, or cover and refrigerate.

Nutmeg

Nutmeg always adds a slight hint of spice and helps bring out the flavor in cheese sauces. You can use a pinch of pre-ground nutmeg, but fresh nutmeg has much more flavor and aroma. Keep a whole nutmeg in a tiny micrograter made just for that purpose, and grate a bit of fresh nutmeg over everything from cheese sauce to potatoes.

Chapter 12

Vegetables and Side Dishes

Citrus Green Beans

Tender and crisp green beans are perked up with lemon and orange juice in this simple side-dish recipe.

1-½ pounds fresh green beans
3 tablespoons butter
3 cloves garlic, minced
2 tablespoons lemon juice
¼ cup orange juice
1 teaspoon grated orange zest
1 teaspoon salt
⅛ teaspoon white pepper

1. Bring a large pot of salted water to a boil. Trim green beans and rinse off. Add to water and bring back to a simmer. Cook for 3 minutes, then drain.

2. In large skillet, melt butter and add garlic. Cook over medium heat until garlic is fragrant, about 2 minutes. Then add green beans; cook and stir for 3 to 5 minutes or until beans are crisp-tender. Stir in lemon juice, orange juice, orange zest, salt, and pepper, and heat through.

Green Beans

When purchasing green beans, look for bright green, firm beans with no wet or dark spots. They should be plump and not shriveled. To prepare them, cut off both ends. You can leave on the blossom end, which is the tapered part, but be sure to cut off the other end, which has a tough stem attached.

Cheesy Home Fries

3 quarts cold water
3 cups ice cubes
4 russet potatoes
⅓ cup grated Parmesan cheese
¼ cup flour
½ teaspoon salt
¼ teaspoon pepper
½ teaspoon dried Italian seasoning
⅓ cup butter

1. Preheat oven to 350°F. Prepare a large bowl full of ice water. Peel potatoes and cut into French fry–size strips, dropping them into the bowl of ice water as you work. When all the potatoes are prepared, remove from ice water and dry, first with kitchen towels, then with paper towels.

2. In large bowl, combine cheese, flour, salt, pepper, and Italian seasoning and mix well. Add potatoes, half at a time, and toss well to coat. Place butter in 15" × 10" jelly roll pan and place in oven to melt. Place coated potatoes on butter in pan and sprinkle with remaining cheese mixture. Bake potatoes for 50 to 60 minutes, turning three times with a spatula, until brown and crisp. Serve immediately.

Cutting Potatoes

There are lots of tools available for cutting potatoes into French-fry strips. You can use the old-fashioned crinkle cut knife, cut them into slices yourself, or use any of the appliances that range from food processors to the manual slicers you see on late-night TV ads. Make sure that you drop the potatoes into ice water as you work to prevent browning.

SERVES 6	
CALORIES	322.74
FAT	12.09 GRAMS
SATURATED FAT	7.51 GRAMS
TRANS FAT	0.30 GRAMS*
CARBOHYDRATES	47.18 GRAMS
CHOLESTEROL	32.00 MG

These fabulous potatoes are tender, crisp, and beautifully seasoned. Don't serve them with ketchup!

Confetti Asparagus

SERVES 4

CALORIES	151.74
FAT	12.61 GRAMS
SATURATED FAT	4.63 GRAMS
TRANS FAT	0.15 GRAMS*
CARBOHYDRATES	9.46 GRAMS
CHOLESTEROL	15.25 MG

Asparagus combined with fresh vegetables is a wonderful and easy side dish that pairs beautifully with any main dish recipe.

1 pound asparagus spears
2 tablespoons butter
¼ cup chopped green onion
½ cup chopped tomato
1 avocado, peeled and chopped

1. Wash asparagus spears and snap off ends. Place in boiling salted water; cook for 3 to 4 minutes or until just crisp-tender. Drain in a colander and arrange on serving plate.

2. Meanwhile, in small saucepan combine butter with green onion; cook and stir over medium heat until crisp-tender, about 3 minutes. Remove from heat and stir in tomato and avocado. Pour over asparagus and serve.

Sautéed Corn

SERVES 6

CALORIES	202.00
FAT	9.38 GRAMS
SATURATED FAT	5.13 GRAMS
TRANS FAT	0.20 GRAMS*
CARBOHYDRATES	29.90 GRAMS
CHOLESTEROL	20.34 MG

In the summer, there's nothing like fresh corn. If you can't find any, substitute 1 (10-ounce) package of frozen whole kernel corn.

6 ears fresh corn
¼ cup butter
1 onion, chopped
½ teaspoon salt
⅛ teaspoon white pepper
2 tablespoons chopped fresh basil

1. Remove leaves and silk from corn and cut kernels from the cobs. In medium saucepan, melt butter over medium heat. Add onion; cook and stir until tender, about 5 minutes. Add corn; cook and stir for 4 to 6 minutes or until corn is hot and tender. Sprinkle with salt, pepper, and basil and serve.

Three-Onion Casserole

3 Vidalia or other sweet onions
1 cup frozen cipollini onions
1 leek
¼ cup butter, divided
1 tablespoon flour
½ teaspoon salt
⅛ teaspoon white pepper
2 tablespoons Dijon mustard
1 cup milk
½ cup grated Parmesan cheese

1. Preheat oven to 400°F. Slice the Vidalia onions, thaw the cipollini onions, and slice and rinse the leek. Melt 2 tablespoons butter in a large skillet and add all of the onions; cook and stir until crisp-tender, about 5 minutes. Remove onions from skillet and set aside.

2. In skillet, combine remaining butter, flour, salt, and pepper; cook and stir over medium heat until bubbly. Add mustard and milk; cook and stir until bubbly, about 4 minutes. Place onions in 2-quart baking dish and pour milk mixture over. Sprinkle with cheese and bake for 20 to 25 minutes until casserole bubbles and cheese browns.

Substituting Onions

If you can't find cipollini onions, which are small globe onions, you can substitute sliced shallots. Almost any onion can be substituted for another. Since the onions are cooked in this recipe, you can substitute ordinary white or yellow onions for the Vidalias. Other sweet onion varieties include Walla Walla, Oso Sweet, and Texas Spring Sweet.

SERVES 8

CALORIES	134.91
FAT	8.37 GRAMS
SATURATED FAT	5.12 GRAMS
TRANS FAT	0.19 GRAMS*
CARBOHYDRATES	10.99 GRAMS
CHOLESTEROL	23.21 MG

Three kinds of onions add fabulous flavor to this easy casserole recipe. Serve it with a pot roast and a green salad for a delicious dinner.

Roasted Vegetables

SERVES 8

CALORIES	86.48
FAT	6.90 GRAMS
SATURATED FAT	0.97 GRAMS
TRANS FAT	0.0 GRAMS
CARBOHYDRATES	6.15 GRAMS
CHOLESTEROL	0.0 GRAMS

Be sure to save some vegetables to use in Easy Antipasto (page 28). This recipe can also be served plain as an appetizer.

½ pound green beans
1 cup baby carrots
1 summer squash, sliced
1 red bell pepper, sliced
1 orange bell pepper, sliced
1 red onion, sliced
¼ cup extra-virgin olive oil
1 tablespoon fresh thyme leaves
1 tablespoon fresh tarragon leaves, minced
1 teaspoon salt
⅛ teaspoon white pepper

1. Cut ends off green beans, and cut baby carrots in half lengthwise. Bring a medium pot of water to a full boil and add green beans and carrots. Simmer for 4 minutes or until crisp-tender. Drain well and arrange on cookie sheet.

2. Preheat oven to 400°F. Add remaining vegetables and drizzle with olive oil. Sprinkle with herbs, salt, and pepper and toss to coat. Arrange evenly on cookie sheet. Roast for 30 to 40 minutes, stirring every 10 minutes, or until vegetables are lightly browned on edges and are tender.

Roasting Vegetables

Almost any vegetable can be roasted. Just be sure that the vegetables you use are all about the same density and are cut approximately the same size, so they cook evenly. For example, root vegetables like potatoes, carrots, and squash would work well roasted together, and thin-skinned vegetables like asparagus and peppers are a good combination.

Brown Rice Stir-Fry

1 cup brown rice
2 cups water
2 tablespoons olive oil
1 onion, chopped
3 cloves garlic, minced
½ cup shredded carrots
½ cup chopped cremini mushrooms
½ teaspoon salt
⅛ teaspoon cayenne pepper
1 cup frozen edamame beans, thawed
1 cup frozen sugar snap peas, thawed
2 tablespoons soy sauce

1. In medium saucepan, combine brown rice and water. Place over medium heat and bring to a boil. Reduce heat, cover, and simmer for 30 to 35 minutes or until rice is almost tender. Set aside.

2. Prepare all vegetables. In large skillet, heat olive oil over medium high heat. When oil shimmers, add onion, garlic, and carrot; stir-fry for 3 minutes. Add mushrooms and sprinkle salt and pepper over; stir-fry for 3 minutes longer. Then stir in rice, beans, and snap peas. Stir-fry for 2 to 4 minutes or until vegetables are hot. Sprinkle with soy sauce, stir gently, and serve.

Rice for Stir-Frying

Typically, stir-fries are made with rice that has been cooked and cooled. The rice can be freshly cooked, but the stir-fry will be softer because the rice has more moisture. If you'd like, you can cook the rice ahead of time, or think about buying it, fully cooked, from a Chinese takeout place in your neighborhood.

SERVES 6

CALORIES	235.77
FAT	8.11 GRAMS
SATURATED FAT	1.20 GRAMS
TRANS FAT	0.0 GRAMS
CARBOHYDRATES	33.33 GRAMS
CHOLESTEROL	0.0 MG

You can substitute just about any frozen vegetable for the edamame (soy beans) and snap peas in this flavorful recipe.

Toasted Crunchy Potatoes

SERVES 8

CALORIES	207.70
FAT	8.96 GRAMS
SATURATED FAT	5.22 GRAMS
TRANS FAT	0.17 GRAMS*
CARBOHYDRATES	25.51 GRAMS
CHOLESTEROL	49.17 MG

For this recipe, make sure that the potatoes are no larger than 2" in diameter so they cook through at the same time.

2 pounds small white potatoes	⅛ teaspoon white pepper
¼ cup butter, melted	1 egg, beaten
¾ cup fine dry bread crumbs	½ teaspoon salt
¼ cup grated Cotija cheese	1 tablespoon milk

1. Preheat oven to 375°F. Spray a 15" × 10" jelly roll pan with nonstick cooking spray and set aside. Wash potatoes and dry thoroughly. Place butter in shallow dish. Combine bread crumbs, cheese, and pepper in another dish. In another dish, beat egg with salt and milk.

2. One at a time, dip potatoes into melted butter, then into crumb mixture, then into egg mixture, then into crumb mixture to coat. Arrange in single layer on prepared pan. Bake for 65 to 75 minutes or until potatoes are tender when pierced with a fork and bread-crumb coating is brown and crisp. Serve immediately.

Hawaiian Carrots

SERVES 6

CALORIES	157.60
FAT	9.81 GRAMS
SATURATED FAT	6.64 GRAMS
TRANS FAT	0.20 GRAMS*
CARBOHYDRATES	17.66 GRAMS
CHOLESTEROL	20.34 MG

The natural sweetness of carrots is complemented by sweet and tart pineapple and lemon juice in this fresh side-dish recipe.

1 (16-ounce) package baby carrots	1 tablespoons cornstarch
¼ cup butter, divided	1 tablespoon lemon juice
1 onion, finely chopped	½ teaspoon salt
1 (8-ounce) can pineapple tidbits	½ cup toasted coconut

1. Wash carrots, place in microwave-safe 2-quart dish along with 1 cup water, cover, and microwave for 3 to 6 minutes on high power, stirring once during cooking, until tender. Drain carrots and set aside.

2. In medium saucepan, combine 2 tablespoons butter and onion; cook and stir over medium heat until crisp-tender, about 4 minutes. Drain pineapple, reserving juice. Add pineapple and drained carrots to saucepan and cook over medium heat for 3 minutes.

3. In small bowl, combine reserved pineapple juice, cornstarch, lemon juice, and salt and stir. Add to saucepan along with remaining 2 tablespoons butter and bring to a simmer. Simmer for 5 minutes, stirring frequently, until thickened. Sprinkle with coconut and serve.

Spinach and Rice

2 tablespoons olive oil
1 onion, chopped
1-½ cups rice
1 teaspoon salt
2-½ cups water
½ teaspoon dried thyme leaves
1 (10-ounce) package frozen spinach
Pinch ground nutmeg
½ cup light cream
1 cup grated Parmesan cheese
½ cup grated Swiss cheese

SERVES 6

CALORIES	366.72
FAT	14.77 GRAMS
SATURATED FAT	6.78 GRAMS
TRANS FAT	0.25 GRAMS*
CARBOHYDRATES	43.75 GRAMS
CHOLESTEROL	30.41 MG

The combination of spinach with rice and cheese is delicious. The touch of nutmeg really brings the flavors together.

1. In large saucepan, heat olive oil over medium heat. Add onion; cook and stir until crisp-tender, about 5 minutes. Add rice; cook and stir for 2 minutes longer. Sprinkle salt over all and add water and thyme leaves. Bring to a boil, reduce heat to low, cover, and simmer for 20 to 25 minutes or until rice is tender.

2. Meanwhile, thaw spinach and drain well in colander, then squeeze with your hands to drain thoroughly. Stir into rice mixture along with nutmeg, cream, and cheeses. Cook and stir until spinach is hot and cheeses are melted, about 5 to 8 minutes.

Thawing Spinach

Frozen chopped spinach and frozen cut-leaf spinach both contain a lot of water. If the recipe calls for draining the spinach, take time to do it properly or the recipe will be ruined. Thaw the spinach, then place it in a colander and squeeze with your hands. Then wrap the spinach in a kitchen towel and twist to remove the last bits of moisture.

Apricot Rice

SERVES 6

CALORIES	302.61
FAT	6.54 GRAMS
SATURATED FAT	2.83 GRAMS
TRANS FAT	0.10 GRAMS*
CARBOHYDRATES	57.42 GRAMS
CHOLESTEROL	10.17 MG

Apricot nectar and dried apricots add flavor to plain white rice in this easy pilaf recipe. Serve it with grilled chicken breasts and a spinach salad for a delicious meal.

1 tablespoon olive oil
2 shallots, finely chopped
3 cloves garlic, minced
1-½ cups long-grain white rice
½ cup finely chopped dried apricots
2 cups apricot nectar
1 cup water
1 teaspoon salt
⅛ teaspoon cayenne pepper
2 tablespoons butter

1. In heavy saucepan, combine olive oil, shallots, and garlic. Cook and stir over medium heat until vegetables are tender, about 4 minutes. Stir in rice; cook and stir for 2 minutes longer. Add apricots along with remaining ingredients except butter. Bring to a boil, then reduce heat, cover, and simmer for 20 to 25 minutes or until rice is tender and liquid is absorbed.

2. Add butter, cover, and remove from heat. Let stand for 5 minutes. Then stir until butter is combined and serve.

Orange-Scented Broccoli

SERVES 4

CALORIES	176.46
FAT	10.79 GRAMS
SATURATED FAT	2.66 GRAMS
TRANS FAT	0.07 GRAMS*
CARBOHYDRATES	17.48 GRAMS
CHOLESTEROL	7.63 MG

Broccoli is one of the best foods you can eat; it's packed full of vitamins, minerals, and antioxidants. This method of cooking yields tender florets scented with orange.

1 bunch fresh broccoli
1 tablespoon olive oil
1 tablespoon butter
2 cloves garlic, minced
1 tablespoon flour
½ cup orange juice
1 teaspoon grated orange zest
2 tablespoons lemon juice
⅓ cup sliced almonds

1. Preheat oven to 400°F. Wash broccoli and cut apart into florets. Peel stems and cut into ½" slices. Bring a large pot of water to a boil. Add broccoli; cook for 3 to 4 minutes or until broccoli is bright green. Drain into a colander and run cold water over; drain well.

2. In saucepan, combine olive oil, butter, and garlic over medium heat. Cook and stir for 2 minutes. Add flour; cook and stir until bubbly. Add orange juice, zest, and lemon juice; cook and stir until mixture simmers for 1 minute.

3. Arrange broccoli in 2-quart casserole dish. Pour sauce over and sprinkle with almonds. Bake for 20 minutes or until broccoli is tender.

Roasted Cauliflower Crunch

1 head cauliflower
¼ cup dried bread crumbs
¼ cup ground walnuts
2 tablespoons grated Parmesan cheese
½ teaspoon dried oregano leaves
½ teaspoon seasoned salt
⅛ teaspoon pepper
⅓ cup butter, melted

1. Preheat oven to 400°F. Remove leaves from cauliflower and discard; cut cauliflower into individual florets. On shallow plate, combine bread crumbs, walnuts, cheese, oregano, salt, and pepper and mix well. Dip cauliflower florets into melted butter, then roll in bread crumb mixture to coat.

2. Arrange in single layer on 15" × 10" jelly roll pan. Roast for 15 to 20 minutes or until cauliflower is tender and coating is browned.

About Dried Bread Crumbs
Read the label carefully when you purchase a package of dried bread crumbs. If it contains the word "hydrogenated" in the ingredient list, it has trans fat. You might want to make your own bread crumbs; simply dry bread in a 300°F oven for 15 to 25 minutes, then cool and grind in a food processor. Store covered for up to 1 week or freeze for longer storage.

SERVES 6

CALORIES	174.53
FAT	13.39 GRAMS
SATURATED FAT	7.17 GRAMS
TRANS FAT	0.28 GRAMS*
CARBOHYDRATES	11.30 GRAMS
CHOLESTEROL	28.95 MG

Roasting cauliflower makes it tender and creamy. The crisp coating is a nice contrast.

Scalloped Mushrooms

SERVES 8

CALORIES	141.23
FAT	6.89 GRAMS
SATURATED FAT	4.14 GRAMS
TRANS FAT	0.15 GRAMS*
CARBOHYDRATES	17.65 GRAMS
CHOLESTEROL	20.27 MG

This elegant side dish is perfect served with some grilled steaks and Cranberry Peach Salad (page 116) for a "steak house" meal.

1 (0.5-ounce) package dried shiitake mushrooms
1 cup boiling water
¼ cup butter
1 onion, chopped
1 (8-ounce) package button mushrooms, sliced
1 cup sliced cremini mushrooms
½ teaspoon salt
½ teaspoon dried thyme leaves
1 tablespoon lemon juice
4 slices Oatmeal Bread (page 43)

1. Preheat oven to 325°F. In small bowl, combine shiitake mushrooms and water; let stand for 15 minutes. Meanwhile, combine butter and onion in large skillet over medium heat. Cook and stir for 4 minutes, until crisp-tender.

2. Add button and cremini mushrooms; sprinkle with salt and thyme leaves. Cook and stir for 4 minutes until mushrooms are glazed. Remove mushrooms from skillet with slotted spoon and place in 2-quart baking dish.

3. Drain shiitake mushrooms, reserving liquid. Strain liquid. Remove stems from shiitake mushrooms and discard; chop tops. Combine with onion-mushroom mixture in baking dish. Add lemon juice and ⅓ cup reserved mushroom liquid to skillet; bring to a boil and remove from heat.

4. Crumble bread to make soft crumbs and sprinkle over mushrooms. Drizzle liquid from skillet over all. Bake for 30 to 40 minutes or until bread crumbs are toasted and mushrooms are tender.

Substituting Mushrooms
Just about any mushroom can be substituted for another. Just be sure they are about the same size so they will cook through and be done at the same time. Other mushrooms include morels (these are easier to find dried), chanterelles, oyster mushrooms, and brown mushrooms. Don't rinse or soak mushrooms to clean; just brush with a soft cloth.

Green Rice Bake

2 tablespoons butter
1 onion, chopped
3 cloves garlic, minced
1 cup brown basmati rice
2 cups Vegetable Broth (page 119)
¾ cup chopped parsley
1 green bell pepper, chopped
½ cup grated Parmesan cheese
1 cup grated Swiss cheese
½ teaspoon dried basil leaves
½ teaspoon dried thyme leaves
½ cup milk
2 eggs, beaten

SERVES 8

CALORIES	229.79
FAT	10.38 GRAMS
SATURATED FAT	5.83 GRAMS
TRANS FAT	0.24 GRAMS*
CARBOHYDRATES	24.05 GRAMS
CHOLESTEROL	78.54 MG

This creamy casserole turns rice into an elegant side dish. Serve it with Baked Fried Chicken (page 153) and Melon Pineapple Salad (page 110).

1. Preheat oven to 375°F. In large ovenproof saucepan, melt butter over medium heat. Add onion and garlic; cook and stir until crisp-tender, about 4 minutes. Stir in rice; cook and stir for 2 minutes. Add Vegetable Broth; bring to a simmer, cover, and simmer for 15 minutes.

2. Stir in parsley, bell pepper, cheeses, and seasonings and mix well. Stir in milk and eggs. Bake, uncovered, for 40 to 50 minutes or until casserole is set and top begins to brown.

Basmati Rice

Basmati rice is a variety of rice grown in India. It is a long-grain rice that cooks up separated and fluffy, so it's perfect for people who have difficulty making fluffy rice. It also smells like popcorn when it's cooking. Other varieties of this rice include Jasmati, Texmati, and Jasmine.

Cheesy Stuffed Potatoes

SERVES 8

CALORIES	351.70
FAT	19.28 GRAMS
SATURATED FAT	9.33 GRAMS
TRANS FAT	0.36 GRAMS*
CARBOHYDRATES	35.93 GRAMS
CHOLESTEROL	43.43 MG

Avocado adds a buttery, nutty richness to these potatoes. It may seem like an odd combination, but it's delicious—and good for you, too!

4 russet potatoes
1 tablespoon olive oil
¼ cup butter, softened
½ cup low-fat sour cream
1 teaspoon salt
⅛ teaspoon white pepper
1-½ cups shredded Gruyère cheese
1 avocado, peeled and diced

1. Preheat oven to 400°F. Wash and dry potatoes, rub with olive oil, and prick with fork. Place potatoes on oven rack and bake for 45 minutes until tender. Let cool on wire rack until cool enough to handle, about 30 minutes.

2. Cut potatoes in half and remove flesh from skin, leaving a quarter-inch of flesh in the potato skin. Put flesh in medium bowl and add butter; beat until combined. Stir in sour cream, salt, and pepper until mixed. Then add cheese and avocado and fold together. Pile potato mixture back into shells. Place on a cookie sheet and bake for 10 to 15 minutes or until potatoes begin to brown on top. Serve immediately.

Lima Beans with Caramelized Onions

SERVES 6

CALORIES	177.32
FAT	4.57 GRAMS
SATURATED FAT	2.57 GRAMS
TRANS FAT	0.10 GRAMS*
CARBOHYDRATES	27.67 GRAMS
CHOLESTEROL	10.17 MG

Lima beans are pillowy and soft and delicious. They're a tasty accompaniment to any chicken or pork dish.

2 tablespoons butter
1 onion, chopped
1 teaspoon sugar
½ teaspoon dried marjoram leaves
½ teaspoon salt
⅛ teaspoon white pepper
½ cup Vegetable Broth (page 119)
2 (10-ounce) packages frozen
   baby lima beans, thawed

1. In small skillet, combine butter with onion; cook and stir over medium heat for 4 minutes. Sprinkle with sugar; continue cooking, stirring frequently, until onions brown around edges, about 5 to 8 minutes longer. Remove from heat and add marjoram, salt, and pepper. Set aside.

2. In large saucepan, bring Vegetable Broth to a boil. Add lima beans; cook over medium heat until lima beans are hot and tender, about 5 to 8 minutes. Drain beans and add onion mixture to beans; cook for 1 minute longer, then serve.

Garlic and Onion Smashed Potatoes

2 pounds white potatoes
¼ cup butter
6 cloves garlic, peeled
1 onion, chopped
1 (3-ounce) package cream cheese, softened
½ cup whole milk
½ teaspoon salt
⅛ teaspoon white pepper

1. Wash potatoes, quarter, and place in large pot of boiling salted water. Simmer over medium low heat for 15 to 20 minutes or until potatoes are tender when tested with a fork. Drain into a colander and immediately return the potatoes to the hot pot. Shake over low heat for 1 minute to evaporate water.

2. Meanwhile, melt butter in small saucepan. Add garlic and onion; cook and stir until onion starts to caramelize, about 8 minutes. When potatoes are cooked and dried, add butter mixture and mash with potato masher or fork until combined. Then add cream cheese, milk, and seasonings; mash and stir until combined, but leave some pieces of potato visible. Cover and turn off heat; let stand for 5 minutes before serving.

Mashed Potatoes

The order you add ingredients to potatoes will ensure a fluffy potato that is tender and creamy. Always add butter or other fats first; the fat coats the starch molecules so they can't combine and make the potatoes sticky. Then add liquids and mash until the mixture is combined and potatoes are creamy.

SERVES 6

CALORIES	251.20
FAT	13.51 GRAMS
SATURATED FAT	8.46 GRAMS
TRANS FAT	0.28 GRAMS*
CARBOHYDRATES	28.73 GRAMS
CHOLESTEROL	38.77 GRAMS

Did you know that most of the nutrients in a potato are located directly under the skin? This recipe uses the whole potato.

Sweet-Potato Mash

SERVES 8

CALORIES	250.56
FAT	10.89 GRAMS
SATURATED FAT	6.09 GRAMS
TRANS FAT	0.08 GRAMS*
CARBOHYDRATES	37.93 GRAMS
CHOLESTEROL	7.63 MG

Try this side dish for Thanksgiving. It's rich and delicious, with a nice crunchy topping.

2 (15-ounce) can sweet potatoes, drained
2 tablespoons butter
1 teaspoon vanilla
½ teaspoon salt
⅛ teaspoon white pepper
2 tablespoons coconut oil
⅓ cup coconut
⅓ cup chopped pecans
½ cup brown sugar

1. Preheat oven to 375°F. Spray a 3-quart baking dish with nonstick cooking spray and set aside. In medium saucepan, heat sweet potatoes until hot. Add butter, vanilla, salt, and pepper and mash with potato masher. Place in prepared dish.

2. In small saucepan, heat coconut oil over medium heat until liquid. Add coconut and pecans; cook and stir until coconut and pecans are toasted, about 3 minutes. Remove from heat and stir in brown sugar. Spoon over mashed potato mixture in baking dish. Bake for 20 to 25 minutes or until topping is crisp and golden brown.

Barley Risotto

3 tablespoons butter, divided
1 tablespoon olive oil
1 onion, chopped
3 cloves garlic, minced
1 cup pearl barley
4 to 5 cups Vegetable Broth (page 119)
1 teaspoon dried thyme leaves
⅛ teaspoon white pepper
1 red bell pepper, chopped
¼ cup heavy cream
¾ cup grated Parmesan cheese

1. In large saucepan, heat 1 tablespoon butter with the olive oil on medium heat. When butter melts, add onion and garlic; cook and stir for 5 minutes. Add barley; cook and stir for 2 minutes. Add 1 cup Vegetable Broth and simmer until broth is absorbed.

2. Stir in another cup Broth along with thyme and white pepper. Simmer, stirring frequently, until Broth is absorbed. Continue adding Broth, ½ cup at a time, until barley is almost tender, about 20 minutes.

3. Stir in red bell pepper, cover, and simmer for 5 minutes, until barley is tender and bell pepper is crisp-tender. Add remaining 2 tablespoons butter, cream, and Parmesan cheese; stir, cover, and remove from heat. Let stand for 5 minutes, then stir and serve.

About Barley
There are several different types of barley. Hulled barley, or barley groats, is the least processed, with just the hull removed. Pearl barley has had the bran layer removed, too; it cooks more quickly and is less nutritious. Barley flakes, or rolled barley, is similar in texture to oatmeal. And quick-cooking barley has been pre-steamed, making it ready in about 10 minutes.

SERVES 6

CALORIES	312.08
FAT	16.87 GRAMS
SATURATED FAT	7.81 GRAMS
TRANS FAT	0.30 GRAMS*
CARBOHYDRATES	32.37 GRAMS
CHOLESTEROL	33.10 MG

This elegant side dish, with chewy, nutty barley in a thyme-scented sauce, is perfect served with a grilled steak.

Real French Fries

SERVES 8

CALORIES	196.76
FAT	10.37 GRAMS
SATURATED FAT	1.35 GRAMS
TRANS FAT	0.03 GRAMS
CARBOHYDRATES	23.90 GRAMS
CHOLESTEROL	0.0 MG

The trick to making the best French fries is to get the potatoes as dry as possible. Dry them in kitchen towels, then in paper towels.

2 teaspoons salt
¼ cup honey
3 quarts cold water
3 cups ice cubes
2 pounds russet potatoes
4 cups canola or corn oil
More salt to taste

1. Place salt, honey, and 1 cup cold water in large bowl; stir until salt and honey are dissolved. Add remaining cold water and ice cubes. Peel potatoes, placing in ice water mixture as you work. Cut potatoes using a mandoline, a knife, or a food processor, being sure to place the cut potatoes back into the ice water to help prevent browning.

2. Preheat oven to 200°F. Place oil in a very large pot; attach a food thermometer. Heat over medium high heat until the temperature reaches 375°F. Meanwhile, dry potatoes, first in a kitchen towel, then with paper towels, until as dry as possible.

3. Carefully drop a couple of handfuls of potatoes into the hot oil at a time. Fry, stirring occasionally, until potatoes are golden brown, about 7 to 11 minutes. Remove from oil and drain on paper towels; sprinkle with salt or other seasonings. Keep potatoes warm in oven until ready to serve.

Chapter 13

Cookies and Candies

Chocolate Almond Meringues

YIELDS 36 COOKIES

CALORIES	69.90
FAT	3.84 GRAMS
SATURATED FAT	1.20 GRAMS
TRANS FAT	0.0 GRAMS
CARBOHYDRATES	8.83 GRAMS
CHOLESTEROL	0.18 MG

These little puffs are perfect for the holidays. Be sure to melt the chocolate exactly as the recipe specifies so it will become firm at room temperature.

3 egg whites
¼ teaspoon cream of tartar
½ teaspoon almond extract
¾ cup sugar
3 tablespoons cocoa powder
1 cup semisweet chocolate chips
¼ cup milk chocolate chips
1 cup finely chopped toasted almonds

1. Preheat oven to 350°F. In large bowl, combine egg whites and cream of tartar; beat until foamy. Add almond extract and a spoonful of sugar; beat until soft peaks form. Then gradually add remaining sugar and cocoa powder, beating until stiff peaks form and sugar is completely dissolved.

2. Drop mixture by teaspoonfuls onto parchment-paper-lined cookie sheets. Bake for 12 to 17 minutes, or until cookies are set and crisp on the outside but still a bit soft inside. Let cool on cookie sheets for 5 minutes, then carefully remove to wire racks to cool completely.

3. When cookies are cool, place 1 cup semisweet chocolate chips in glass measuring cup. Microwave on 50 percent power for 1 minute, remove and stir. Microwave at 50 percent power for 30 seconds longer, then remove and stir until completely melted. Add milk chocolate chips; stir until melted. Dip bottoms of cookies into chocolate mixture, then into chopped almonds to coat. Place on parchment paper; let stand until firm.

Leftover Melted Chocolate

If you have leftover melted chocolate after dipping cookies and candies, just save it! Let the chocolate cool until it hardens, then remove from the cup or bowl and coarsely chop. Store in an airtight container in the pantry for up to 2 months. Use as a substitute for chocolate chips in any recipe. Don't re-melt because the chocolate may become too grainy.

Applesauce Brownies

⅓ cup butter

2 (1-ounce) squares unsweetened chocolate

½ cup sugar

½ cup brown sugar

2 eggs

⅔ cup applesauce

1-½ teaspoons vanilla

1-¼ cups flour

½ teaspoon baking powder

¼ teaspoon salt

1 (8-ounce) package cream cheese, softened

2 tablespoons butter

2-½ cups powdered sugar

2 tablespoons apple juice

1. Preheat oven to 350°F. Grease a 9" × 9" pan with unsalted butter and set aside. In heavy saucepan, melt ⅓ cup butter with the chocolate until smooth. Beat in sugar and brown sugar until blended. Then beat in eggs, one at a time. Add applesauce and vanilla and mix until smooth.

2. Add flour, baking powder, and salt, mixing well, and pour into prepared pan. Bake for 20 to 30 minutes or until brownies are just set. Do not over-bake. While brownies cool, prepare frosting. In large bowl, beat cream cheese with 2 tablespoons butter until smooth. Add powdered sugar, then enough apple juice to make desired spreading consistency. When brownies are cooled but still slightly warm, frost. Let stand until cool, then cut into bars.

YIELDS 25 BROWNIES

CALORIES	186.25
FAT	8.24
SATURATED FAT	5.02 GRAMS
TRANS FAT	0.14 GRAMS*
CARBOHYDRATES	27.47 GRAMS
CHOLESTEROL	35.85 MG

The apple cream cheese frosting is the perfect finish to these moist and chewy brownies.

Gingersnaps

YIELDS 36 COOKIES

CALORIES	95.36
FAT	4.36 GRAMS
SATURATED FAT	2.99 GRAMS
TRANS FAT	0.07 GRAMS*
CARBOHYDRATES	13.34 GRAMS
CHOLESTEROL	12.62 MG

Wheat germ adds a bit of nutty crunch to these crisp cookies. Store overnight before serving to let the flavor develop. And save some to make Gingerbread Trifle (page 283).

½ cup butter, softened
¼ cup coconut oil
1 cup brown sugar
¼ cup light molasses
1 egg
1-¾ cups flour
¼ cup whole-wheat flour
¼ cup wheat germ
1-½ teaspoons ginger
½ teaspoon cinnamon
¼ teaspoon cardamom
1 teaspoon baking soda
½ teaspoon baking powder
¼ teaspoon salt

1. In large bowl, combine butter, coconut oil, and brown sugar and beat until fluffy. Add molasses and egg and beat until blended. Stir in flour, whole wheat flour, wheat germ, ginger, cinnamon, cardamom, baking soda, baking powder, and salt until a dough forms. Cover dough and chill in refrigerator for at least 3 hours.

2. When ready to bake, preheat oven to 350°F. Form dough into 1" balls and place 2" apart on ungreased cookie sheets. Flatten slightly with the bottom of a drinking glass dipped in sugar. Bake for 12 to 15 minutes or until cookies are light brown on the bottom and crisp. Cool on sheets for 3 minutes, then remove to wire racks to cool completely.

Chilling Cookie Dough

Rolled cookie dough is usually chilled before use to make it easier to handle. But chilling dough has other advantages. It lets you use a bit less flour, which results in a more tender cookie. And it lets the gluten in the flour relax, so the dough is easier to handle and rolls without springing back.

Peanut Butter Creams

¾ cup butter, softened, divided
1 cup natural peanut butter, divided
½ cup brown sugar
¼ cup sugar
1 egg
1 teaspoon vanilla
1-¾ cups flour
¼ cup ground oatmeal
¼ teaspoon salt
1 egg white
1 cup finely chopped peanuts
2-½ cups powdered sugar
2-3 tablespoons milk

1. In large bowl, combine ½ cup butter, ¾ cup peanut butter, brown sugar, and sugar and beat until smooth. Stir in egg and vanilla until combined. Then add flour, ground oatmeal, and salt. Cover and chill dough for at least 3 hours in the refrigerator.

2. When ready to bake, preheat oven to 350°F. Place egg white in shallow bowl and beat with fork until foamy. Place peanuts in another bowl. Roll dough into 1" balls. Roll each ball into egg white, then into peanuts to coat. Place on parchment-paper-lined cookie sheets and gently press your thumb into each cookie to form a depression. Bake for 5 minutes, remove from oven and press in the depression again. Return to oven and bake 3 to 6 minutes longer or until cookies are just set and light golden brown on bottom.

3. Cool cookies completely. In medium bowl, combine ¼ cup butter, ¼ cup peanut butter, and 1 cup powdered sugar; beat well. Alternately add remaining powdered sugar with enough milk to form a frosting. Fill the depression in each cookie with a spoonful of the peanut butter mixture. Let stand until set; store covered at room temperature.

YIELDS 48 COOKIES

CALORIES	138.26
FAT	8.04 GRAMS
SATURATED FAT	2.74 GRAMS
TRANS FAT	0.08 GRAMS*
CARBOHYDRATES	14.59 GRAMS
CHOLESTEROL	12.08 MG

Peanutty thumbprint cookies are rolled in peanuts before baking, then topped with a spoonful of peanut cream. Yum!

Cranberry Crisps

YIELDS 60 COOKIES

CALORIES	115.23
FAT	5.38 GRAMS
SATURATED FAT	2.27 GRAMS
TRANS FAT	0.04 GRAMS
CARBOHYDRATES	16.19 GRAMS
CHOLESTEROL	11.32 MG

Coconut oil adds a nice crispness and tenderness to these little cookies. You could make them with currants or raisins if you'd like.

½ cup butter, softened
¼ cup coconut oil
¼ cup canola oil
2 cups sugar
2 eggs
2 teaspoons vanilla
2-¾ cups flour
½ teaspoon cream of tartar
½ teaspoon salt
1 teaspoon baking powder
½ cup white chocolate, ground
2 cups dried sweetened cranberries
1 cup finely chopped pecans
⅓ cup granulated sugar

1. Preheat oven to 350°F. In large bowl, combine butter, coconut oil, and canola oil and beat until blended. Gradually add 2 cups sugar, beating until fluffy. Add eggs, one at a time, beating well after each addition. Then stir in vanilla. Place flour, cream of tartar, salt, and baking powder in sifter and sift over batter. Stir until a dough forms.

2. Stir in white chocolate, cranberries, and pecans. Chill dough, if necessary, for easier handling. Roll dough into ¾" balls then roll in ⅓ cup granulated sugar. Place on ungreased cookie sheets and flatten with fork. Bake for 10 to 12 minutes or until cookies are light golden brown around edges. Cool on cookie sheets for 3 minutes, then remove to wire racks to cool.

Cream of Tartar

Cream of tartar is a white powder; it's an acid ingredient used in home-made baking powder. It decreases the pH of these cookies, making them tender and quite crisp. Don't use tartar sauce instead (that is a common mistake)! You can find cream of tartar in the spice aisle or baking aisle of any supermarket.

Chocolate Truffles

1 cup heavy whipping cream
1 (1-ounce) square unsweetened chocolate
7 (1-ounce) squares semisweet chocolate
1-½ cups milk chocolate chips
2 tablespoons butter
1 teaspoon vanilla
1 pound white chocolate candy coating

1. In heavy saucepan, heat cream until it just begins to simmer around the edges. Meanwhile, chop the squares of chocolate into chip-size bits. When the cream begins to simmer, remove from the heat and add all of the chocolates and the butter. Stir until chocolate melts and mixture is smooth. Add vanilla, cover, and chill until firm.

2. When mixture is firm, scoop out balls with a small cookie scoop or melon baller; place on parchment paper. Chill again until firm. Cut candy coating into small pieces and melt as package directs. Dip the truffles into the candy coating and place on parchment paper; chill until hardened. Store at room temperature.

YIELDS 36 TRUFFLES

CALORIES	155.05
FAT	9.86 GRAMS
SATURATED FAT	5.74 GRAMS
TRANS FAT	0.06 GRAMS*
CARBOHYDRATES	15.59 GRAMS
CHOLESTEROL	9.80 MG

Be sure to read the label of the candy coating package carefully to make sure it doesn't contain partially hydrogenated vegetable oil. Many varieties have no trans fat.

Coconut Oatmeal Macaroons

YIELDS 36 COOKIES

CALORIES	62.12
FAT	3.32 GRAMS
SATURATED FAT	1.09 GRAMS
TRANS FAT	0.0 GRAMS
CARBOHYDRATES	7.68 GRAMS
CHOLESTEROL	0.0 MG

Macaroons can be crisp or chewy. These cookies are the chewy kind; brown sugar and ground oatmeal make them so.

3 egg whites
½ cup sugar
¼ cup brown sugar
1 cup quick oats, ground
1-½ cups coconut
1 cup chopped pecans
1 teaspoon vanilla

1. Preheat oven to 350°F. In large bowl, beat egg whites until foamy. Gradually add sugar, beating until stiff peaks form. Then add brown sugar slowly, beating until combined. Fold in remaining ingredients.

2. Drop dough by teaspoonfuls onto parchment-paper-lined cookie sheets. Bake for 12 to 17 minutes or until cookies are light golden brown and set. Cool on cookie sheets for 3 minutes, then slide paper onto wire racks to cool. When macaroons are cool, carefully peel off the paper. Store covered at room temperature.

About Nuts

Nuts are so good for you! They contain a lot of monounsaturated oils, which can help contribute to heart health. Buy nuts in small quantities, because they can become rancid fairly quickly. You can store nuts in the freezer, but be sure to thaw them completely before chopping, or they will become oily.

Honey Oatmeal Spice Cookies

1-½ cups quick-cooking oatmeal, divided
½ cup butter, softened
⅓ cup brown sugar
¼ cup honey
1 teaspoon vanilla
1 egg
1 cup flour
½ teaspoon baking soda
¼ teaspoon salt
1 teaspoon cinnamon
½ teaspoon ginger
¼ teaspoon nutmeg
1 cup chopped pecans

YIELDS 36 COOKIES

CALORIES	98.33
FAT	5.36 GRAMS
SATURATED FAT	1.93 GRAMS
TRANS FAT	0.07 GRAMS*
CARBOHYDRATES	11.31 GRAMS
CHOLESTEROL	12.65 MG

Honey adds a flowery aroma to these spicy cookies, and helps keep the cookies moist and chewy for days. You can increase the spice amounts if you'd like.

1. Preheat oven to 350°F. Place ½ cup of the oatmeal in a food processor and process until ground; mix with remaining oatmeal and set aside. In large bowl, combine butter and brown sugar; beat until fluffy. Add honey, vanilla, and egg and beat until combined.

2. Stir in flour, baking soda, salt, cinnamon, ginger, nutmeg, and the combined oatmeal and stir well. Add pecans and mix in. Drop by teaspoonfuls onto ungreased cookie sheets and bake for 8 to 12 minutes or until cookies are just set and light golden brown around the edges. Let cool on cookie sheets for 3 minutes, then carefully remove to wire racks to cool completely.

Frosted Lemon Bars

YIELDS 48 BARS

CALORIES	109.75
FAT	4.49 GRAMS
SATURATED FAT	2.94 GRAMS
TRANS FAT	0.07 GRAMS*
CARBOHYDRATES	16.70 GRAMS
CHOLESTEROL	25.25 MG

These delicious bars have a fluffy filling and an intense lemon frosting. They're for lemon lovers!

2-¼ cups flour, divided
¾ cup butter, divided
¼ cup coconut oil
2-¼ cups powdered sugar, divided
1 tablespoon lemon rind
4 eggs
1-½ cups sugar
¼ teaspoon salt
1 teaspoon baking powder
⅔ cup fresh lemon juice
2 tablespoons lemon juice for frosting

1. Preheat oven to 350°F. In large bowl, combine 2 cups flour, ½ cup butter, coconut oil, ¼ cup powdered sugar, and lemon rind. Mix at low speed until crumbs form. Press into bottom of 9" × 13" baking pan. Bake for 20 minutes.

2. While crust is baking, beat eggs in large bowl until foamy. Gradually add sugar, beating until mixture is thick and very light yellow. Sift ¼ cup flour, salt, and baking powder over the mixture; beat in just until combined, then beat in ⅔ cup lemon juice. Remove crust from oven and immediately pour egg mixture over crust. Return to oven and bake for 25 to 35 minutes or until filling is set and beginning to turn light golden brown. Cool.

3. In small bowl, combine 2 cups powdered sugar, ¼ cup butter, and enough lemon juice to make a frosting; beat well. Spread over cooled bars. Store, covered, in the refrigerator.

Lemons

An average-size lemon will yield about 3 tablespoons of juice. Remove the peel, or zest, from the lemon before you squeeze the juice. To get the most juice out of each lemon, prick them with a fork and microwave each for 10 seconds on high. Or, using the palm of your hand, firmly roll the lemons on the countertop before slicing.

Almond Pineapple Bars

1 cup blanched almonds
½ cup candied pineapple
½ cup coconut

2 tablespoons butter, softened
2 tablespoons honey
1-½ cups dark chocolate chips

1. Grease a 9" × 13" pan with unsalted butter and set aside. In food processor, combine almonds and pineapple; grind until fine. Spread coconut in a small microwave-safe pan; microwave on high for 3 to 6 minutes or until golden brown, stirring once during cooking time. Add to almond mixture.

2. Add butter and honey and mix well. Press into prepared pan. In small microwave-safe bowl, place dark chocolate chips. Microwave on 50 percent power for 1 minute, remove and stir. Continue microwaving chips at 30-second intervals, stirring after each interval, until chocolate melts. Pour over bars and spread to coat. Chill until firm, then cut into bars.

YIELDS 36 BARS

CALORIES	74.25
FAT	5.24 GRAMS
SATURATED FAT	2.21 GRAMS
TRANS FAT	0.02 GRAMS*
CARBOHYDRATES	7.23 GRAMS
CHOLESTEROL	1.70 MG

This chewy bar tastes like toffee, but it's very low in fat. You can find candied pineapple in bulk bins or at health food stores.

Chocolate Walnut Fingers

½ cup unsalted butter
1 cup chopped walnuts
4 eggs
¾ cup sugar
¼ cup brown sugar

1 teaspoon vanilla
½ cup flour
½ teaspoon salt
1 cup semisweet chocolate chips
¼ cup powdered sugar

1. Preheat oven to 375°F. In small saucepan, melt butter. Pour into 9" × 13" pan and sprinkle with walnuts; set aside. In large bowl, beat eggs for 5 minutes until light. Gradually add sugars and beat for 5 minutes longer. Beat in vanilla, then fold in flour and salt.

2. Spoon egg mixture over nut mixture in pan and spread evenly. Bake for 20 to 25 minutes, until bars are light golden brown and set. Let cool for 10 minutes, then invert onto parchment paper that has been sprinkled with half of the powdered sugar. Replace any nuts that may have stuck to pan. Sprinkle with chocolate chips, then with powdered sugar. Cool completely and cut into rectangles.

YIELDS 36 BARS

CALORIES	106.03
FAT	6.58 GRAMS
SATURATED FAT	2.74 GRAMS
TRANS FAT	0.07 GRAMS*
CARBOHYDRATES	11.14 GRAMS
CHOLESTEROL	30.28 MG

Be sure to only use unsalted butter in this recipe so the bar cookies don't stick to the pan when inverted.

Sour Cream Chocolate Bars

These unusual bar cookies have no butter or other fat; sour cream provides the fat needed for good structure. They're cake like and velvety smooth.

1 cup sour cream
1 cup sugar
1 egg
1 teaspoon vanilla
1-½ cups flour
½ teaspoon baking soda
½ teaspoon baking powder
¼ teaspoon nutmeg
1 cup milk chocolate chips
1 cup chopped walnuts
¼ cup brown sugar

1. Preheat oven to 350°F. Grease 9" × 13" pan with unsalted butter and set aside. In large bowl, combine sour cream, sugar, egg, and vanilla and mix well. Add flour, baking soda, baking powder, and nutmeg and mix well.

2. Spoon dough into prepared pan and spread evenly. Sprinkle top with chocolate chips, walnuts, and brown sugar. Bake for 20 to 25 minutes or until bars are set and golden brown around edges. Cool in pan, then cut into bars.

Why Unsalted Butter for Pans?

Never use salted butter for greasing pans; the salt in the fat will make the cookies or bars stick! You can use cooking sprays, especially those containing flour, but they can leave a slightly artificial aftertaste. You can make your own cooking and baking sprays by purchasing an oil mister and filling it with the oil of your choice.

Lemon Meringues

3 egg whites
Pinch salt
1 teaspoon lemon juice
1 cup sugar
1 teaspoon lemon zest
5 round lemon candies, finely crushed

1. Preheat oven to 250°F. In large bowl, beat egg whites with salt and lemon juice until foamy. Gradually beat in sugar until stiff peaks form and sugar is dissolved. Fold in lemon zest and the finely crushed candies.

2. Drop by teaspoonfuls onto a baking sheet lined with parchment paper. Bake for 50 to 60 minutes or until meringues are set and crisp and very light golden brown. Cool on the cookie sheets for 3 minutes, then carefully peel off the parchment paper and place on wire racks to cool.

YIELDS 30 COOKIES

CALORIES	30.83
FAT	0.01 GRAMS
SATURATED FAT	0.0 GRAMS
TRANS FAT	0.0 GRAMS
CARBOHYDRATES	7.52 GRAMS
CHOLESTEROL	0.0 GRAMS

Make sure that the lemon candies are very finely crushed. And save some cookies (or make another batch!) to make Lemon Meringue Parfaits (page 282).

Apricot Bars

1 cup chopped dried apricots
1 cup sugar
1 cup water
1 cup chopped walnuts, divided
½ cup apricot preserves
2 cups flour

2 cups quick-cooking oatmeal
1-¼ cups brown sugar
1 teaspoon baking soda
¼ teaspoon salt
1 cup butter, melted

1. Preheat oven to 350°F. In medium saucepan, combine apricots, sugar, and water. Bring to a simmer over medium heat, then reduce heat to low and cook, stirring frequently, until mixture is thick, about 20 minutes. Stir in ½ cup walnuts and apricot preserves and set aside.

2. In bowl, combine flour, oatmeal, brown sugar, baking soda, salt, and remaining walnuts. Stir in melted butter until crumbs form. Place half of the crumbs into a 9" × 13" pan and press down. Top with apricot mixture and spread to cover. Sprinkle with remaining oat mixture. Bake for 25 minutes or until crumbs are golden brown around edges. Cool, then cut into bars.

YIELDS 48 BARS

CALORIES	133.76
FAT	5.67 GRAMS
SATURATED FAT	2.56 GRAMS
TRANS FAT	0.10 GRAMS*
CARBOHYDRATES	20.13 GRAMS
CHOLESTEROL	10.17 MG

Remember date bars? Those old-fashioned cookies are updated with a tangy apricot filling that combines cooked dried apricots with preserves.

Date Nut Chews

Finely ground oatmeal and white chocolate chips add chewy texture to these fabulous bar cookies.

3 eggs
½ cup sugar
½ cup powdered sugar
2 tablespoons corn syrup
1 teaspoon vanilla
¾ cup flour
½ teaspoon salt
1 tablespoon cornstarch
1 teaspoon baking powder
½ cup oatmeal, ground
½ cup white chocolate chips, ground
1 cup chopped dates
1 cup chopped pecans
Powdered sugar

1. Preheat oven to 350°F. Grease a 9" × 13" pan with unsalted butter and set aside. In large bowl, beat eggs until frothy. Gradually add sugar and powdered sugar, beating until mixture becomes very thick and light-colored. Beat in corn syrup and vanilla. Then stir in flour, salt, cornstarch, and baking powder and mix well.

2. Stir in ground oatmeal, ground white chocolate chips, dates, and pecans. Spoon batter into prepared pan. Bake for 25 to 35 minutes or until bars are just set and light golden brown. Cool for 30 minutes, or until cool enough to handle, then cut into bars. Roll bars in powdered sugar to coat; place on wire rack to cool completely.

White Chocolate Chips

White chocolate chips, also known as vanilla milk chips, are actually not true chocolate at all. They don't contain any chocolate liqueur so can't be classified as actual chocolate. If you can't find the white chocolate chips, you can buy a white chocolate candy bar and chop it to use in this or any other recipe.

Carrot Pecan Bars

4 eggs
1 cup sugar
½ cup brown sugar
½ cup caramel ice cream topping, divided
1-½ cups canola oil
2 cups finely grated carrots
2 teaspoons vanilla, divided
2 cups flour
½ cup whole-wheat flour
½ teaspoon salt
1 teaspoon baking soda
1 teaspoon baking powder
1 teaspoon cinnamon
¼ teaspoon nutmeg
1-½ cups chopped pecans
1 (8-ounce) package low-fat cream cheese, softened
3 cups powdered sugar

YIELDS 48 BARS

CALORIES	185.48
FAT	10.61 GRAMS
SATURATED FAT	1.76 GRAMS
TRANS FAT	0.02 GRAMS
CARBOHYDRATES	21.51 GRAMS
CHOLESTEROL	20.31 MG

These bars are like a dense and chewy carrot cake. The cream cheese frosting adds the perfect finishing touch.

1. Preheat oven to 350°F. Grease a 10" × 15" jelly roll pan with unsalted butter and set aside. In large bowl, place eggs; beat at high speed until light-colored and thick. Gradually add sugar and brown sugar, beating thoroughly. Add ¼ cup caramel ice cream topping, canola oil, carrots, and 1 teaspoon vanilla.

2. Stir in flour, whole-wheat flour, salt, baking soda and powder, cinnamon, and nutmeg and mix well. Stir in pecans. Spoon and spread batter into prepared pan. Bake for 30 to 40 minutes or until bars are light golden brown and spring back when touched. Let cool on wire rack.

3. For frosting, in large bowl combine cream cheese and ¼ cup caramel ice cream topping; beat until fluffy. Add powdered sugar and 1 teaspoon vanilla; beat until smooth. Frost cooled bars. Store covered at room temperature.

Crisp Icebox Cookies

You can substitute any nut you'd like in these delicious little crisp cookies. Finely chopped macadamia nuts would be an excellent choice.

¾ cup butter, softened
¼ cup coconut oil
1 cup brown sugar
1 cup sugar
2 eggs
2 teaspoons vanilla
2-¼ cups flour
1 teaspoon baking soda
½ teaspoon salt
1 cup finely chopped cashews

1. In large bowl, beat butter and coconut oil until blended. Gradually add brown sugar and sugar; beat until fluffy. Add eggs and vanilla and mix well. Stir in flour, baking soda, and salt.

2. Shape dough into 3 long rolls, about 1-½" in diameter. Roll the cookie rolls in the chopped cashews, gently pressing nuts into dough to adhere. Wrap well in wax paper, then put rolls into plastic food-storage bags. Chill for at least 24 hours.

3. Preheat oven to 375°F. Cut the dough into slices about ¼" thick and place on ungreased cookie sheets. Bake for 6 to 8 minutes or until cookies are very light golden brown and set. Cool on cookie sheets for 3 minutes, then remove to wire racks to cool.

About Icebox Cookies
If you're pressed for time, icebox cookies are a great choice. You can make the dough one day, then chill it in the refrigerator and bake the next day, or the next. These cookie doughs also freeze very well. Wrap them in freezer wrap then place in freezer plastic bags. You can slice and bake the dough frozen; just add a few minutes to the baking time.

Browned Butter Granola Cookies

½ cup butter
¼ cup coconut oil
1 cup brown sugar
½ cup sugar
1 egg
¼ cup orange juice
1 teaspoon grated orange rind
1-½ teaspoons vanilla
2 cups flour
1 teaspoon baking powder
1 teaspoon baking soda
1 teaspoon cinnamon
¼ teaspoon cardamom
1-½ cups granola
½ cup milk chocolate chips, chopped

YIELDS 36 COOKIES

CALORIES	134.92
FAT	6.21 GRAMS
SATURATED FAT	3.55 GRAMS
TRANS FAT	0.07 GRAMS*
CARBOHYDRATES	18.29 GRAMS
CHOLESTEROL	13.19 MG

Buy granola from a natural-foods store and read the label carefully to make sure that partially hydrogenated oil isn't in the ingredient list.

1. In heavy saucepan, melt butter over medium heat. Continue to cook butter, watching carefully, until brown flecks form in the butter, about 7 to 10 minutes. Remove from heat and cool, then refrigerate until solid.

2. Preheat oven to 350°F. In large bowl, combine chilled butter, coconut oil, brown sugar, and sugar and beat well. Stir in egg, orange juice, orange rind, and vanilla. Then add flour, baking powder and soda, cinnamon, and cardamom until a dough forms. Stir in granola and chopped chocolate chips.

3. Drop dough by teaspoons onto ungreased cookie sheet. Bake for 10 to 13 minutes or until cookies are set and light golden brown on the bottoms. Cool on cookie sheets for 3 minutes, then carefully remove to wire racks to cool completely.

Oatmeal Pumpkin Nut Bars

YIELDS 36 BARS

CALORIES	200.52
FAT	11.23 GRAMS
SATURATED FAT	2.05 GRAMS
TRANS FAT	0.05 GRAMS
CARBOHYDRATES	23.26 GRAMS
CHOLESTEROL	28.59 MG

A buttery oatmeal crust is topped with a smooth pumpkin cake-like filling, then finished with chopped pecans. This is a great choice for Thanksgiving dessert.

¾ cup quick-cooking oatmeal
2-¾ cups flour, divided
1 cup brown sugar, divided
6 tablespoons butter, melted
4 eggs
1 cup canola oil
1-½ cups sugar
1 (15-ounce) can solid-pack pumpkin
1 teaspoon baking powder
1 teaspoon baking soda
½ teaspoon salt
1 teaspoon cinnamon
¼ teaspoon cardamom
1 cup chopped pecans

1. Preheat oven to 350°F. In large bowl, combine oatmeal, ¾ cup flour, and ½ cup brown sugar and mix well. Add butter and mix thoroughly. Press crumbs into a 9" × 13" pan. Bake for 10 minutes, then remove from oven and set aside.

2. Meanwhile, in large bowl combine eggs, canola oil, sugar, ½ cup brown sugar, and pumpkin and beat until smooth. Add 2 cups flour, baking powder, baking soda, salt, cinnamon, and cardamom and beat until mixture is combined. Pour over baked crust and sprinkle with pecans. Return to oven and bake for 25 to 30 minutes or until bars are set. Sprinkle with powdered sugar, if desired. Store bars in refrigerator.

Baking Powder Versus Baking Soda

Some recipes call for baking powder, others for soda, and others for a combination. Why? It depends on the acidity of the batter or dough. If acidic ingredients like brown sugar, lemon juice, buttermilk, or sour cream are used, the baking soda helps even out the pH so the texture of the product is even and consistent. Don't substitute one for the other!

Banana Milk-Chocolate Bars

⅓ cup butter, softened
½ cup sugar
½ cup brown sugar
1 cup sour cream
1 cup mashed bananas
1-½ teaspoons vanilla
1-¾ cups flour
1 teaspoon baking soda
½ teaspoon baking powder
¼ teaspoon salt
½ teaspoon cinnamon
2 cups milk chocolate chips, divided
2 cups mini marshmallows

YIELDS 36 BARS

CALORIES	133.53
FAT	5.90 GRAMS
SATURATED FAT	3.26 GRAMS
TRANS FAT	0.06 GRAMS*
CARBOHYDRATES	18.88 GRAMS
CHOLESTEROL	9.48 MG

You'll need about two very ripe bananas to make the cup of mashed bananas needed in this delicious, velvety bar-cookie recipe.

1. Preheat oven to 350°F. Grease a 9" × 13" pan with unsalted butter and dust with flour; set aside. In large bowl, combine butter and sugars; beat until light and fluffy. Beat in sour cream, bananas, and vanilla. Then stir in flour, baking soda, baking powder, salt, and cinnamon. Chop ½ cup milk chocolate chips and stir into batter.

2. Pour batter into prepared pan. Bake for 30 to 40 minutes or until bars are set and golden brown. When bars come out of oven, immediately sprinkle with remaining 1-½ cups milk chocolate chips and marshmallows. Return to oven for 3 minutes or until marshmallows are puffed. Place on wire rack and let cool for 20 minutes; using the tip of a knife, swirl the chocolate and marshmallows together. Let cool and cut into bars.

Ripening Bananas
Many of us have ripe bananas on hand because not all of the bananas in a bunch get eaten when they're at the perfect texture. But if you want ripe bananas and none are available, place bananas in a closed paper bag along with an apple or tomato. Those fruits give off ethylene gas, which helps hasten the ripening process.

Brown Sugar Drop Cookies

YIELDS 42 COOKIES

CALORIES	120.31
FAT	4.75 GRAMS
SATURATED FAT	2.89 GRAMS
TRANS FAT	0.11 GRAMS*
CARBOHYDRATES	18.59 GRAMS
CHOLESTEROL	21.25 MG

Brown sugar cookies are frosted with a browned butter frosting. These little cookies are deliciously soft and chewy.

¾ cup butter, divided

1 cup brown sugar

½ cup sugar

2 eggs

2 teaspoons vanilla, divided

2-¼ cups flour

1 teaspoon baking soda

½ teaspoon baking powder

¼ teaspoon salt

1 cup sour cream

2 cups powdered sugar

2 to 3 tablespoons milk

1. In heavy saucepan over medium heat, melt the butter. Reduce heat to low and cook butter, stirring frequently, until brown flecks form, about 8 minutes. Chill butter until firm. When ready to bake, preheat oven to 350°F.

2. In large bowl, combine ½ cup of the chilled butter, brown sugar, and sugar and beat well. Add eggs and 1 teaspoon vanilla. Place flour, baking soda, baking powder, and salt in a sifter. Sift one-third of flour mixture over butter mixture and stir in. Then add half of the sour cream. Repeat until all of the flour mixture and sour cream are added.

3. Drop batter by teaspoons onto parchment-paper-lined cookie sheet. Bake for 8 to 11 minutes or until cookies are set. Remove to wire rack to cool. For frosting, place remaining chilled butter in medium bowl. Beat in powdered sugar, 1 teaspoon vanilla, and enough milk for desired consistency. Frost cooled cookies.

Chilling Melted Butter

Butter forms the structure of cookies and baked goods. When sugar is beaten into butter, the crystals form small air pockets, which expand with the CO_2 the leavening creates. Unless the recipe calls for it, do not melt the butter and rechill; it will change the texture of the finished product. These cookies were developed with melted and rechilled butter.

Chapter 14

Sweet Pies

Traditional Pie Crust

**YIELDS 2 CRUSTS
(20 SERVINGS)**

CALORIES	129.74
FAT	8.76 GRAMS
SATURATED FAT	5.62 GRAMS
TRANS FAT	0.12 GRAMS*
CARBOHYDRATES	11.44 GRAMS
CHOLESTEROL	12.28 MG

Butter adds flavor to this pie crust, the coconut oil makes it light and flaky, and the shortening gives it body. It's just about perfect.

½ cup butter
¼ cup coconut oil
2 tablespoons trans fat–free shortening
2-¼ cups flour
1 tablespoon sugar
½ teaspoon salt
2 tablespoons milk
2 to 3 tablespoons cold water

1. In medium bowl, combine butter, coconut oil, and shortening with 1 tablespoon flour. Beat until combined; place in refrigerator for 20 minutes. Meanwhile, in large bowl, combine remaining flour, sugar, and salt and mix well.

2. When butter mixture has chilled, cut into pieces over flour mixture. Using a pastry blender or two knives, cut butter mixture into flour mixture until particles are fine. Sprinkle milk over mixture, tossing with fork. Then add enough water, tossing with fork, until particles just come together when pressed with fingers.

3. Form into a ball and flatten slightly. Wrap in plastic wrap and chill for at least 1 hour. When ready to bake, divide dough in half. On lightly floured surface, roll each half to a 12" circle. Ease gently into 9" pie plate, press down, and flute edges. For single crust pie, prick crust with fork and bake at 425°F for 10 to 12 minutes or until lightly browned. For double crust pie, follow directions in recipe.

Purchased Pie Crusts
Read labels carefully if you choose to use purchased, premade pie crusts. Not all labels currently have trans fat information, so look for the words "hydrogenated" or "partially hydrogenated" in the list of ingredients. Some manufacturers have switched to lower trans fat oils and fats; they may still contain some trans fat.

Oatmeal Pie Crust

2 cups quick-cooking oatmeal, divided
¼ cup all-purpose flour
¼ cup brown sugar
¼ teaspoon salt

7 tablespoons butter, softened
2 tablespoons coconut oil
1 to 3 tablespoons cold water

1. Preheat oven to 350°F. In blender or food processor, process 1 cup of the oatmeal until fine. Place in large bowl along with remaining oats, flour, brown sugar, and salt and mix well. Add butter and coconut oil and work with fingers until crumbs are fine. Sprinkle water over crust and work with fingers until it forms a dough.

2. Crumble dough into 9" pie plate and press so it covers bottom and sides of plate. Bake for 14 to 21 minutes or until crust is light golden brown and firm. You can fill the crust before baking if using a baked filling.

YIELDS 1 CRUST (10 SERVINGS)

CALORIES	188.97
FAT	11.83 GRAMS
SATURATED FAT	7.64 GRAMS
TRANS FAT	0.21 GRAMS*
CARBOHYDRATES	18.60 GRAMS
CHOLESTEROL	21.35 MG

Oatmeal adds a nice crunch to this simple pie crust. It's perfect for any sweet filling; it's especially good in Brown Sugar Pecan Pie (page 270).

Cookie Pie Crust

1-½ cups flour
2 tablespoons sugar
3 tablespoons brown sugar
6 tablespoons butter, melted
2 egg yolks
¼ teaspoon salt

1. Preheat oven to 375°F. In large bowl, combine flour, sugar, and brown sugar and mix well. In small bowl, combine melted butter and egg yolks and mix well. Sprinkle over flour mixture and stir with a fork until combined and a dough forms. Crumble dough onto a cookie sheet, spreading evenly. Bake for 10 to 15 minutes or until crumbs are light golden brown.

2. Cool for 10 to 20 minutes, or until crumbs are cool enough to handle. Press into bottom and up sides of 9" pie plate. Cool completely.

YIELDS 1 PIE CRUST (10 SERVINGS)

CALORIES	165.46
FAT	7.99 GRAMS
SATURATED FAT	4.73 GRAMS
TRANS FAT	0.18 GRAMS*
CARBOHYDRATES	20.95 GRAMS
CHOLESTEROL	60.26 MG

This simple pie-crust recipe is perfect for beginning cooks. You don't have to worry about rolling out dough and handling that fragile thin crust.

Cream Cheese Pie Crust

YIELDS 1 CRUST (10 SERVINGS)

CALORIES	130.92
FAT	8.98 GRAMS
SATURATED FAT	5.07 GRAMS
TRANS FAT	0.17 GRAMS*
CARBOHYDRATES	10.60 GRAMS
CHOLESTEROL	21.63 MG

Using cream cheese helps cut the fat in this pie crust recipe, and it adds flakiness and a nice flavor.

1 (3-ounce) package cream cheese, softened
¼ cup butter, softened
1 tablespoon trans fat–free shortening
1 cup all-purpose flour
1 tablespoon cornstarch
Pinch salt
1 to 2 tablespoons milk
½ teaspoon lemon juice

1. In medium bowl, combine cream cheese, butter, and shortening and mix well until combined. Place in refrigerator until hard. Then in large bowl, combine flour, cornstarch, and salt and mix well. Cut cream cheese mixture into small pieces and cut into flour mixture until particles are fine. Sprinkle 1 tablespoon milk and the lemon juice over flour mixture and toss. If necessary, add enough more milk until dough just holds together.

2. Gather dough together and press into a ball. Wrap in plastic wrap and flatten into a disk. Refrigerate for at least two hours. When ready to bake, preheat oven to 350°F. Roll out pastry between two sheets of wax paper. Ease into a 9" pie plate and press pastry to bottom and up sides. Flute edges, prick with fork, and bake for 8 to 13 minutes or until pastry is light golden brown. Cool completely.

Filling a Pie Crust
Any pie crust is the start of an easy dessert. You can fill a crust with scoops of ice cream and toppings ranging from candied nuts to crushed cookies to ice cream toppings. Make a simple pudding, fold in 1 cup of whipped heavy cream, pour into the pie crust, and chill, and you have a mousse pie. Use your imagination!

Crumb Crust

⅓ cup butter
2 tablespoons coconut oil
2 tablespoons sugar
1-½ cups cookie crumbs
¼ cup finely chopped walnuts

1. Preheat oven to 350°F. In medium bowl, combine butter, coconut oil, and sugar, and mix until blended. Stir in crumbs and walnuts and mix until crumbs are coated. Press into the bottom and up sides of a 9" pie plate. Bake for 10 to 15 minutes or until crust is set. Cool completely and fill as directed in recipe.

YIELDS 1 CRUST (SERVES 10)

CALORIES	216.30
FAT	14.57 GRAMS
SATURATED FAT	8.36 GRAMS
TRANS FAT	0.16 GRAMS*
CARBOHYDRATES	20.59 GRAMS
CHOLESTEROL	24.47 MG

Crumbs made from these cookies work well in this recipe: Honey Graham Crackers (page 64), Crisp Icebox Cookies (page 254), and Gingersnaps (page 242).

Cantaloupe Ice Cream Tart

1 Crumb Crust (above)
2 cups cubed cantaloupe
1 tablespoon lemon juice
2 cups vanilla frozen yogurt
1-½ cups lemon sherbet

1. Make Crumb Crust using Honey Graham Crackers (page 64) and press into bottom and up sides of 10" deep-dish pie pan. Bake at 350°F for 8 to 12 minutes or until set. Cool completely.

2. Purée cantaloupe with lemon juice in food processor or blender. Combine with frozen yogurt in medium bowl; let stand for 10 minutes to soften yogurt. Stir to marble. Spread lemon sherbet in bottom of pie crust and top with cantaloupe mixture. Freeze for at least 4 hours before serving.

SERVES 10

CALORIES	306.47
FAT	16.69 GRAMS
SATURATED FAT	9.62 GRAMS
TRANS FAT	0.16 GRAMS*
CARBOHYDRATES	37.05 GRAMS
CHOLESTEROL	25.04 MG

This delicious pie can be made with just about any fruit. Strawberries, raspberries, or peaches would all be nice choices.

Angel Pie Crust

YIELDS 1 CRUST (SERVES 8)

CALORIES	92.90
FAT	1.46 GRAMS
SATURATED FAT	0.91 GRAMS
TRANS FAT	0.04 GRAMS*
CARBOHYDRATES	19.09 GRAMS
CHOLESTEROL	3.81 MG

This practically fat-free pie crust is perfect piled high with ice cream balls and different types of ice cream topping.

3 egg whites
½ teaspoon lemon juice
¾ cup sugar
¼ teaspoon salt
1 teaspoon vanilla
1 tablespoon unsalted butter
1 teaspoon flour

1. Preheat oven to 275°F. Separate eggs while cold; let egg whites stand at room temperature for 45 minutes before beating (for better volume). Beat egg whites with lemon juice until foamy. Gradually add ¼ cup sugar, beating until soft peaks form. Add salt and vanilla and beat well. Then gradually add remaining ½ cup sugar, beating until stiff peaks form.

2. Heavily butter a 9" pie plate and dust with flour. Place meringue in prepared plate and form a shell, building up the sides to about ½" over top rim of pie plate. Bake for 1 hour, until crust is very light golden. Turn off oven and let meringue cool for 1 hour in closed oven, then cool completely on wire rack.

3. You can also shape this pie on a Silpat-lined cookie sheet. Spread meringue into a 10" circle at least 1" thick, then spoon more meringue on the edges and build up a 2" rim that is 2" wide. Bake at 275°F for 45 minutes, then cool for 30 minutes in closed, turned-off oven; remove and cool completely on wire rack.

Leftover Egg Yolks

Leftover egg yolks can be frozen. Just beat slightly and divide into ice cube trays. Freeze until solid, then package into freezer bags. To thaw, let stand in the refrigerator overnight. You can use egg yolks to make Cookie Pie Crust (page 261) and Kringla (page 98). They're also great fried, then chopped and added to egg salad.

Chocolate Oatmeal Pie

½ recipe Traditional Pie Crust (page 260)
½ cup butter
1-½ cups semisweet chocolate chips, divided
¾ cup brown sugar
¼ cup corn syrup
3 eggs
2 tablespoons flour
1 cup chopped walnuts
1 cup quick-cooking oatmeal

1. Preheat oven to 350°F. Do not prebake pie crust. In large saucepan, combine butter with ¾ cup of the chocolate chips, brown sugar, and corn syrup. Cook and stir over low heat until butter and chocolate chips melt. Remove from heat. Beat in eggs, one at a time, beating well after each addition.

2. Stir in flour, walnuts, oatmeal, and remaining ¾ cup of chocolate chips. Pour into prepared crust. Bake for 40 to 50 minutes or until pie is set and pie crust is golden brown. Cool for 45 minutes, then serve warm or cool.

SERVES 12

CALORIES	486.53
FAT	29.58 GRAMS
SATURATED FAT	14.17 GRAMS
TRANS FAT	0.30 GRAMS*
CARBOHYDRATES	52.36 GRAMS
CHOLESTEROL	83.44 MG

Oatmeal takes the place of nuts in this simple yet very rich pie. Serve it with a scoop of ice cream or a dollop of whipped cream.

Cherry Orange Meringue Pie

SERVES 10

CALORIES	475.44
FAT	20.74 GRAMS
SATURATED FAT	11.76 GRAMS
TRANS FAT	0.18 GRAMS*
CARBOHYDRATES	66.43 GRAMS
CHOLESTEROL	106.10 MG

Cherry preserves and oranges make this simple creamy pie delicious. Note: pasteurized eggs may take longer to beat into peaks.

1 Crumb Crust (page 263)
¼ cup cherry preserves
1 teaspoon orange zest
1 (14-ounce) can sweetened condensed milk
3 pasteurized eggs, separated
⅓ cup orange juice
3 tablespoons lemon juice, divided
½ cup sugar

1. Preheat oven to 350°F. Make the Crumb Crust with trans fat–free vanilla wafers or Honey Graham Crackers (page 64); bake for 10 minutes at 350°F and cool completely. In small bowl, combine cherry preserves with orange zest and blend well; spread over cooled pie crust.

2. In medium bowl, combine sweetened condensed milk, 3 egg yolks, orange juice, and all but ½ teaspoon lemon juice; mix until thickened. Spoon into pie crust. In large bowl, combine egg whites with ½ teaspoon lemon juice; beat until foamy.

3. Gradually add sugar, beating until very stiff peaks form. Spoon onto filling and spread gently to cover, making sure to seal meringue to edges of pie crust. Bake for 10 to 15 minutes or until meringue is lightly browned. Cool for 30 minutes, then chill in refrigerator until ready to serve, at least 4 hours.

Preserves, Jams, or Jelly?

The difference between these three forms of fruit jelly lies in the way the fruit is used. In jellies, the fruit juice only is used; it is thickened with sugar and pectin. Jams are made from the whole fruit, usually puréed or mashed. And preserves are made from pieces of fruit mixed with a purée, so it most closely resembles the fresh fruit.

Cranberry Almond Pie

½ recipe Traditional Pie Crust (page 260)
2 cups cranberries
¾ cup orange juice
1 teaspoon orange zest
½ cup sugar
2 tablespoons cornstarch
2 tablespoons water
½ cup flour
½ cup brown sugar
½ teaspoon cinnamon
⅛ teaspoon allspice
⅓ cup butter
¾ cup slivered almonds
½ cup sliced almonds

SERVES 10	
CALORIES	381.06
FAT	21.26 GRAMS
SATURATED FAT	10.01 GRAMS
TRANS FAT	0.28 GRAMS*
CARBOHYDRATES	45.00 GRAMS
CHOLESTEROL	28.55 MG

Tart cranberries are cooked with orange juice to make the filling for this festive pie. The almond topping is crunchy and sweet, for a nice contrast.

1. Bake and cool pie crust. In large saucepan, combine cranberries, orange juice, orange zest, and sugar. Bring to a boil over medium high heat. Cook until cranberries start to pop, about 15 minutes. In small bowl, combine cornstarch and water and mix well. Stir into cranberry mixture, bring to a boil, and cook until thick. Cool for 1 hour, then pour into pie shell.

2. Preheat oven to 375°F. In small bowl, combine flour, brown sugar, cinnamon, and allspice and mix well. Cut in butter until crumbs form. Stir in slivered almonds. Sprinkle sliced almonds over cranberry mixture in pie shell. Sprinkle with brown sugar mixture. Bake for 20 to 25 minutes or until streusel is light brown. Cool completely, then chill for at least 4 hours before serving.

Free-Form Apple Pie

SERVES 10

CALORIES	349.48
FAT	16.62 GRAMS
SATURATED FAT	8.19 GRAMS
TRANS FAT	0.21 GRAMS*
CARBOHYDRATES	48.71 GRAMS
CHOLESTEROL	21.43 MG

This pie is called "free form" because it isn't baked in a pie plate. It's rustic and beautiful in its simplicity.

½ recipe Traditional Pie Crust (page 260)
¼ cup almond paste
4 apples, peeled and sliced
2 tablespoons lemon juice
⅔ cup sugar
2 tablespoons flour
¼ teaspoon salt
½ teaspoon cinnamon
½ cup brown sugar
½ cup chopped almonds
½ teaspoon cinnamon
¼ cup flour
3 tablespoons butter

1. Preheat oven to 400°F. Roll out pie crust to 13" circle and place on cookie sheet. Grate almond paste over the crust, leaving a 2-½" border around the edge. In large bowl, combine apples with lemon juice and toss; then sprinkle sugar, 2 tablespoons flour, salt, and cinnamon over apples; toss again. Set aside.

2. For streusel, in small bowl, combine brown sugar, almonds, cinnamon, and ¼ cup flour and mix well. Cut in butter until particles are fine. Place apple mixture in center of pie crust over almond paste. Fold edges of pie crust over the filling, leaving a 4" space open in the center. Sprinkle streusel over top of pie.

3. Place in oven and bake for 25 minutes. Reduce heat to 350°F and bake for 25 to 35 minutes longer or until pie crust is golden brown and juices are bubbling in center of pie.

Preparing Apples

Place an unpeeled apple on work surface. Using a sharp knife, cut down into apple on all four sides, leaving the core behind. Peel the pieces, then slice or chop as directed for recipe. Sprinkle the apple with lemon or lime juice as you work to prevent enzymatic browning.

Fresh Peach Pie

1 Cookie Pie Crust (page 261)
6 peaches, peeled
½ cup peach nectar
1 cup sugar
3 tablespoons cornstarch
4 tablespoons butter, divided
1 egg white
⅓ cup sugar
1-⅓ cups chopped pecans

SERVES 10

CALORIES	450.29
FAT	23.21 GRAMS
SATURATED FAT	8.55 GRAMS
TRANS FAT	0.28 GRAMS*
CARBOHYDRATES	59.19 GRAMS
CHOLESTEROL	72.46 MG

This excellent pie made from fresh peaches is topped with meringue-coated nuts. Omit the nut topping for just 281.66 calories and 8.14 grams of fat per serving.

1. Prepare Cookie Pie Crust; bake and cool. Dice three of the peaches and combine in large saucepan with peach nectar, 1 cup sugar, cornstarch, and 1 tablespoon butter. Cook over medium heat, stirring frequently, until thick and mixture boils, about 8 to 10 minutes. Chop remaining peaches and stir into cornstarch mixture. Cool for 30 minutes, then pour into pie crust. Place in refrigerator; chill for at least four hours.

2. Preheat oven to 325°F. In small bowl, beat egg white until foamy. Gradually add ⅓ cup sugar, beating until stiff peaks form. Fold in pecans. In 9" × 9" square pan, place 3 tablespoons butter; melt in oven. Remove pan from oven and spoon pecan mixture over butter. Bake for 30 minutes, stirring every 10 minutes, until nuts are light golden brown. Cool completely, then break into pieces. When serving pie, sprinkle pecans over each piece.

Brown Sugar Pecan Pie

SERVES 12

CALORIES	455.12
FAT	27.42 GRAMS
SATURATED FAT	11.55 GRAMS
TRANS FAT	0.30 GRAMS*
CARBOHYDRATES	51.84 GRAMS
CHOLESTEROL	84.79 MG

This pie doesn't contain any corn syrup, so it is denser and richer than traditional pecan pie, with a more intense pecan taste.

1-½ cups coarsely chopped pecans
½ recipe Traditional Pie Crust (page 260), unbaked
½ cup semisweet chocolate chips
2 cups brown sugar
3 eggs
½ cup heavy cream
⅓ cup butter, melted
2 teaspoons vanilla

1. Preheat oven to 350°F. Spread pecans on a cookie sheet and toast in oven for 5 to 9 minutes or until fragrant. Cool completely. Chop chocolate chips and sprinkle in bottom of prepared pie crust.

2. When ready to bake, in large bowl combine brown sugar, eggs, cream, butter, and vanilla and beat well with wire whisk to blend. Stir in pecans and pour over chocolate chips in pie crust. Bake for 30 to 40 minutes or until pie is set around edges but still slightly loose in center. Cool on wire rack.

Toasting Pecans

Nuts are toasted to help bring out their flavor so they are more intense and you can use less of them. You can toast nuts before or after chopping them. If toasting before chopping, let the nuts cool completely; if they are chopped while hot, they will become mushy. Let the nuts cool completely before adding them to any recipe.

German Chocolate Pie

1 teaspoon cocoa powder
½ cup butter
½ cup sugar
½ cup brown sugar
2 eggs, separated
1-½ cups semisweet chocolate chips, divided
⅓ cup flour
1 teaspoon vanilla
1 cup quick-cooking oatmeal
2 tablespoons sugar
3 tablespoons butter, melted
¼ cup chopped walnuts
½ cup flaked coconut
2 tablespoons heavy cream
1 teaspoon vanilla
⅓ cup brown sugar

SERVES 12

CALORIES	381.49
FAT	21.61 GRAMS
SATURATED FAT	12.31 GRAMS
TRANS FAT	0.29 GRAMS*
CARBOHYDRATES	47.42 GRAMS
CHOLESTEROL	66.64 MG

This is a crustless pie. The filling is more like a brownie than a pie filling. And the broiled topping is chewy and rich. It's divine!

1. Preheat oven to 325°F. Grease a 9" pie plate with unsalted butter and dust with cocoa powder; set aside. In large bowl, combine ½ cup butter, ½ cup sugar, and ½ cup brown sugar and beat well. Add egg yolks and beat until combined. Melt 1 cup chocolate chips in small pan over low heat; beat into butter mixture. Add flour, vanilla, and oatmeal and mix well.

2. In small bowl, combine egg whites with 2 tablespoons sugar and beat until stiff peaks form. Fold into chocolate mixture and spoon into prepared pie plate. Bake for 25 to 30 minutes or until just set.

3. While pie is in oven, prepare topping. In small bowl, combine 3 tablespoons melted butter, walnuts, coconut, cream, 1 teaspoon vanilla, and ⅓ cup brown sugar; mix well. When pie is done, remove from oven. Carefully spoon walnut mixture evenly over pie; gently spread to cover. Turn oven to broil. Broil pie 6" from the heat for 2 to 4 minutes, watching constantly and turning the pie, until mixture bubbles all over and begins to brown. Cool completely.

Chocolate Peanut Butter Truffle Tart

SERVES 16

CALORIES	389.12
FAT	23.30 GRAMS
SATURATED FAT	10.76 GRAMS
TRANS FAT	0.13 GRAMS*
CARBOHYDRATES	42.42 GRAMS
CHOLESTEROL	30.81 MG

Wow—this super-rich tart should be saved for a special occasion. You have to cut it into tiny pieces because it's so rich.

¼ cup butter, softened
¾ cup peanut butter, divided
½ cup sugar
1 teaspoon vanilla
1 egg
1-⅓ cups flour
1 (12-ounce) package semisweet chocolate chips
1 (11.5-ounce) package milk chocolate chips
½ cup heavy cream

1. Preheat oven to 350°F. In medium bowl, combine butter, ¼ cup peanut butter, and sugar and beat until combined. Add vanilla and egg and mix well. Stir in flour until a dough forms. Press dough into bottom and up sides of 10-inch tart pan with removable bottom. Bake for 15 to 20 minutes or until set and light golden brown. Cool completely.

2. In large microwave-safe bowl, combine ½ cup peanut butter, semisweet chocolate chips, milk chocolate chips, and cream. Microwave on high for 2 minutes; remove and stir. Continue microwaving for 30-second intervals, stirring after each interval, until chocolate is melted and mixture is smooth. Pour into cooled pie crust. Cover and chill for at least 4 hours. Let stand at room temperature for 15 to 20 minutes before serving to make cutting easier.

Measuring Brown Sugar
Brown sugar is measured differently than other sugars. Because it has a high moisture content, it must be packed firmly into the measuring cup, not spooned in like granulated or powered sugar. When the sugar is turned out of the cup, it should retain the shape of the cup. Measure tablespoons and teaspoons the same way.

Citrus Angel Pie

1 Angel Pie Crust (page 264)
⅓ cup all-purpose flour
1 cup sugar
¼ teaspoon salt
1-½ cups milk
1 (8-ounce) package cream cheese
3 egg yolks
3 tablespoons butter
½ teaspoon lemon zest
½ teaspoon orange zest
½ teaspoon lime zest
¼ cup lemon juice
¼ cup orange juice
3 tablespoons lime juice

1. Bake and cool the Angel Pie Crust. In large saucepan, combine flour, sugar, and salt and blend well with wire whisk. Gradually add milk, stirring constantly. Place over medium heat and cook and stir until mixture thickens and comes to a full boil. Reduce heat to low and cook for 2 minutes longer, stirring constantly. Cut cream cheese into cubes and add to milk mixture along with egg yolks. Cook and stir for 2 more minutes.

2. Remove from heat and stir in remaining ingredients, beating well until combined. Cool for 30 minutes, then chill for 1 hour until mixture mounds when dropped from a spoon. Stir again if necessary and spoon into pie shell. Cover and chill for at least 4 hours before serving.

SERVES 10

CALORIES	313.77
FAT	14.30 GRAMS
SATURATED FAT	8.62 GRAMS
TRANS FAT	0.11 GRAMS*
CARBOHYDRATES	42.60 GRAMS
CHOLESTEROL	101.91

The creamy citrus filling is piled into a meringue crust for a decadent pie perfect for summer entertaining. Follow directions to the letter so the filling sets properly.

Strawberry Meringue Pie

SERVES 8

CALORIES	213.86
FAT	1.66 GRAMS
SATURATED FAT	0.92 GRAMS
TRANS FAT	0.04 GRAMS*
CARBOHYDRATES	48.92 GRAMS
CHOLESTEROL	3.81 MG

A hard meringue for the shell and a soft meringue on top make this delicious and gorgeous pie unique. And it's very low in fat!

1 Angel Pie Crust (page 264), baked and cooled
3 cups sliced strawberries
1 cup sugar, divided
¼ teaspoon salt
1 (0.25-ounce) package unflavored gelatin
3 tablespoons water
2 teaspoons vanilla, divided
2 pasteurized egg whites
½ teaspoon lemon juice

1. Bake and cool the Angel Pie Crust. Place 1 cup of the strawberries in a large saucepan; mash with potato masher or fork. Add ½ cup sugar and the salt and let stand for 10 minutes. Meanwhile, in small bowl sprinkle gelatin over water and let stand.

2. Cook strawberry mixture over medium heat until it comes to a boil; stir until sugar dissolves. Remove from heat and add gelatin mixture. Cool for 30 minutes, then stir in 1 teaspoon vanilla and remaining strawberries. Chill in refrigerator until set.

3. When strawberry mixture is set, spoon into the pie crust and return to refrigerator. In medium bowl, beat egg whites with lemon juice until foamy. Gradually add ½ cup sugar, beating until stiff peaks form and sugar dissolves. Spoon on top of strawberry mixture, sealing the meringue to the pie-crust edges. Using a propane torch, brown the meringue, being careful not to overbrown the pie-crust edges. Chill for at least four hours before serving.

Using a Propane Torch

You must use a propane torch when browning a meringue on a pie that can't go into the oven, like an ice cream pie or Strawberry Meringue Pie (this page). You can find them at baking supply stores or even large grocery stores. Follow the instructions carefully. The meringue browns very quickly, so keep the flame moving constantly.

Peanut Butter Ice Cream Pie

½ recipe Traditional Pie Crust (page 260)
⅔ cup powdered sugar
⅔ cup natural peanut butter, divided
3 cups vanilla frozen yogurt
½ cup whipping cream
2 tablespoons powdered sugar
¼ cup grated milk chocolate

1. Prepare, bake, and cool the pie crust. In small bowl, combine powdered sugar and ⅓ cup peanut butter and mix until crumbly; set aside. In large bowl, combine ⅓ cup peanut butter and frozen yogurt; let stand for 10 minutes. In small bowl, combine whipping cream and powdered sugar and beat until stiff peaks form. With same beaters, beat peanut butter and frozen yogurt mixture until smooth. Fold in whipped cream.

2. Sprinkle half the grated chocolate in the pie shell. Top with half of the frozen yogurt mixture, then half of the powdered sugar mixture. Repeat layers and sprinkle top with remaining chocolate. Cover and freeze for at least six hours before serving.

SERVES 12

CALORIES	337.04
FAT	20.50 GRAMS
SATURATED FAT	9.55 GRAMS
TRANS FAT	0.19 GRAMS*
CARBOHYDRATES	33.28 GRAMS
CHOLESTEROL	19.43 MG

This pie is perfect to serve after a summer barbecue in the backyard. Be sure to remove it from the freezer 30 minutes before slicing for best results.

Apricot Cream Pie

SERVES 8

CALORIES	308.15
FAT	15.39 GRAMS
SATURATED FAT	9.13 GRAMS
TRANS FAT	0.25 GRAMS*
CARBOHYDRATES	40.62 GRAMS
CHOLESTEROL	33.36 MG

Apricots taste like a cross between peaches and mandarin oranges. This gorgeous pie is excellent topped with some whipped cream and chocolate sauce.

1 Cream Cheese Pie Crust (page 262)
1 (16-ounce) can apricot halves
3 tablespoons lemon juice
¾ cup sugar
1 (0.25-ounce) package unflavored gelatin
½ cup sour cream
¼ cup coconut, toasted

1. Prepare and bake the pie crust; cool completely. Drain the apricots, reserving the liquid. Purée apricots in blender or food processor along with lemon juice and sugar; set aside. In small microwave-safe bowl, combine gelatin with ½ cup of the reserved apricot liquid; let stand for 5 minutes. Microwave mixture on 30 percent power for 1 to 2 minutes or until gelatin is completely dissolved.

2. Add gelatin and sour cream to apricot mixture. Blend or process until mixture is smooth. Pour into pie crust and chill for 2 hours; sprinkle with coconut. Chill for at least 2 more hours before serving. Store in refrigerator.

Toasting Coconut
You can toast coconut several ways. With either method, spread the coconut in a thin even layer in a small pan. Microwave at high power for 1 to 2 minutes, then stir. Repeat at 30-second intervals until coconut is light golden brown. To toast in the oven or toaster oven, bake for 20 to 30 minutes at 325°F, stirring occasionally, until brown.

Caramel Apple Meringue Pie

½ recipe Traditional Pie Crust (page 260)
3 tablespoons butter, melted
⅔ cup brown sugar, divided
⅓ cup pecans
6 large apples
3 tablespoons lemon juice
1 cup sugar, divided
2 tablespoons flour
1 teaspoon cinnamon
¼ teaspoon nutmeg
3 pasteurized egg whites
¼ teaspoon cream of tartar

SERVES 10	
CALORIES	366.90
FAT	14.96 GRAMS
SATURATED FAT	8.05 GRAMS
TRANS FAT	0.21 GRAMS*
CARBOHYDRATES	57.67 GRAMS
CHOLESTEROL	21.43 MG

This fabulous pie has a pecan caramel layer under the tender and tart apples, and is topped with a fluff of meringue.

1. Preheat oven to 400°F. Do not bake pie crust; place crust in freezer while preparing filling. In small bowl, combine 3 tablespoons melted butter with ⅓ cup brown sugar and ⅓ cup pecans and mix well. Set aside. Peel apples and slice into large bowl, sprinkling with lemon juice as you work.

2. Sprinkle apples with ½ cup sugar, ⅓ cup brown sugar, flour, cinnamon, and nutmeg and toss to coat. Remove pie crust from freezer and sprinkle crust with pecan mixture, pressing into pastry. Spoon apples into pie crust. Loosely cover with aluminum foil and place in oven. Bake for 10 minutes, then reduce heat to 350°F and bake for 40 to 50 minutes longer, until apples are tender and juices are bubbling in center of pie. Remove from oven. Turn oven temperature to 325°F.

3. In medium bowl, beat egg whites with cream of tartar until foamy. Gradually add remaining ½ cup of sugar, beating until stiff peaks form. Carefully spoon meringue onto hot pie, sealing meringue to pie crust and using the back of your spoon to make peaks. Bake at 325°F for 10 to 15 minutes or until meringue is lightly browned. Cool completely.

Banana-Split Pie

SERVES 10

CALORIES	492.64
FAT	26.50 GRAMS
SATURATED FAT	15.59 GRAMS
TRANS FAT	0.28 GRAMS*
CARBOHYDRATES	64.98 GRAMS
CHOLESTEROL	49.41 MG

Top this spectacular pie with caramel and chocolate ice cream topping, and sprinkle with toasted nuts and coconut.

1 Crumb Crust (page 263)
30 large marshmallows
½ cup milk
¾ cup heavy cream
2 tablespoons powdered sugar
2 bananas
⅓ cup seedless raspberry jam
1 cup chocolate chips

1. Make Crumb Crust using Crisp Icebox Cookies (page 254). Bake and cool completely. In large microwave-safe bowl, combine marshmallows and milk. Microwave on 50 percent power for 1 to 2 minutes, stirring once during cooking time, until marshmallows melt. Beat until smooth. In small bowl, combine heavy cream and powdered sugar and beat until stiff.

2. Fold whipped cream mixture into marshmallow mixture. Place half in bottom of pie crust. Peel bananas and slice; arrange over marshmallow filling. Drizzle jam over banana slices.

3. In small microwave-safe bowl, place chocolate chips. Microwave on 50 percent power for 2 minutes; remove and stir until smooth. Let cool for 20 minutes. Fold into remaining marshmallow mixture until marbled, and spread over bananas. Chill pie for at least 4 hours before serving.

Marbling

Marbling *is a cooking term that means to combine two mixtures, but not completely, so streaks of both still appear in the mixture. Usually the two mixtures have about the same consistency, so the marbling will hold and one won't melt into the other. Be sure that both mixtures are approximately the same temperature.*

Chapter 15

Desserts and Cakes

Caramel Gingerbread

SERVES 20

CALORIES	381.35
FAT	12.74 GRAMS
SATURATED FAT	8.63 GRAMS
TRANS FAT	0.21 GRAMS*
CARBOHYDRATES	65.71 GRAMS
CHOLESTEROL	43.93 MG

Golden Syrup is an English product that is a cross between corn syrup and molasses. Look for it in the baking aisle. If you can't find it, use ½ cup honey instead.

1-½ cups brown sugar, divided
½ cup sugar
½ cup butter, melted
⅓ cup coconut oil, melted
½ cup honey
½ cup Golden Syrup
½ cup orange juice
2 eggs
2-½ cups flour
½ cup whole-wheat flour
2-½ teaspoons cinnamon, divided
2 teaspoons ground ginger, divided
½ teaspoon salt
½ teaspoon ground nutmeg
1 (8-ounce) package low-fat cream cheese, softened
¼ cup butter, softened
2-½ cups powdered sugar

1. Preheat oven to 350°F. Spray a 9" × 13" pan with nonstick baking spray containing flour and set aside.

2. In large bowl, combine 1 cup brown sugar, sugar, ½ cup melted butter, melted coconut oil, honey, Golden Syrup, orange juice, and eggs and beat until smooth and blended. Stir in flour, whole-wheat flour, 2 teaspoons cinnamon, 1-½ teaspoons ginger, salt, and nutmeg and stir just until blended. Pour into prepared pan. Bake for 50 to 60 minutes, or until a toothpick inserted in cake comes out clean. Cool on wire rack.

3. For the Caramel Frosting, in medium bowl, combine cream cheese, ¼ cup butter, ½ cup brown sugar, powdered sugar, ½ teaspoon cinnamon, and ½ teaspoon ground ginger and beat until fluffy. Frost gingerbread. Store tightly covered at room temperature.

Devil's Food Cupcakes

1 cup sugar
½ cup brown sugar
½ cup cocoa powder
1 egg
⅔ cup butter, melted
1 cup buttermilk
½ cup brewed coffee
2 teaspoons vanilla
2-¼ cups flour
½ teaspoon salt
2 teaspoons baking soda
1 teaspoon baking powder

YIELDS 24 CUPCAKES

CALORIES	149.80
FAT	5.77 GRAMS
SATURATED FAT	3.52 GRAMS
TRANS FAT	0.15 GRAMS*
CARBOHYDRATES	23.31 GRAMS
CHOLESTEROL	22.78 MG

Using cocoa powder instead of chocolate not only reduces the saturated fat content, but makes cupcakes that are velvety and smooth.

1. Preheat oven to 350°F. Line 24 muffin cups with paper liners and set aside. In large mixing bowl, combine sugar, brown sugar, cocoa powder, egg, butter, buttermilk, coffee, and vanilla and mix well until smooth.

2. Sift together flour, salt, baking soda, and baking powder and add all at once to sugar mixture. Stir with a wire whisk until batter is smooth. Using a ¼ cup measure, pour batter into prepared muffin cups. Bake for 15 to 20 minutes or until cakes spring back when lightly touched in center. Cool in pans for 5 minutes, then remove to wire racks to cool completely. Frost with Buttercream Frosting (page 295) or sprinkle with powdered sugar.

Decorating Cupcakes

It's fun to decorate cupcakes; let your imagination run wild. You can place a doily on the top and sift powdered sugar over; carefully remove the doily for a lacy design. Frost cupcakes with just about any frosting; decorate with sprinkles or add chopped candies. For a fun birthday-party theme, top each frosted cupcake with an animal cracker.

Lemon Meringue Parfaits

SERVES 6

CALORIES	472.48
FAT	26.95 GRAMS
SATURATED FAT	9.06 GRAMS
TRANS FAT	0.33 GRAMS*
CARBOHYDRATES	56.09 GRAMS
CHOLESTEROL	139.79 MG

This spectacular dessert is perfect for a special occasion. You have to make it ahead of time, so all you have to do is take it out of the fridge.

3 eggs
⅓ cup lemon juice
¾ cup sugar
¼ cup butter, divided
⅓ cup brown sugar
1 cup coarsely chopped pecans
½ cup heavy whipping cream
12 Lemon Meringues (page 251)

1. In heavy saucepan, combine eggs with lemon juice and sugar. Beat with wire whisk until smooth. Cook over low heat, stirring constantly, until mixture thickens and bubbles, about 10 to 15 minutes. Remove from heat and strain into a small bowl. Stir in 2 tablespoons butter, then place a sheet of plastic wrap directly on the surface and chill until cold.

2. In medium microwave-safe bowl, combine 2 tablespoons butter and brown sugar. Microwave on high until melted and stir until blended. Stir in chopped pecans and microwave on high for 2 to 3 minutes, stirring once during cooking time, until pecans are glazed. Spread on wax paper and cool completely.

3. In small bowl, beat cream until stiff peaks form. With the same beaters, beat the chilled lemon mixture and fold in cream. Break Lemon Meringues into pieces. In four parfait glasses, layer the lemon cream, pecans, and Meringues. Cover and chill for at least 3 hours before serving.

Gingerbread Trifle

⅓ cup brown sugar
3 tablespoons cornstarch
2 cups milk
1 egg, beaten
1 teaspoon vanilla
½ cup whipping cream
2 tablespoons powdered sugar
½ pan Caramel Gingerbread (page 280)
1 cup dried cranberries
6 Gingersnaps (page 242), crumbled

Yes, frosted gingerbread is used in this unusual trifle recipe; it adds a nice touch of sweetness and creaminess that contrasts with the custard.

1. In heavy saucepan, combine brown sugar and cornstarch and mix well with wire whisk. Add about ½ cup of the milk and stir until smooth. Gradually add remaining milk, beating with whisk as you add. Then add egg. Bring to a simmer over medium heat; cook and stir for 7 to 8 minutes or until mixture is thickened. Remove from heat, stir in vanilla, and let cool.

2. In small bowl, combine whipping cream and powdered sugar; beat until stiff peaks form. Fold into brown sugar custard. Cut Caramel Gingerbread into 1" squares (some will have frosting and some will not). In large glass dish, layer one-third of the Gingerbread squares, custard, cranberries, and Gingersnaps. Repeat layers. Cover trifle and chill for 2 to 3 hours before serving.

Making Custards

Making your own custards and puddings is one way to enjoy this treat without having to rely on commercial mixes and blends, which can be high in trans fat. To make the best custard, stir constantly while the mixture is cooking. Use a wire whisk instead of a spoon to make sure there are no lumps.

Peanut Butter Crunch Cake

SERVES 16

CALORIES	463.62
FAT	23.95 GRAMS
SATURATED FAT	8.73 GRAMS
TRANS FAT	0.10 GRAMS*
CARBOHYDRATES	58.40 GRAMS
CHOLESTEROL	49.82 MG

Applesauce replaces some of the butter in this delicious cake with the built-in streusel topping.

⅓ cup butter, softened
1 cup natural peanut butter
1-½ cups brown sugar
½ cup sugar
2 cups flour
1 cup applesauce
3 eggs
1 teaspoon baking powder
½ teaspoon baking soda
1-½ teaspoons vanilla
2 cups semisweet chocolate chips
1 cup chopped peanuts

1. Preheat oven to 350°F. Spray a 9" × 13" baking pan with nonstick cooking spray containing flour and set aside. In large bowl, combine butter, peanut butter, brown sugar, sugar, and flour and mix until crumbly. Reserve 1 cup of this mixture and place in medium bowl.

2. To crumbs remaining in large bowl, add applesauce, eggs, baking powder, baking soda, and vanilla. Stir until combined, then beat for 3 minutes at medium speed. Pour batter into prepared pan. Add chocolate chips and peanuts to crumbs reserved in medium bowl and mix well. Sprinkle over batter.

3. Bake for 35 to 45 minutes or until cake begins to pull away from edges of pan and springs back when touched lightly in center. Cool completely; store covered at room temperature.

Natural Peanut Butter Versus Processed
Here's where you can make a choice about your trans fat consumption. Processed peanut butters do contain very small amounts of artificial trans fat, because partially hydrogenated oils are added to them so the oil in the peanuts doesn't separate out. Natural peanut butters will always separate unless you keep them refrigerated. It's up to you!

Chocolate Cream–Filled Cupcakes

¾ cup butter, softened
1 cup sugar
¼ cup brown sugar
2 teaspoons vanilla, divided
2 eggs
2-¼ cups flour, divided
1 teaspoon baking powder
½ teaspoon salt, divided
1-½ cups milk, divided
2 (1-ounce) squares unsweetened chocolate, chopped
⅓ cup butter, softened
3-4 cups powdered sugar

1. Preheat oven to 375°F. Line 24 muffin cups with paper liners. In large bowl, combine ¾ cup butter, 1 cup sugar, brown sugar, and 1 teaspoon vanilla and beat until fluffy. Add eggs, one at a time, beating well after each addition. Add 2 cups flour, baking powder, ¼ teaspoon salt, and 1 cup milk; beat until blended, then beat at medium speed for 2 minutes.

2. Fill prepared muffin cups ⅔ full with cake batter. Bake for 20 to 25 minutes or until cupcakes are light golden brown and top springs back when lightly touched with finger. Remove from muffin tins and cool completely.

3. In medium saucepan, combine ¼ cup flour and ½ cup milk; cook over medium low heat, stirring constantly, until the mixture thickens. When milk mixture begins to boil, add chopped chocolate and remove from heat. Stir until chocolate melts and mixture is smooth. Cool completely.

4. For chocolate cream, in large bowl, combine ⅓ cup butter with 1 teaspoon vanilla, ¼ teaspoon salt, and milk mixture and beat until fluffy. Gradually add enough powdered sugar for desired spreading consistency. Place half of mixture in a pastry bag with large round tip. Insert tip into the top of each cupcake; gently squeeze bag until cupcake expands slightly. Repeat with remaining cupcakes. Frost cupcake tops with remaining cream mixture.

Apple Spice Meringue Pie

SERVES 8

CALORIES	249.27
FAT	0.12 GRAMS
SATURATED FAT	0.02 GRAMS
TRANS FAT	0.0 GRAMS
CARBOHYDRATES	62.32 GRAMS
CHOLESTEROL	0.0 MG

Canned commercial pie fillings can have lots of trans fat. Make your own filling and layer it in a crisp meringue shell for a fabulous healthy dessert.

4 egg whites
¼ teaspoon cream of tartar
2 cups sugar, divided
4 cups peeled sliced apples
1 tablespoon lemon juice
¼ cup cornstarch
1 teaspoon cinnamon
¼ teaspoon salt
2 cups water

1. Preheat oven to 250°F. Grease a 9" pie pan with unsalted butter and set aside. In large bowl, beat egg whites with cream of tartar until foamy. Gradually add 1 cup sugar, beating until stiff peaks form and meringue is glossy. Make sure that the sugar is completely dissolved. Place in prepared pie pan; spread into bottom and up sides to form a shell. Bake for 55 to 70 minutes or until shell is crisp and very light golden brown around edges. Cool completely.

2. Toss apples with lemon juice and set aside. In large heavy saucepan, combine 1 cup sugar, cornstarch, cinnamon, and salt and mix well. Add water and stir to blend. Bring to a boil over medium heat, then boil for 1 minute. Stir in apples and bring back to a boil. Reduce heat to low, cover, and simmer for 6 to 9 minutes or until apples are tender when pierced with fork. Let cool until warm; then cover and chill.

3. When apple filling is cold and thick, stir gently and spoon into meringue crust. Cover and chill for 2 to 6 hours before serving.

The Best Meringues

Meringue can be tricky to make. Separate your eggs while they are cold and let the whites stand at room temperature for 30 minutes before you start beating. Make sure the bowl and beaters are completely dry and free of fat. Add the sugar gradually, and keep beating until you can't feel any sugar crystals when you rub a bit of meringue between your fingers.

Olive Oil Cake

3 eggs
1 cup sugar
1 teaspoon vanilla
½ teaspoon almond extract
½ cup extra-virgin olive oil
½ cup pineapple-orange juice
1 tablespoon grated orange rind
½ cup ground slivered almonds
1-¼ cups flour
½ teaspoon baking powder
½ teaspoon baking soda
¼ teaspoon salt

1. Preheat oven to 350°F. Grease a 9" square pan with unsalted butter and set aside. In large bowl, beat eggs until light. Gradually add sugar, beating until light yellow in color and thick. Stir in vanilla and almond extract.

2. Stir in olive oil, juice, and orange rind until blended. Then add ground almonds, flour, baking powder, baking soda, and salt. Beat at medium speed for 1 minute or until blended. Pour batter into prepared pan. Bake for 25 to 35 minutes or until cake springs back when lightly touched in center. Cool on wire rack; store covered at room temperature.

About Olive Oil

There are several grades and types of olive oil; all depend on the method used to produce it and the acidity level of the oil. Premium cold-pressed extra-virgin olive oil is the finest; it is made by simply pressing the olives. It has an acidity level of around 0.22 percent. Extra-virgin has an acidity level less than 1 percent. Regular olive oil is best used for frying.

SERVES 9	
CALORIES	314.63
FAT	16.54 GRAMS
SATURATED FAT	2.41 GRAMS
TRANS FAT	0.0 GRAMS
CARBOHYDRATES	37.66 GRAMS
CHOLESTEROL	70.50 MG

This cake, which originated in Italy, is less sweet than most cakes. It has a nice fine texture and a slightly nutty flavor from the ground almonds. Be sure to choose cold-pressed extra-virgin olive oil.

Meringue Peaches

SERVES 8

CALORIES	111.24
FAT	0.21 GRAMS
SATURATED FAT	0.01 GRAMS
TRANS FAT	0.0 GRAMS
CARBOHYDRATES	26.37 GRAMS
CHOLESTEROL	0.0 MG

Poached peaches are surrounded by a simple meringue, then baked until the meringue is browned. With less than a gram of fat (would you believe peaches have fat?) you have a fabulous dessert.

6 peaches
3 tablespoons lemon juice, divided
2 cups water
1-½ cups sugar, divided
4 egg whites
¼ teaspoon cream of tartar
1 teaspoon vanilla
1 tablespoon brown sugar

1. Peel peaches and cut in half; remove pits. As you work, sprinkle the fruit with 2 tablespoons lemon juice. In large saucepan, combine water and 1 cup sugar; bring to a simmer. Carefully add peaches; bring back to a simmer, then lower heat and cook peaches for 3 to 6 minutes, until tender when pierced with a knife. Remove from heat; let peaches cool in liquid.

2. Preheat oven to 350°F. In large bowl, beat egg whites with cream of tartar. Gradually add ½ cup sugar, beating until stiff peaks form and sugar dissolves. Beat in vanilla. Line a baking sheet with parchment paper. Drain peaches thoroughly and place, cut-side down, on parchment paper. Spoon meringue over peaches, spreading gently with knife to completely coat fruit.

3. Sprinkle meringue with brown sugar. Bake for 10 to 15 minutes or until meringue is light golden brown. Carefully remove each peach from baking sheet and place on serving plates. Serve immediately.

Caramel Sour Cream Cake

1 cup sour cream
½ cup sugar
½ cup brown sugar
2 eggs
2 teaspoons vanilla
1-¾ cups flour
1 teaspoon baking powder
1 teaspoon baking soda
¼ teaspoon salt
¼ teaspoon ground nutmeg

1. Preheat oven to 350°F. Grease 9" × 13" pan with unsalted butter and set aside. In large bowl, combine sour cream and sugar; beat well. Then add brown sugar and beat. Add eggs, one at a time, beating well after each addition. Stir in vanilla.

2. Sift flour with baking powder, baking soda, salt, and nutmeg. Stir into sour cream mixture and beat at medium speed for 1 minute. Pour into prepared pan.

3. Bake for 25 to 35 minutes or until cake pulls away from sides of pan and top springs back when lightly touched in center. Cool completely on wire rack; store covered at room temperature. Frost with Buttercream Frosting (page 295) or the Caramel Frosting used for Caramel Gingerbread (page 280).

What Is Caramel?

Caramel is created when sugar is melted. When sugar is melted and reaches 338°F, the molecules in the sugar begin to break down and recombine to form other compounds. These new compounds create the color and complex, rich flavor of caramel. Brown sugar does not contain caramel; it's regular granulated sugar combined with molasses.

SERVES 16

CALORIES	139.82
FAT	3.77 GRAMS
SATURATED FAT	2.09 GRAMS
TRANS FAT	0.04 GRAMS*
CARBOHYDRATES	24.04 GRAMS
CHOLESTEROL	32.76 MG

Drizzle this cake with some purchased caramel ice cream topping for a decadent dessert with only a minute amount of natural trans fat!

Carrot Cake

SERVES 20

CALORIES	356.93
FAT	16.69 GRAMS
SATURATED FAT	11.37 GRAMS
TRANS FAT	0.16 GRAMS*
CARBOHYDRATES	49.60 GRAMS
CHOLESTEROL	62.62 MG

This delicious cake is usually made with vegetable oil. One slice of this creamy cake provides 80 percent of the Daily Recommended Value of vitamin A!

1 (16-ounce) bag baby carrots
⅓ cup coconut oil
¾ cup butter, softened, divided
1 cup sugar
¾ cup brown sugar
3 eggs
3 teaspoons vanilla, divided
2-½ cups all-purpose flour
2 teaspoons baking soda
½ teaspoon baking powder
1 (8-ounce) can crushed pineapple
1 cup flaked coconut, divided
1 (8-ounce) package cream cheese, softened
3 cups powdered sugar
2 to 4 tablespoons milk

1. Preheat oven to 350°F. Grease a 9" × 13" pan with unsalted butter and set aside. Place baby carrots in food processor. Process until very finely chopped and set aside.

2. In large bowl, combine coconut oil with ½ cup butter and granulated sugar; beat until smooth and fluffy. Add brown sugar and beat until combined. Beat in eggs and 2 teaspoons vanilla.

3. By hand, stir in flour, baking soda, and baking powder (batter will be stiff). Stir in carrots, undrained pineapple, and ½ cup coconut. Pour batter into prepared pan. Bake for 40 to 50 minutes or until cake is dark golden brown and set. Cool completely on wire rack.

4. For frosting, combine cream cheese with ¼ cup butter in medium bowl. Add powdered sugar, 1 teaspoon vanilla, and 2 tablespoons milk; beat until combined. Add more milk if necessary to reach spreading consistency. Add ½ cup coconut and frost cake.

Classic Pound Cake

⅔ cup butter, softened
1 (3-ounce) package cream cheese, softened
½ cup coconut oil
2-½ cups sugar
2 teaspoons vanilla
5 eggs
2-½ cups flour
2 tablespoons cornstarch
½ teaspoon baking soda
¼ teaspoon salt
1 cup light cream

SERVES 16

CALORIES	379.74
FAT	19.82 GRAMS
SATURATED FAT	13.52 GRAMS
TRANS FAT	0.28 GRAMS*
CARBOHYDRATES	47.07 GRAMS
CHOLESTEROL	97.87 MG

Yes, classic pound cake is high in fat. But for a once-in-a-while treat, you really should eat the original. Bakery pound cakes usually have lots of trans fat. This one doesn't!

1. Preheat oven to 325°F. Grease a 12-cup Bundt pan with unsalted butter and dust with flour; set aside. In large bowl, beat butter, cream cheese, and coconut oil until fluffy, about 5 minutes. Gradually add sugar, beating until very light. This process should take at least 10 minutes.

2. Beat in vanilla, then add eggs, beating for 1 minute after each addition. Place flour, cornstarch, baking soda, and salt in a sifter. Sift one-quarter of the flour mixture over the batter and beat in. Then add one-third of the light cream and beat until combined. Repeat until all ingredients are combined.

3. Spoon batter into prepared pan and smooth top. Bake for 70 to 90 minutes or until cake is deep golden brown and toothpick inserted near center comes out clean. Watch after 60 minutes; you may need to tent the cake with foil to prevent overbrowning. Loosen cake from pan and invert onto wire rack. Cool completely.

Using Pound Cake

There are so many ways to use pound cake. You can top slices with crushed strawberries and some whipped cream for a variation on strawberry shortcake. Cut the cake into cubes and dunk into melted chocolate for a chocolate fondue. Or toast slices on the grill or griddle and serve with a fruit salsa for a wonderful dessert.

Glazed Cinnamon Apple Cake

SERVES 10

CALORIES	325.46
FAT	13.11
SATURATED FAT	8.04 GRAMS
TRANS FAT	0.30 GRAMS*
CARBOHYDRATES	50.98 GRAMS
CHOLESTEROL	54.30 MG

Lots of apples add great flavor and moistness to this delicious dessert that's a cross between apple pie and cake.

10 tablespoons butter, softened, divided
½ cup brown sugar
1 egg
1 teaspoon vanilla
1-¼ cups flour
1-½ teaspoons baking powder
¼ teaspoon salt

2-½ teaspoons cinnamon, divided
½ cup milk
5 apples, peeled and chopped
2 tablespoons lemon juice
1 cup sugar, divided
1 tablespoon cornstarch
¾ cup water

1. Preheat oven to 350°F. Grease a 10" springform pan with unsalted butter and set aside. In large bowl, combine 6 tablespoons butter and brown sugar; beat until fluffy. Add egg and vanilla and beat until combined. Place flour, baking powder, salt, and ½ teaspoon cinnamon in a sifter. Sift ⅓ of flour mixture over butter mixture and beat. Then add ⅓ of the milk. Repeat, beating after each addition.

2. Spread batter into prepared pan. Prepare apples and sprinkle with lemon juice, ¼ cup sugar and 1 teaspoon cinnamon; toss. Spread over batter in pan.

3. In small heavy saucepan, combine ¾ cup sugar, cornstarch, and water and mix well. Add 4 tablespoons butter and 1 teaspoon cinnamon; cook over medium heat, stirring constantly, until thick. Spoon over apples. Bake for 40 to 50 minutes or until cake pulls away from sides of pan and apples are glazed. Cool for 30 minutes; serve warm.

Working with Butter
When butter is used in baked goods, it needs to be softened. If any of the butter melts during the softening process, the texture of the final product will change. To soften butter properly, let it stand at room temperature for about an hour before using. Do not use the microwave; the hot and cold spots means part of the butter always melts.

Date Torte

3 eggs
½ cup sugar
1 teaspoon vanilla
3 tablespoons flour
1 teaspoon baking powder
3 tablespoons white chocolate chips, ground
½ cup finely chopped dates
½ cup chopped pecans

1. Preheat oven to 350°F. Grease a 9" pie pan with unsalted butter and set aside. In large bowl, beat eggs until light in color. Gradually add sugar, beating until mixture is light and fluffy. Stir in vanilla, then fold in flour and baking powder. Add white chocolate, dates, and pecans.

2. Spread mixture into prepared pan. Bake for 25 to 35 minutes or until torte begins to pull away from sides of pan. Cool for 1 hour, then cut into wedges and serve warm.

Chopping Dates

When a recipe calls for chopped dates, choose whole pitted dates and chop them yourself for best results. You can use kitchen scissors to chop dates, or a chef's knife. To minimize sticking, toss dates with a teaspoon of flour before you begin, or dip the scissors or knife blade in hot water in between cuts.

SERVES 6

CALORIES	248.70
FAT	10.82 GRAMS
SATURATED FAT	2.38 GRAMS
TRANS FAT	0.0 GRAMS
CARBOHYDRATES	35.37 GRAMS
CHOLESTEROL	106.49 MG

This recipe isn't a layered torte. It's a simple dessert with a light and chewy texture made by beating eggs until very light and fluffy. Serve it with whipped cream or ice cream.

Lemon Apple Rice Pudding

SERVES 6

CALORIES	198.80
FAT	7.35 GRAMS
SATURATED FAT	3.76 GRAMS
TRANS FAT	0.06 GRAMS*
CARBOHYDRATES	27.55 GRAMS
CHOLESTEROL	122.23 MG

Rice pudding is one of the ultimate comfort foods. Add apples and lemon and it becomes a trendy dessert that's good for you, too.

½ cup rice
1-¼ cups water
2 cups whole milk
3 eggs
⅓ cup sugar
¼ teaspoon salt
2 apples, peeled and diced
1 teaspoon lemon zest
3 tablespoons lemon juice
1 tablespoon butter, melted

1. In heavy saucepan, combine rice and water; bring to a boil. Reduce heat, cover pan, and simmer for 20 minutes until rice is tender.

2. Preheat oven to 350°F. Grease a 2-quart casserole dish with unsalted butter. Add milk, eggs, sugar, salt, diced apples, lemon zest, and lemon juice to cooked rice and mix well.

3. Pour into prepared baking dish and drizzle the top with melted butter. Bake for 45 to 55 minutes or until pudding is set and beginning to brown on top. Serve warm.

Buttercream Frosting

1 cup butter, softened
5 cups powdered sugar
1 teaspoon vanilla
3 to 5 tablespoons whole milk

1. In large bowl, beat butter until fluffy. Gradually add 1 cup powdered sugar, beating until combined. Stir in vanilla. Then add remaining powdered sugar alternately with the whole milk, until desired spreading consistency is reached. Fills and frosts two 9" cake layers, or frosts one 9" × 13" cake.

Buttercream Frosting Flavorings
To this recipe, add 2 squares of melted unsweetened chocolate or ⅓ cup cocoa powder for Chocolate Frosting. For a Peanut Butter Frosting, reduce the butter amount to ⅔ cup and add ⅓ cup peanut butter (you may need more milk). For Peppermint Frosting, fold crushed peppermint candies into the frosting. For Caramel Frosting, add ¼ cup caramel ice cream topping; reduce milk to 2 tablespoons.

YIELDS 48 TABLESPOONS (SERVING SIZE 2 TABLESPOONS)

CALORIES	176.44
FAT	7.79 GRAMS
SATURATED FAT	4.92 GRAMS
TRANS FAT	0.10 GRAMS*
CARBOHYDRATES	27.53
CHOLESTEROL	20.69 GRAMS

Tubs of prepared buttercream frosting are loaded with artificial trans fat. All of the trans fat in this recipe comes from the butter; it's the natural version, which is good for you.

Mango Angel Fluff

SERVES 12

CALORIES	148.39
FAT	5.74 GRAMS
SATURATED FAT	4.07 GRAMS
TRANS FAT	0.13 GRAMS*
CARBOHYDRATES	23.73 GRAMS
CHOLESTEROL	13.70 MG

This light dessert is delicious served with a raspberry sauce made by puréeing frozen thawed raspberries with a little lemon juice.

4 pasteurized egg whites
1 cup sugar
1 tablespoon lemon juice
Half of a 15-ounce bag of frozen mangoes, thawed
1 cup heavy whipping cream
2 tablespoons powdered sugar
1 teaspoon vanilla
1 cup flaked coconut

1. In large bowl, place egg whites; let stand for 30 minutes at room temperature. Add sugar, lemon juice, and mangoes. Beat until combined, then beat for 15 minutes at high speed, until mixture is thick and triples in volume.

2. In medium bowl, beat cream with powdered sugar and vanilla until stiff. Fold into meringue along with coconut. Rinse a 10-inch ring mold with water and shake out over sink; do not dry mold. Pour coconut mixture into mold. Cover and freeze until firm.

3. To unmold, rinse a kitchen towel in hot water and wring out. Place mold on serving plate. Drape hot towel over mold for 10 to 15 seconds to loosen dessert. Remove mold, let stand at room temperature for 15 minutes, slice, and serve with raspberry sauce.

About Pasteurized Egg Whites
When using eggs in recipes that are not cooked, you should consider using pasteurized eggs. They are more expensive but worth it. Be sure to watch the expiration date on these eggs and discard them after that date has passed. It does take longer for pasteurized whites to whip, but just keep working; they will fluff up.

Apple Raisin Cake

⅓ cup butter, softened
1 cup brown sugar
⅓ cup sugar
1 egg
½ cup water
1 cup applesauce
1-⅔ cups flour
1 teaspoon baking soda
½ teaspoon baking powder
½ teaspoon salt
½ teaspoon cinnamon
¼ teaspoon allspice
½ cup raisins
2 cups powdered sugar
2 tablespoons butter, melted
2 tablespoons orange juice

SERVES 16

CALORIES	250.15
FAT	5.78 GRAMS
SATURATED FAT	3.47 GRAMS
TRANS FAT	0.14 GRAMS*
CARBOHYDRATES	49.14 GRAMS
CHOLESTEROL	27.20 MG

Applesauce is a good way to add moistness and flavor to cakes while reducing the fat content. This old-fashioned cake is great for packing lunchboxes.

1. Preheat oven to 350°F. Grease a 9" × 13" pan with unsalted butter. In large bowl, combine ⅓ cup butter with brown sugar and sugar; beat until fluffy. Add egg and beat well. Stir in water and applesauce and mix well. Add flour, baking soda, baking powder, salt, cinnamon, and allspice; beat for 2 minutes. Stir in raisins.

2. Pour batter into prepared pan. Bake for 40 to 50 minutes or until cake begins to pull away from sides of pan and toothpick inserted in center comes out clean. Let cool completely.

3. In small bowl, combine powdered sugar, 2 tablespoons melted butter, and orange juice and mix well. Drizzle over cooled cake.

Crumb Cake

SERVES 16

CALORIES	282.99
FAT	11.99 GRAMS
SATURATED FAT	5.98 GRAMS
TRANS FAT	0.23 GRAMS*
CARBOHYDRATES	41.82 GRAMS
CHOLESTEROL	49.93 MG

This classic cake was inspired by a now-defunct frozen crumb cake by a famous company. It's light yet rich, velvety smooth, and crunchy all at the same time!

2 cups brown sugar
2 cups flour
¾ cup butter
1 cup buttermilk
1 teaspoon baking soda
2 eggs
¼ teaspoon salt
1 teaspoon cinnamon
¼ teaspoon nutmeg
2 teaspoons vanilla
½ cup chopped pecans
¼ cup powdered sugar

1. Preheat oven to 350°F. Grease a 9" × 13" pan with unsalted butter and set aside. In large bowl, combine brown sugar and flour and mix well. Cut butter into small pieces and add to flour mixture, mixing with pastry blender or two knives until crumbs form. Remove ¾ cup crumb mixture and set aside.

2. To remaining crumb mixture, add buttermilk, baking soda, eggs, salt, cinnamon, nutmeg, and vanilla and stir until combined. Then beat at medium speed for 2 minutes. Spoon into prepared pan. To reserved crumbs, add pecans and mix well. Sprinkle over cake.

3. Bake for 25 to 35 minutes or until cake begins to pull away from sides of pan and top springs back when lightly touched. Cool cake completely, then place powdered sugar in small strainer and sprinkle heavily over cake.

Baked Stuffed Apples

6 whole medium apples
3 tablespoons lemon juice, divided
½ cup brown sugar
2 tablespoons butter
2 tablespoons honey
½ teaspoon cinnamon
½ cup raisins
½ cup chopped walnuts
2 cups water
¼ cup sugar

SERVES 6

CALORIES	330.15
FAT	10.49 GRAMS
SATURATED FAT	3.07 GRAMS
TRANS FAT	0.10 GRAMS*
CARBOHYDRATES	62.57 GRAMS
CHOLESTEROL	10.18 MG

Apples are so good for you! And this recipe turns them into an indulgent yet healthy dessert packed full of flavor.

1. Preheat oven to 350°F. Using a sharp knife or apple corer, cut out the core of each apple from the top. Do not cut all the way through the apple. Peel the top quarter of each apple to help prevent splitting as it cooks. Sprinkle the prepared apples with 1 tablespoon lemon juice.

2. In small bowl, combine brown sugar, butter, honey, and cinnamon and mix well. Stir in raisins and walnuts. Stuff the apple centers with this mixture. Place apples in 9" × 13" glass baking dish. In heavy saucepan, combine water, sugar, and 2 tablespoons lemon juice and bring to a boil, stirring occasionally. Pour this mixture over the apples.

3. Bake apples, uncovered, for 45 to 55 minutes, basting occasionally with pan juices, until apples are tender when pierced with a knife. Let the apples cool for 30 minutes, spooning pan juices over them as they cool. Serve warm.

Apples for Baking
You do have to carefully choose the apples you use in baking recipes. Some apples, including Red Delicious, Fuji, and Gala, break down too much when cooked. The apples that hold their shape in baking include Granny Smith, Golden Delicious, Winesap, and Jonagold. McIntosh apples are best for making applesauce or puddings.

Pumpkin Bread Pudding

SERVES 12

CALORIES	389.45
FAT	18.33 GRAMS
SATURATED FAT	7.23 GRAMS
TRANS FAT	0.08 GRAMS*
CARBOHYDRATES	49.62 GRAMS
CHOLESTEROL	77.18 MG

Bread pudding is a classic comfort food. Adding pumpkin to the recipe gives it a nice boost of flavor (and vitamin A). The white chocolate chips add a sweet contrast.

3 eggs
½ cup sugar
½ cup brown sugar
1 teaspoons cinnamon
½ teaspoon ginger
1 cup canned pumpkin
1 cup milk
1 (13-ounce can) evaporated milk
2 teaspoons vanilla
2 tablespoons butter, melted
8 slices Oatmeal Bread (page 43), cubed
1 cup white chocolate chips
1 cup chopped pecans

1. Preheat oven to 375°F. Grease a 9" × 13" glass baking dish with unsalted butter and set aside. In large bowl, combine eggs and sugar. Beat until light and fluffy. Add brown sugar, cinnamon, and ginger and beat well. Gradually beat in pumpkin until smooth.

2. Add milk, evaporated milk, vanilla, and butter and mix well. Place Bread cubes in baking dish and sprinkle with white chocolate chips and nuts. Pour egg mixture over all. Let stand for 30 minutes, pressing bread down into egg mixture as necessary.

3. Bake for 40 minutes, then increase heat to 400°F and bake for 10 to 15 minutes longer or until pudding is golden brown and set. Let cool for at least 30 minutes; serve warm.

Canned Pumpkin

When a recipe calls for canned pumpkin, be sure that you buy and use what is called "solid pack" pumpkin. If you use canned pumpkin-pie pudding, the recipe will fail because that ingredient contains sugar, emulsifiers, and liquids in addition to pumpkin. If you're feeling ambitious, you could cook and purée a fresh pumpkin and use that.

Buttermilk Cocoa Cake

1 cup buttermilk
½ cup canola oil
½ cup butter, melted
2 eggs
1-½ cups sugar
½ cup brown sugar
½ cup cocoa
2-½ cups flour
½ teaspoon salt
2 teaspoons baking soda
1 cup boiling water
3 tablespoons cornstarch
1 cup sugar
1 cup water
⅓ cup cocoa
¼ cup butter
¼ teaspoon salt
2 teaspoons vanilla

SERVES 16

CALORIES	385.45
FAT	17.19 GRAMS
SATURATED FAT	6.59 GRAMS
TRANS FAT	0.05 GRAMS
CARBOHYDRATES	57.02 GRAMS
CHOLESTEROL	49.93 MG

Cooked frostings are old-fashioned and delicious. They're also a way to have a creamy frosting with less butter or other fats.

1. Preheat oven to 350°F. In large bowl, combine buttermilk, oil, melted butter, and eggs and beat well until combined. Add 1-½ cups sugar and brown sugar and mix well. In medium bowl, combine ½ cup cocoa, flour, salt, and baking soda. Add alternately to buttermilk mixture with boiling water.

2. Pour into ungreased 9" × 13" pan and bake for 45 to 55 minutes or until cake springs back when lightly touched. Cool completely.

3. In large saucepan, combine cornstarch, 1 cup sugar, 1 cup water, ⅓ cup cocoa, ¼ cup butter, and ¼ teaspoon salt. Cook over medium heat, stirring constantly with wire whisk, until mixture thickens and comes to a boil. Remove from heat and add vanilla. Cool, stirring occasionally, until mixture is thick. Frost cake.

Classic Apple Crisp

SERVES 12

CALORIES	412.46
FAT	15.99 GRAMS
SATURATED FAT	5.85 GRAMS
TRANS FAT	0.20 GRAMS*
CARBOHYDRATES	64.41 GRAMS
CHOLESTEROL	37.96 MG

This hearty apple crisp has a chewy, candylike topping that pairs perfectly with the tart apples. You could substitute pears and cranberries for the apples.

8 cups sliced, peeled apples
¼ cup honey
2 tablespoons lemon juice
1 teaspoon cinnamon
1-½ cups quick oatmeal
1 cup flour
½ teaspoon salt
½ teaspoon baking powder
1-½ cups brown sugar
1 cup chopped walnuts
½ cup butter
1 egg, beaten

1. Preheat oven to 350°F. Prepare apples and place in 9" × 13" pan. Drizzle with honey, lemon juice, and cinnamon and toss to coat. In large bowl, combine oatmeal, flour, salt, baking powder, brown sugar, and walnuts and mix well.

2. Melt butter in small saucepan over medium heat. Let cool for 10 minutes, then beat in egg until mixture is combined. Pour over oatmeal mixture and mix until crumbly. Sprinkle over apples in pan.

3. Bake for 40 to 50 minutes or until apples are bubbling and top is golden brown and crisp. Let cool for 45 minutes; serve warm.

Why Apples Turn Brown
When apples are peeled and sliced, cells are broken open and exposed to air. The cells in the apple contain an enzyme that reacts with the oxygen in the air, forming compounds that cause the color change. There are two ways to stop this process; add an acid (like lemon juice) to denature the enzyme, or cook the apples, which also denatures the enzyme.

Pecan Caramel Angel Food Cake

1 cup powdered sugar, divided
1 cup brown sugar
½ cup granulated sugar
12 egg whites
1 teaspoon cream of tartar
2 teaspoons vanilla
1 cup flour
½ teaspoon salt
¼ teaspoon nutmeg
½ cup finely ground pecans

SERVES 16

CALORIES	181.81
FAT	3.80 GRAMS
SATURATED FAT	0.33 GRAMS
TRANS FAT	0.0 GRAMS
CARBOHYDRATES	33.95 GRAMS
CHOLESTEROL	0.0 MG

To make this a regular angel food cake, omit the pecans and use all granulated sugar instead of the combination of powdered and brown sugar.

1. Preheat oven to 350°F. In medium bowl, combine ½ cup powdered sugar, brown sugar, and granulated sugar and beat with electric mixer until blended. In large bowl, combine egg whites, cream of tartar, and vanilla. Beat until soft peaks form. Gradually add the brown sugar mixture, beating until stiff peaks form.

2. In small bowl, combine flour, salt, nutmeg, pecans, and remaining ½ cup powdered sugar and mix well. Sprinkle one-quarter of this mixture over the egg white mixture and carefully fold in. Repeat until all the flour mixture is added. Spoon batter into ungreased angel food cake pan.

3. Bake for 40 to 50 minutes or until cake is deep golden brown and set. Invert onto wire rack and let cool in pan for 1 hour; remove from pan and cool on wire rack.

Glossary

Active dry yeast

This is a small plant that has been preserved by drying. When rehydrated, the yeast activates and begins producing carbon dioxide and alcohols.

Al dente

A term used in Italian cooking that refers to the texture of cooked pasta. When cooked "al dente," the pasta is tender, but still firm in the middle. The term literally means "to the tooth."

Bake

To cook in dry heat, usually in an oven, until proteins denature, starches gelatinize, and water evaporates to form a structure.

Bagel

A large round chewy roll, usually made with a hole in the center. The dough is first boiled, then baked to produce the characteristic texture and crisp crust.

Beat

To combine two mixtures and to incorporate air by manipulating with a spoon or an electric mixer until fluffy.

Biscotti

A crisp cookie or biscuit made by twice-baking a dough or batter.

Butter

A natural fat obtained by churning heavy cream to consolidate and remove some of the butterfat.

Calorie

A unit of measurement in nutrition, a calorie is the amount of energy needed to raise the temperature of 1 gram of water by 1 degree Celsius. The number of calories in a food is measured by chemically analyzing the food.

Cholesterol

Cholesterol is not a fat, but a sterol, an alcohol and fatty acid, a soft, waxy substance used by your body to make hormones. Your body makes cholesterol and you eat foods containing cholesterol. Only animal fats have cholesterol.

Cis

This Latin word means "same," referring to hydrogen molecules being bonded to carbon molecules on the same side of a fatty acid chain.

Confectioner's sugar
This sugar is finely ground and mixed with cornstarch to prevent lumping; it is used mostly in icings and frostings. It is also known as powdered sugar and 10X sugar.

Corn oil
An oil obtained from the germ of the corn kernel. It has a high smoke point and contains a small amount of artificial trans fat.

Cornmeal
Coarsely ground corn, used to make polenta, also to coat foods to make a crisp crust.

Cornstarch
Very finely ground powder made from the starch in the endosperm of corn; used as a thickener.

Deep-fry
To fry in a large amount of oil or melted shortening, lard, or butter so the food is completely covered. In this dry-heat method of cooking, about 10 percent of the fat is absorbed into the food.

Dice
To cut food into very small, even pieces.

Diet
All of the foods and liquids one person eats; also, to cut down on calories in order to lose weight.

Dissolve
To immerse a solid in a liquid and heat or manipulate to form a solution in which none of the solid remains.

Dredge
To dip a food into another mixture, usually made of flour, bread crumbs, or cheese, to completely coat.

Edamame
The word for edible soybeans, a green pea encased in a pod.

Egg substitute
A blend of egg whites, starch, corn oil, skim milk powder, tofu, food coloring, and additives sold in a carton. It contains no cholesterol and can be used for scrambling and baking in place of whole eggs.

En papillote
French term meaning "in paper"; food wrapped in parchment paper or foil and baked in a hot oven or grilled.

Emulsify
To combine an oil and a liquid, either through manipulation or the addition of another ingredient, so they remain suspended in each other.

Evaporated milk
Milk that has been reduced by removing some of the water. It can be found whole-fat, reduced-fat, and nonfat.

Fat substitutes
Artificial substances created to replace natural fats. Some names include Simplesse, Olestra, and Leanesse.

Fatty acids
A fatty acid is a long chain of carbon molecules bonded to each other and to hydrogen molecules, attached to an alcohol or glycerol molecule. They are short-chain, medium-chain, and long-chain, always with an even number of carbon molecules.

Flaky
A word describing food texture, usually a pie crust or crust on meat, which breaks apart into flat layers.

Flax seed
This small oil-rich seed is used primarily to make linseed oil, but is also a valuable source of nutrients like calcium, iron, and omega-3 fatty acids.

Focaccia
An Italian flat bread, usually topped with olive oil and herbs, used to make sandwiches.

Fry
To cook the food in hot oil, a dry heat environment.

Gluten
A protein in flour made by combining glutenin and gliadin with a liquid and physical manipulation.

Golden
The color of food when it is browned or quickly sautéed.

HDL
High-density lipoproteins, the "good" type of cholesterol that carries fat away from the bloodstream.

Herbs
The aromatic leafy part of an edible plant; herbs include basil, parsley, chives, thyme, tarragon, oregano, and mint.

Hummus
A combination of puréed chickpeas with garlic, lemon juice, and usually tahini; used as an appetizer or sandwich spread.

Hydrogenation
The process of adding hydrogen molecules to carbon chains in fats and fatty acids.

Irish soda bread
A quick bread shaped into a round loaf, usually flavored with caraway.

Italian salad dressing
A dressing made of olive oil and vinegar or lemon juice, combined into an emulsion, usually with herbs like basil and thyme.

Jelly
A congealed mixture made from fruit juice, sugar, and pectin.

Julienne
To cut food into very thin, even strips that are about 2" long.

Kebab
Meats, fruits, and/or vegetables threaded onto skewers, usually barbecued over a wood or coal fire.

Kidney bean
A legume, either white or dark red, used for making chili and soups.

Knead
To manipulate a dough, usually a bread dough, to help develop the gluten in the flour so the bread has the proper texture.

Lard
The fat from pork, used to fry foods and as a substitute for margarine or butter.

LDL
Low-density lipoproteins, the "bad" cholesterol, which carries fat from the liver and intestines to the bloodstream.

Lecithin
A substance made of fatty acids that is a natural emulsifier, found in eggs and legumes.

Lipid
Lipids are organic molecules insoluble in water, consisting of a chain of hydrophobic carbon and hydrogen molecules and an alcohol or glycerol molecule. They include fats, oil, waxes, steroids, and cholesterol.

Lipid hypothesis
The theory, first put forth in the 1950s, that saturated fat and cholesterol in the diet cause heart disease. Data and conclusions of the theory have been questioned.

Long-chain fatty acids
These fatty acids have 12 to 24 carbon molecules bonded to hydrogen molecules and to a glycerol molecule.

Margarine
A fat made by hydrogenating polyunsaturated oils, colored with yellow food coloring to resemble butter.

Marinate
To coat foods in an acidic liquid or dry mixture to help break down protein bonds and tenderize the food.

Mayonnaise
An emulsification of egg yolks, lemon juice or vinegar, and oil, blended into a thick white creamy dressing.

Meat thermometer
A thermometer specially labeled to read the internal temperature of meat.

Medium-chain fatty acids

These fatty acids have 6 to 12 carbon molecules bonded to each other and to hydrogen molecules. Coconut and palm oils contain these fatty acids and they are used in infant formulas.

Monounsaturated oil

A fatty acid that has two carbons double-bonded to each other, missing two hydrogen molecules. These very stable oils are good for frying, but can have low smoke points. Examples include olive, almond, avocado, canola, and peanut oils.

Mortar and pestle

A mortar is a bowl-shaped tool, sometimes made of stone or marble, and a pestle is the round instrument used to grind ingredients in the mortar.

Mouthfeel

A food science term that describes the action of food in the mouth; descriptors range from gummy to dry to slippery to smooth to chewy to tender.

Neufchatel cheese

The original French cheese is a soft unripened cow's milk cheese. The American version is low-fat cream cheese.

Nuts

The edible fruit of some trees, consisting of a kernel in a hard shell. Most edible nuts are actually seeds and are a good source of monounsaturated fats.

Omega-3 fatty acids

A polyunsaturated fat named for the position of the first double bond. The body cannot make Omega-3 fatty acids; they must be consumed.

Omega-6 fatty acids

A polyunsaturated fat name for the position of the first double bond. Too much of this fatty acid in the body can cause heart disease. Like HDL with LDL cholesterol, this fat works in concert with Omega-3 fatty acids.

Organic food

Food that has been grown and processed without pesticides, herbicides, insecticides, fertilizers, artificial coloring, artificial flavoring, or additives. Currently, there are no consistent regulations in the United States regarding the term "organic."

Orzo

A tiny, rice-shaped pasta.

Paillards

A very thinly cut and quick-cooking piece of beef, pork, or chicken, which may or may not be pounded to make it even thinner.

Pan-fry

To quickly fry in a small amount of oil in a saucepan or skillet.

Polyunsaturated oil

A fatty acid that has more than two carbon molecules double-bonded to each other; it is missing at least four hydrogen molecules. Examples include corn, soybean, safflower, and sunflower oils.

Processed food

Any food that has been manipulated by chemicals or otherwise treated, such as frozen, canned, and enriched foods.

Rancid

Fats can become rancid over time and through exposure to oxygen. The fats oxidize, or break down, and free radicals form, which then exacerbate the process. Rancid fats smell and taste unpleasant.

Reduction

Quickly boiling or simmering liquid to evaporate the water and concentrate the flavor.

Risotto

An Italian rice dish made by slowly cooking rice in broth, stirring to help release starch that thickens the mixture.

Roast

To cook food at relatively high heat in an oven. This is a dry-cooking method, usually used for vegetables and meats.

Roux

A mixture of flour and oil or fat, cooked until the starches in the flour can absorb liquid. It is used to thicken sauces, from white sauce to gumbo.

Saturated fat

A fatty acid that has no double-bonded carbons, but has all the carbons bonded to hydrogen molecules. Butter, coconut oil, and palm oil are all high in saturated fats.

Sauté

To quickly cook food in a small amount of fat over relatively high heat.

Season

To change the flavor of food by adding ingredients like salt, pepper, herbs, and spices.

Short-chain fatty acid

A fat that contains 2 to 6 carbon molecules; examples include lauric and octanoic acids.

Shortening

A partially hydrogenated oil that is solid at room temperature, used to make everything from frostings to cakes to pastries and breads.

Smoke point

The temperature at which fats begin to break down under heat. The higher the smoke point, the more stable the fat will be while frying and cooking. Butter's smoke point is 350°F, olive oil's 375°F, and refined oil's around 440°F.

Sole

Sole is a large flatfish with a mild taste, part of the flounder family.

Sour cream

A milk product that contains about 20 percent fat, made by treating milk with a lactic acid culture. It may also contain gelatin and rennin to help stabilize the mixture.

Spices

Aromatic seasonings from seeds, bark, roots, and stems of edible plants. Spices include cinnamon, cumin, turmeric, ginger, and pepper, among others.

Tart

A pastry or pie made in a shallow pan, usually with a removable bottom. A tart is thinner than a pie.

Tortellini

A small stuffed pasta, usually folded into a round shape. Tortellini is smaller than tortelloni.

Trans

Latin word means "across," referring to the positioning of the hydrogen molecules on the carbon chain of a fatty acid.

Trans fat

A specific form of fatty acid, where hydrogen molecules are positioned across from each other, in the "trans" position, as opposed to the "cis" position.

Tropical oils

Oils from plants grown in the tropic region; the most common are coconut oil and palm oil. These oils are usually fully saturated and are solid at room temperature.

Unsalted butter

Sometimes known as "sweet butter," this is butter that contains no salt or sodium chloride. It's used for greasing pans, since salt in butter will make batter or dough stick.

Unsaturated fat

Fatty acids that have two or more carbon molecules double-bonded to each other; an unsaturated fat is missing at least two hydrogen molecules.

Vanilla

The highly aromatic seeds contained in a long pod, or fruit, of the vanilla plant, a member of the orchid family.

Vegetable oil

Oils made by pressing or chemically extracting lipids from a vegetable source, whether seeds, nuts, or fruits of a plant.

Vitamins

Vitamins are molecules that are used to promote and facilitate chemical reactions in the body. Most vitamins must be ingested, as your body cannot make them.

Suggested Menus

Menu planning is an art that takes some experience. Think about the color wheel as you plan your menu, and try to choose foods that are as colorful as possible. Balance taste, texture, and temperature, too, and always consider foods that contrast and complement each other.

Dinner for the Boss

Spinach Pesto Spread

Crisp Cheese Crackers

Butterflake Rolls

Salad with French Dressing

Garlic and Onion Pot Roast

Hawaiian Carrots

Lemon Meringue Parfaits

Breakfast on the Run

Raspberry Cinnamon Muffins

Health Bread

Popped Tarts

Open-Faced Breakfast Waffle Sandwiches

Lunch on the Porch

Oatmeal Streusel Muffins

Egg and Mushroom Luncheon Rolls

Creamy Date and Nut Salad

Peanut Butter Creams

Christmas Eve Dinner

Cream and Cranberry Spread

Yeast Knot Rolls

Orange-Scented Broccoli

Scampi Roasted Chicken

Melon Pineapple Salad

Pecan Caramel Angel Food Cake

Simple Entertaining

Pesto Guacamole

Sesame Corn Wafers

Pizza Burgers by the Yard

Sautéed Corn

Crumb Cake

Dessert Party

Gingerbread Trifle

Brown Sugar Pecan Pie

Banana Milk-Chocolate Bars

Lemon Meringues

Mango Angel Fluff

Chocolate Peanut Butter Truffle Tart

Last-Minute Get-Together

Stir-Fried Chicken Tahiti

Glazed Honey Rolls

Cauliflower Radish Salad

Coconut Oatmeal Macaroons

Appetizer Buffet

Fresh and Spicy Salsa

Herbed Potato Chips

Cheesy Filo Rolls

Tex-Mex Popcorn

Brown Sugar Glazed Salmon

Chicken "Wings"

Chocolate Truffles

Birthday Dinner

Spice and Honey Nuts

Salad with Thousand Island Dressing

Country-Style Pork Kiev

Roasted Vegetables

Chocolate Cream–Filled Cupcakes

Fourth of July Cookout

Red Gazpacho

Four-Bean Salad

Real French Fries

Grilled Steaks with Romesco Sauce

Date Nut Chews

Picnic in the Park

Peanut Butter Apple Wraps

Orzo Vegetable Cheese Salad

Crisp and Healthy Fried Chicken

Brown Sugar Drop Cookies

Cozy Dinner at Home

Pumpkin Wild Rice Chowder

Carrot and Tomato Salad

Cranberry Peach Salad

Apricot Bars

Christmas Morning Breakfast

Lemon Meringue Coffeecake

Peach Cranberry Spice Turnovers

Wild Rice Crab Quiche

Apple and Onion Strata

Brown Bag Lunch

Apple and Almond Sandwich Spread

Curried Chicken Rice Salad

Honey Oatmeal Spice Cookies

Resources

Web Resources

Ban Trans Fats

www.bantransfats.com

This organization sued Kraft and McDonald's in 2003 to eliminate trans fat in Oreo cookies and McDonald's French fries; they are working to rid America's food supply of trans fat.

Eat Trans Fat, Get Big Belly

www.webmd.com/content/article/123/ 115139.htm

WebMD addresses the obesity risks of consuming trans fat.

Hidden Trans Fat Exposed

www.hsph.harvard.edu/nutritionsource/ transfats.html

Harvard School of Public Health addresses the trans fat controversy.

New York City's Ban on Trans Fat

www.nyc.gov/html/doh/html/pr2006/ pr114-06.shtml

The New York City Department of Health gives details about the 2006 ban on trans fat.

Revealing Trans Fats

www.fda.gov/fdac/features/2003/ 503_fats.html

The FDA's page all about trans fat and how you can identify it in the food you eat.

The Skinny on Fats

www.westonaprice.org/knowyourfats/ skinny.html

The Weston A. Price Foundation's Web site about good fats and bad fats.

Trans Fat 101

www.umm.edu/features/transfats.html

Answers to some of the most common questions about trans fat from the University of Maryland Medical Center.

Trans Fat Overview

www.americanheart.org/presenter.jhtml? identifier=4776

The American Heart Association's page about trans fat and how to avoid it.

USDA Food Pyramid

www.mypyramid.gov

The Pyramid, updated in 2005, recommends basing your diet on whole grains, fruits, and vegetables, with moderate exercise.

Books

Demaria, Dr. Robert, and Laura Meyer. *Dr. Bob's Trans Fat Survival Guide.* Elyria, OH: Drugless Healthcare Solutions, 2005.

Enig, Dr. Mary. *Know Your Fats: The Complete Primer for Understanding the Nutrition of Fats, Oils and Cholesterol.* Silver Spring, MD: Bethesda Press, 2000.

Enig, Dr. Mary, and Sally Fallon. *Eat Fat to Lose Fat.* New York: Penguin Group, 2006.

Fallon, Sally. *Nourishing Traditions: The Cookbook that Challenges Politically Correct Nutrition and the Diet Dictocrats.* Winona Lake, IN: New Trends Publishing Inc., 1999.

Hobbs, Suzanne Havala. *Get the Trans Fat Out.* New York: Three Rivers Press, 2006.

Severson, Kim, and Cindy Burke. *The Trans Fat Solution: Cooking and Shopping to Eliminate the Deadliest Fat from Your Diet.* Berkeley, CA: Ten Speed Press, 2003.

Shaw, Judith. *Trans Fats: The Hidden Killer in Our Food.* New York: Pocket Books, 2004.

Index

THE EVERYTHING SERIES!

BUSINESS & PERSONAL FINANCE

Everything® Accounting Book
Everything® Budgeting Book
Everything® Business Planning Book
Everything® Coaching and Mentoring Book
Everything® Fundraising Book
Everything® Get Out of Debt Book
Everything® Grant Writing Book
Everything® Guide to Personal Finance for Single Mothers
Everything® Home-Based Business Book, 2nd Ed.
Everything® Homebuying Book, 2nd Ed.
Everything® Homeselling Book, 2nd Ed.
Everything® Improve Your Credit Book
Everything® Investing Book, 2nd Ed.
Everything® Landlording Book
Everything® Leadership Book
Everything® Managing People Book, 2nd Ed.
Everything® Negotiating Book
Everything® Online Auctions Book
Everything® Online Business Book
Everything® Personal Finance Book
Everything® Personal Finance in Your 20s and 30s Book
Everything® Project Management Book
Everything® Real Estate Investing Book
Everything® Retirement Planning Book
Everything® Robert's Rules Book, $7.95
Everything® Selling Book
Everything® Start Your Own Business Book, 2nd Ed.
Everything® Wills & Estate Planning Book

COOKING

Everything® Barbecue Cookbook
Everything® Bartender's Book, $9.95
Everything® Cheese Book
Everything® Chinese Cookbook
Everything® Classic Recipes Book
Everything® Cocktail Parties and Drinks Book
Everything® College Cookbook
Everything® Cooking for Baby and Toddler Book
Everything® Cooking for Two Cookbook
Everything® Diabetes Cookbook
Everything® Easy Gourmet Cookbook
Everything® Fondue Cookbook
Everything® Fondue Party Book
Everything® Gluten-Free Cookbook
Everything® Glycemic Index Cookbook
Everything® Grilling Cookbook

Everything® Healthy Meals in Minutes Cookbook
Everything® Holiday Cookbook
Everything® Indian Cookbook
Everything® Italian Cookbook
Everything® Low-Carb Cookbook
Everything® Low-Fat High-Flavor Cookbook
Everything® Low-Salt Cookbook
Everything® Meals for a Month Cookbook
Everything® Mediterranean Cookbook
Everything® Mexican Cookbook
Everything® No Trans Fat Cookbook
Everything® One-Pot Cookbook
Everything® Pizza Cookbook
Everything® Quick and Easy 30-Minute, 5-Ingredient Cookbook
Everything® Quick Meals Cookbook
Everything® Slow Cooker Cookbook
Everything® Slow Cooking for a Crowd Cookbook
Everything® Soup Cookbook
Everything® Stir-Fry Cookbook
Everything® Tex-Mex Cookbook
Everything® Thai Cookbook
Everything® Vegetarian Cookbook
Everything® Wild Game Cookbook
Everything® Wine Book, 2nd Ed.

GAMES

Everything® 15-Minute Sudoku Book, $9.95
Everything® 30-Minute Sudoku Book, $9.95
Everything® Blackjack Strategy Book
Everything® Brain Strain Book, $9.95
Everything® Bridge Book
Everything® Card Games Book
Everything® Card Tricks Book, $9.95
Everything® Casino Gambling Book, 2nd Ed.
Everything® Chess Basics Book
Everything® Craps Strategy Book
Everything® Crossword and Puzzle Book
Everything® Crossword Challenge Book
Everything® Crosswords for the Beach Book, $9.95
Everything® Cryptograms Book, $9.95
Everything® Easy Crosswords Book
Everything® Easy Kakuro Book, $9.95
Everything® Easy Large Print Crosswords Book
Everything® Games Book, 2nd Ed.
Everything® Giant Sudoku Book, $9.95
Everything® Kakuro Challenge Book, $9.95
Everything® Large-Print Crossword Challenge Book

Everything® Large-Print Crosswords Book
Everything® Lateral Thinking Puzzles Book, $9.95
Everything® Mazes Book
Everything® Movie Crosswords Book, $9.95
Everything® Online Poker Book, $12.95
Everything® Pencil Puzzles Book, $9.95
Everything® Poker Strategy Book
Everything® Pool & Billiards Book
Everything® Sports Crosswords Book, $9.95
Everything® Test Your IQ Book, $9.95
Everything® Texas Hold 'Em Book, $9.95
Everything® Travel Crosswords Book, $9.95
Everything® Word Games Challenge Book
Everything® Word Scramble Book
Everything® Word Search Book

HEALTH

Everything® Alzheimer's Book
Everything® Diabetes Book
Everything® Health Guide to Adult Bipolar Disorder
Everything® Health Guide to Controlling Anxiety
Everything® Health Guide to Fibromyalgia
Everything® Health Guide to Postpartum Care
Everything® Health Guide to Thyroid Disease
Everything® Hypnosis Book
Everything® Low Cholesterol Book
Everything® Massage Book
Everything® Menopause Book
Everything® Nutrition Book
Everything® Reflexology Book
Everything® Stress Management Book

HISTORY

Everything® American Government Book
Everything® American History Book, 2nd Ed.
Everything® Civil War Book
Everything® Freemasons Book
Everything® Irish History & Heritage Book
Everything® Middle East Book

HOBBIES

Everything® Candlemaking Book
Everything® Cartooning Book
Everything® Coin Collecting Book
Everything® Drawing Book
Everything® Family Tree Book, 2nd Ed.
Everything® Knitting Book
Everything® Knots Book
Everything® Photography Book

Everything® Quilting Book
Everything® Scrapbooking Book
Everything® Sewing Book
Everything® Soapmaking Book, 2nd Ed.
Everything® Woodworking Book

HOME IMPROVEMENT

Everything® Feng Shui Book
Everything® Feng Shui Decluttering Book, $9.95
Everything® Fix-It Book
Everything® Home Decorating Book
Everything® Home Storage Solutions Book
Everything® Homebuilding Book
Everything® Organize Your Home Book

KIDS' BOOKS

All titles are $7.95
Everything® Kids' Animal Puzzle & Activity Book
Everything® Kids' Baseball Book, 4th Ed.
Everything® Kids' Bible Trivia Book
Everything® Kids' Bugs Book
Everything® Kids' Cars and Trucks Puzzle
   & Activity Book
Everything® Kids' Christmas Puzzle
   & Activity Book
Everything® Kids' Cookbook
Everything® Kids' Crazy Puzzles Book
Everything® Kids' Dinosaurs Book
Everything® Kids' First Spanish Puzzle and
   Activity Book
Everything® Kids' Gross Cookbook
Everything® Kids' Gross Hidden Pictures Book
Everything® Kids' Gross Jokes Book
Everything® Kids' Gross Mazes Book
Everything® Kids' Gross Puzzle and
   Activity Book
Everything® Kids' Halloween Puzzle
   & Activity Book
Everything® Kids' Hidden Pictures Book
Everything® Kids' Horses Book
Everything® Kids' Joke Book
Everything® Kids' Knock Knock Book
Everything® Kids' Learning Spanish Book
Everything® Kids' Math Puzzles Book
Everything® Kids' Mazes Book
Everything® Kids' Money Book
Everything® Kids' Nature Book
Everything® Kids' Pirates Puzzle and Activity Book
Everything® Kids' Presidents Book
Everything® Kids' Princess Puzzle and Activity Book
Everything® Kids' Puzzle Book
Everything® Kids' Riddles & Brain Teasers Book
Everything® Kids' Science Experiments Book
Everything® Kids' Sharks Book
Everything® Kids' Soccer Book
Everything® Kids' States Book
Everything® Kids' Travel Activity Book

KIDS' STORY BOOKS

Everything® Fairy Tales Book

LANGUAGE

Everything® Conversational Japanese Book with
   CD, $19.95
Everything® French Grammar Book
Everything® French Phrase Book, $9.95
Everything® French Verb Book, $9.95
Everything® German Practice Book with CD,
   $19.95
Everything® Inglés Book
**Everything® Intermediate Spanish Book with
   CD, $19.95**
**Everything® Learning Brazilian Portuguese
   Book with CD, $19.95**
Everything® Learning French Book
Everything® Learning German Book
Everything® Learning Italian Book
Everything® Learning Latin Book
**Everything® Learning Spanish Book with
   CD, 2nd Edition, $19.95**
Everything® Russian Practice Book with CD, $19.95
Everything® Sign Language Book
Everything® Spanish Grammar Book
Everything® Spanish Phrase Book, $9.95
Everything® Spanish Practice Book
   with CD, $19.95
Everything® Spanish Verb Book, $9.95
Everything® Speaking Mandarin Chinese Book
   with CD, $19.95

MUSIC

Everything® Drums Book with CD, $19.95
**Everything® Guitar Book with CD, 2nd
   Edition, $19.95**
Everything® Guitar Chords Book with CD, $19.95
Everything® Home Recording Book
Everything® Music Theory Book with CD, $19.95
Everything® Reading Music Book with CD, $19.95
Everything® Rock & Blues Guitar Book
   with CD, $19.95
**Everything® Rock and Blues Piano Book
   with CD, $19.95**
Everything® Songwriting Book

NEW AGE

Everything® Astrology Book, 2nd Ed.
Everything® Birthday Personology Book
Everything® Dreams Book, 2nd Ed.
Everything® Love Signs Book, $9.95
Everything® Numerology Book
Everything® Paganism Book
Everything® Palmistry Book
Everything® Psychic Book
Everything® Reiki Book

Everything® Sex Signs Book, $9.95
Everything® Tarot Book, 2nd Ed.
Everything® Toltec Wisdom Book
Everything® Wicca and Witchcraft Book

PARENTING

Everything® Baby Names Book, 2nd Ed.
Everything® Baby Shower Book
Everything® Baby's First Year Book
Everything® Birthing Book
Everything® Breastfeeding Book
Everything® Father-to-Be Book
Everything® Father's First Year Book
Everything® Get Ready for Baby Book
Everything® Get Your Baby to Sleep Book, $9.95
Everything® Getting Pregnant Book
Everything® Guide to Raising a One-Year-Old
Everything® Guide to Raising a Two-Year-Old
Everything® Homeschooling Book
Everything® Mother's First Year Book
**Everything® Parent's Guide to Childhood
   Illnesses**
Everything® Parent's Guide to Children
   and Divorce
Everything® Parent's Guide to Children
   with ADD/ADHD
Everything® Parent's Guide to Children
   with Asperger's Syndrome
Everything® Parent's Guide to Children
   with Autism
Everything® Parent's Guide to Children with
   Bipolar Disorder
**Everything® Parent's Guide to Children with
   Depression**
Everything® Parent's Guide to Children
   with Dyslexia
**Everything® Parent's Guide to Children with
   Juvenile Diabetes**
Everything® Parent's Guide to Positive Discipline
Everything® Parent's Guide to Raising a
   Successful Child
Everything® Parent's Guide to Raising Boys
Everything® Parent's Guide to Raising Girls
Everything® Parent's Guide to Raising Siblings
Everything® Parent's Guide to Sensory
   Integration Disorder
Everything® Parent's Guide to Tantrums
Everything® Parent's Guide to the Strong-Willed
   Child
Everything® Parenting a Teenager Book
Everything® Potty Training Book, $9.95
Everything® Pregnancy Book, 3rd Ed.
Everything® Pregnancy Fitness Book
Everything® Pregnancy Nutrition Book
Everything® Pregnancy Organizer, 2nd Ed., $16.95
Everything® Toddler Activities Book
Everything® Toddler Book

Everything® Tween Book
Everything® Twins, Triplets, and More Book

PETS

Everything® Aquarium Book
Everything® Boxer Book
Everything® Cat Book, 2nd Ed.
Everything® Chihuahua Book
Everything® Dachshund Book
Everything® Dog Book
Everything® Dog Health Book
Everything® Dog Obedience Book
Everything® Dog Owner's Organizer, $16.95
Everything® Dog Training and Tricks Book
Everything® German Shepherd Book
Everything® Golden Retriever Book
Everything® Horse Book
Everything® Horse Care Book
Everything® Horseback Riding Book
Everything® Labrador Retriever Book
Everything® Poodle Book
Everything® Pug Book
Everything® Puppy Book
Everything® Rottweiler Book
Everything® Small Dogs Book
Everything® Tropical Fish Book
Everything® Yorkshire Terrier Book

REFERENCE

Everything® American Presidents Book
Everything® Blogging Book
Everything® Build Your Vocabulary Book
Everything® Car Care Book
Everything® Classical Mythology Book
Everything® Da Vinci Book
Everything® Divorce Book
Everything® Einstein Book
Everything® Enneagram Book
Everything® Etiquette Book, 2nd Ed.
Everything® Inventions and Patents Book
Everything® Mafia Book
Everything® Philosophy Book
Everything® Pirates Book
Everything® Psychology Book

RELIGION

Everything® Angels Book
Everything® Bible Book
Everything® Buddhism Book
Everything® Catholicism Book
Everything® Christianity Book
Everything® Gnostic Gospels Book
Everything® History of the Bible Book
Everything® Jesus Book

Everything® Jewish History & Heritage Book
Everything® Judaism Book
Everything® Kabbalah Book
Everything® Koran Book
Everything® Mary Book
Everything® Mary Magdalene Book
Everything® Prayer Book
Everything® Saints Book, 2nd Ed.
Everything® Torah Book
Everything® Understanding Islam Book
Everything® World's Religions Book
Everything® Zen Book

SCHOOL & CAREERS

Everything® Alternative Careers Book
Everything® Career Tests Book
Everything® College Major Test Book
Everything® College Survival Book, 2nd Ed.
Everything® Cover Letter Book, 2nd Ed.
Everything® Filmmaking Book
Everything® Get-a-Job Book, 2nd Ed.
Everything® Guide to Being a Paralegal
Everything® Guide to Being a Personal Trainer
Everything® Guide to Being a Real Estate Agent
Everything® Guide to Being a Sales Rep
Everything® Guide to Careers in Health Care
Everything® Guide to Careers in Law Enforcement
Everything® Guide to Government Jobs
Everything® Guide to Starting and Running a Restaurant
Everything® Job Interview Book
Everything® New Nurse Book
Everything® New Teacher Book
Everything® Paying for College Book
Everything® Practice Interview Book
Everything® Resume Book, 2nd Ed.
Everything® Study Book

SELF-HELP

Everything® Dating Book, 2nd Ed.
Everything® Great Sex Book
Everything® Self-Esteem Book
Everything® Tantric Sex Book

SPORTS & FITNESS

Everything® Easy Fitness Book
Everything® Running Book
Everything® Weight Training Book

TRAVEL

Everything® Family Guide to Cruise Vacations
Everything® Family Guide to Hawaii
Everything® Family Guide to Las Vegas, 2nd Ed.
Everything® Family Guide to Mexico
Everything® Family Guide to New York City, 2nd Ed.
Everything® Family Guide to RV Travel & Campgrounds
Everything® Family Guide to the Caribbean
Everything® Family Guide to the Walt Disney World Resort®, Universal Studios®, and Greater Orlando, 4th Ed.
Everything® Family Guide to Timeshares
Everything® Family Guide to Washington D.C., 2nd Ed.

WEDDINGS

Everything® Bachelorette Party Book, $9.95
Everything® Bridesmaid Book, $9.95
Everything® Destination Wedding Book
Everything® Elopement Book, $9.95
Everything® Father of the Bride Book, $9.95
Everything® Groom Book, $9.95
Everything® Mother of the Bride Book, $9.95
Everything® Outdoor Wedding Book
Everything® Wedding Book, 3rd Ed.
Everything® Wedding Checklist, $9.95
Everything® Wedding Etiquette Book, $9.95
Everything® Wedding Organizer, 2nd Ed., $16.95
Everything® Wedding Shower Book, $9.95
Everything® Wedding Vows Book, $9.95
Everything® Wedding Workout Book
Everything® Weddings on a Budget Book, $9.95

WRITING

Everything® Creative Writing Book
Everything® Get Published Book, 2nd Ed.
Everything® Grammar and Style Book
Everything® Guide to Magazine Writing
Everything® Guide to Writing a Book Proposal
Everything® Guide to Writing a Novel
Everything® Guide to Writing Children's Books
Everything® Guide to Writing Copy
Everything® Guide to Writing Research Papers
Everything® Screenwriting Book
Everything® Writing Poetry Book
Everything® Writing Well Book